# NOLS Wilderness Educator Notebook
## 11th edition, 2015
### Edited By John Gookin, PhD and Adam Swisher

### Acknowledgements

The NOLS Wilderness Educator Notebook is written by the NOLS field staff. The primary authors and editors since the first edition in 1989 include Molly Absolon, Drew Leemon, Tod Schimelpfenig, Craig Stebbins, Maria Timmons, Darran Wells, Adam Swisher, and John Gookin.

Others who have authored or reviewed parts of this book include Susan Benepe, Rich Brame, Susan Brame, Mark Bruscino, Adrienne Cachelin, John Cederquist, Barb Cestero, Michael Cheek, Mihaly Csikszentmihalyi, Patrick Clark, Mark Cole, Colby Coombs, Carrie Cox, Willy Cunningham, Brian DeBolt, Debbie Derbish, Bill Dunbar, John Gans, Dave Glenn, Steve Goryl, Pippa Gowen, Molly Hampton, Brian Harper, Chad Henderson, Nan Henderson, Scott Kane, Chavawn Kelly, Jennifer Lamb, Christi Larsen, Ed Lee, Ian McCammon, Kevin McGowan, Jono McKinney, Melissa Meuller, Kirk Nichols, Lianne Owen, Karen Paisley, Paul Petzoldt, Tom Reed, Peggy Savanick, Eric Sawyer, Marit Sawyer, Jim Sibthorp, Del Smith, Tom Smith, Bruce Smithhammer, Abby Warner, Willy Warner, Don Webber, Tiana White, Willie Williams, Lynne Wolfe, Thelma Young, Mike Zawaski, Ariel Greene, Drew Seitz, and many others.

The illustrations are by John McMullen, Hannah Hinchman, Alisha Bube, Eryn Pierce, and John Gookin. The illustrations supplied by the Brunton Corporation are by John Cox.

Thousands of people have created and refined the techniques in this book. The people who have the biggest effect on advancing this profession aren't those who merely improve their own field practices and teaching techniques—the biggest advances come from those who refine techniques and share them with the rest of us. Those little notes brought from the field on rain-warped paper, smeared with dirt and smashed mosquitoes, are what has advanced this book, and this profession. To all of you who help the rest of us advance, thank you.

John Gookin,
NOLS Curriculum & Research Manager

**Cover Photos**
Front Cover: Stéphane Terrier
Back Cover: Paul Petzoldt teaches to a group of NOLS students. NOLS Archives

Copyright ©2015 National Outdoor Leadership School

Published by
National Outdoor Leadership School
284 Lincoln Street
Lander, WY 82520
www.nols.edu

All rights reserved. No part of this book may be reproduced in any form without the written consent of the National Outdoor Leadership School. All inquiries should be addressed to the National Outdoor Leadership School, 284 Lincoln Street, Lander, WY 82520, or books@nols.edu

ISBN-13: 978-1-882045-04-4

# NOLS Wilderness Educator Notebook
# Table of Contents

## Chapter One: Introduction to NOLS
Our Mission — 4
NOLS Values — 4
What is NOLS? — 4
NOLS' Philosophy of Education — 4
The Instructor Role in Excellence — 5

## Chapter Two: Teaching at NOLS
The NOLS Core Curriculum — 6
Neurobiology—The Science Behind Learning — 7
Maslow's Hierarchy of Needs — 7
Learner Motivation — 7
Challenge — 8
Flow — 8
Reflection — 9
The Myth of Sensory-based Learning Styles — 9
Teaching Styles — 9
Teaching Tips — 12

## Chapter Three: Personalizing Education
Developmental Psychology — 14
Advancement and Enrichment — 14
Reaching Adolescent Learners — 14
Education in the Stages of Adulthood — 16
Working with Students from Backgrounds Underrepresented at NOLS — 16
English Language Learners (ELL) — 17

## Chapter Four: Holistic Education
Non-cognitive Skills — 19
Human Development — 19
Training, Teaching, & Educating — 19
Educational Scaffolding — 20
Standards-based Education at NOLS — 20
Objective Evaluation versus Personal Growth — 20
Habits of Mind—Four Levels of Education — 20
Maslow's Hierarchy Expanded — 21
Resiliency Education (Tolerance for Adversity) — 21
Awakening Genius — 21
Piaget's Developmental Theory — 22
Emotional Intelligence — 22
Cooperative Learning — 22
Building Community — 22
Service Learning — 23
Teaching for Transfer — 23
Nurturing Spirituality — 23

## Chapter Five: Empowering and Engaging Students
Empowering NOLS Students — 25
Ways We Empower NOLS Students — 25
Styles that Empower NOLS Students — 26
Engaging NOLS Students — 26
Intrinsic Motivation — 26
Self-efficacy — 27

## Chapter Six: Teaching Basic Outdoor Living Skills
Leave No Trace — 28
Pack Packing — 29
Campsite Selection — 30
Tent and Fly Pitching — 31
Waste Disposal — 31
Water Disinfection and Hygiene — 32
Stove Use and Care — 33
Basic Cooking and Food Identification — 34
Baking — 35
Nutrition — 35
Staying Warm and Dry — 36
Staying Found — 37
Fire Building — 37
Fishing — 38
Trout Habitat and Behavior — 39
NOLS Grizzly Bear Practices — 40
Bear Spray — 43
Bear Encounters — 44
Food Storage in Bear Country — 45
NOLS Black Bear Practices — 46
NOLS Backcountry Swimming Practices & Guidelines — 46
Meteorology — 48
Backcountry Lightning Safety — 49

## Chapter Seven: Teaching Basic Wilderness Travel and Navigation
Trail Technique — 53
Hazard Evaluation — 54
Map Reading — 55
Route Finding — 56
Compass Navigation — 57
Using UTM Coordinates — 58
Using Latitude/Longitude Coordinates — 59
Travel Plans — 59
Using The Global Positioning System (GPS) — 60
River Crossings — 61
The Tyrolean Traverse — 65

## Chapter Eight: Teaching Environmental Studies and Biology

| | |
|---|---|
| Teaching Ecological Principles | 67 |
| Teaching Biology on Semester Courses | 67 |
| Environmental Studies at NOLS Flowchart | 68 |

## Chapter Nine: Teaching Leadership

| | |
|---|---|
| Using The NOLS Leadership Model | 69 |
| Student Teaching | 69 |
| Expedition Planning | 70 |

## Chapter Ten: Teaching Risk Management

| | |
|---|---|
| Risk Management—A Three-Part Framework | 71 |
| NOLS Risk Management Goals | 71 |
| Incident Reporting | 72 |
| Teaching Risk Management | 73 |
| Risk Assessment Tools | 73 |
| Situational Awareness | 75 |
| Teaching Risk Management on Outdoor Educator Courses | 76 |

## Chapter Eleven: Emergency Procedures

| | |
|---|---|
| Basic Procedures | 78 |
| Finding Lost Students | 78 |
| Lost Group Response Action Chart | 80 |
| Improvised Litters | 81 |
| Helicopter Evacuations | 82 |

## Chapter Twelve: Course Management Skills

| | |
|---|---|
| Designing a NOLS Course | 84 |
| NOLS Student Supervision Practices | 84 |
| The Progression to Student Independence | 84 |
| Guidelines for Conducting Solos on NOLS Courses | 87 |
| Visiting Student Camps | 88 |
| Staff Guidelines for Grades and Diplomas at NOLS | 88 |

## Chapter Thirteen: Helping All Students Succeed by Closing the Gap Between Behaviors and Expectations

| | |
|---|---|
| The Management Spectrum | 91 |
| Instructor Response Methodology | 91 |
| Student Performance Agreements | 92 |
| Documenting Student Non-Medical Incidents | 92 |
| NOLS' Responses to Specific Behaviors | 93 |

# Chapter One
# Introduction to NOLS

## Our Mission
The mission of the National Outdoor Leadership School is to be the leading source and teacher of wilderness skills and leadership that serve people and the environment.

## NOLS Values
The NOLS community—its staff, students, trustees, and alumni—shares a commitment to wilderness, education, leadership, safety, community, and excellence. These values define and direct who we are, what we do, and how we do it.

### Wilderness
We define wilderness as a place where nature is dominant and situations and their consequences are real. Living in these conditions, away from the distractions of modern civilization, fosters self-reliance, judgment, respect, and a sense of responsibility for our actions. It can also be a profoundly moving experience that leads to inspiration, joy and commitment to an environmental ethic.

### Education
We believe that education should be exciting, fun, and challenging. With this in mind, our courses are designed to help people develop and practice the skills they need to live, travel, and play safely in the outdoors. On our expeditions, people learn by accepting and meeting real challenges. Our instructors are educators, not guides. They are committed to inspiring students to explore and develop their understanding of wilderness ethics, leadership, teamwork, natural history, and technical skills.

### Leadership
We believe that leadership is a skill that can be learned and practiced. With students and staff we encourage the evolution of judgment, personal responsibility, and awareness of group needs—key leadership traits—through practical experience and timely feedback. We value integrity, experience, accountability, and humility in our leaders.

### Safety
We accept risk as an integral part of the learning process and of the environments through which we travel. The recognition and management of risk is critical to both the development of leadership and to the safety and health of our students and staff. We believe successful risk management stems from good judgment based on experience, training, and knowledge.

### Community
NOLS is an international community composed of talented individuals who care deeply about what they do. We value diversity, integrity, and personal responsibility while recognizing that our strength lies in teamwork and commitment to our mission and each other. We appreciate creativity, individuality, and passion among our staff and as an institution. We take our jobs seriously and pursue our mission with enthusiasm, and we cherish our sense of humor and our ability to laugh at ourselves.

### Excellence
We seek excellence in all we do. We recognize that maintaining excellence requires that we question decisions, learn from failures, and celebrate successes. We are committed to high quality experiences where every moment and every relationship counts. We evolve and adapt with new technology, changing techniques, and differing circumstances.

## What is NOLS?
NOLS is a school rooted in wilderness and leadership education. Founder Paul Petzoldt led the first NOLS expedition on June 8, 1965, the year after the Wilderness Act was signed into law. Petzoldt's goal for the newly created school was to train leaders to serve the growing number of people spending time in the wilderness. Since the first NOLS course stepped into the Wyoming wilderness in 1965, NOLS has expanded to include operating locations around the world and a variety of course offerings including semesters, customized field courses, wilderness medicine courses, and professional consulting. Our expedition courses take students away from the distractions of civilization into the mountains, deserts, and oceans to learn the skills they need to lead their own expeditions.

NOLS graduates are leaders who have an understanding of team building, self-confidence, problem solving, competence, and good judgment. Research about what transfers from NOLS to life back home shows that the leadership skills gained on a NOLS course last long after you leave the school and are transferable to everyday life (Sibthorp, 2008). These include the ability to function effectively under difficult circumstances, the ability to work as a team member, the ability to plan and organize, the ability to get along with different types of people, and the ability to make informed and thoughtful decisions, to mention a few.

From our founding, NOLS has promoted the protection of our wilderness classrooms through environmental education and stewardship. NOLS and the US Forest Service cofounded the national Leave No Trace program in the United States in 1990, and has a long-standing reputation for developing practical conservation practices.

In a world dominated by humans, the lessons available from the direct experience of nature and wilderness expedition have become increasingly rare and important. We seek to be open to these lessons as individuals, to apply them to the organization and management of our school, and to share them with the world community.

## NOLS' Philosophy of Education
The experiential learning process is core to the NOLS philosophy of education. NOLS field courses are designed to give students the tools to travel safely through wild places, to lead others in a variety of situations, and to appreciate and protect the natural world. NOLS field courses take students away from the distractions of civilization and immerse them in the wilderness of mountains, deserts, and oceans to develop the skills necessary to plan and lead their own expeditions. In the backcountry classroom, students quickly recognize the applicability of information as it is presented to them. The wilderness is a powerful teacher, providing illustration for key concepts, reinforcing lessons with real consequences, and ultimately cultivating a wildland ethic. Activities and experiences enhance learning by providing opportunities to practice new skills and examine new theories. Attaining tangible goals provides illuminating lessons that last a lifetime. Immersion in the grandeur and adventure of wilderness provides an experience that can profoundly affect one's overall perspective.

NOLS students are expected to take care of themselves, to hold group goals above their own, to respect others, and to respect the environment. Each expedition member is expected to contribute to a positive and productive expedition.

NOLS instructors teach classes and develop challenging learning opportunities. Instructors use teaching progressions that start with basic rules, which then develop into principles, and culminate in the form of situational judgment. They look for opportunities for students to explore the Earth, their group, and themselves. They model the principles they expect students to develop. They coach students to help them attain mastery and independence.

## The NOLS Core Curriculum

**Leadership education** is the hallmark of the NOLS curriculum. NOLS uses four roles, seven skills, and one signature style as a framework to help students practice leadership and teamwork with peers in real situations. Our progression starts with learning to be a contributing team member, and rapidly progresses into *leader of the day* exercises that focus on setting and attaining group goals. Coaching by the NOLS staff, feedback from peers, and natural consequences help students progress quickly. NOLS uses diverse leadership types to help students practice styles appropriate for varied situations. Our alumni say these lessons transfer well to their personal lives and work.

**Environmental Studies** is an integral part of the NOLS curriculum. It permeates many classes and activities, whether learning Leave No Trace camping, observing ecological systems, pausing to enjoy beautiful scenery, exploring new environs, or adapting your schedule to nature's rhythms. It is based on both practical needs and developing a sense of place. A NOLS student is expected to go home with the basic knowledge, leadership skills, conservation ethic, and can-do attitude to be a more responsible steward and citizen.

**Risk Management** is a fundamental part of the NOLS curriculum. It is our top priority in every class and activity, whether learning how to pack your pack or how to navigate the coast in a kayak. Instruction begins with basic tenets that help novices succeed. Coached application helps students learn context and patterns. New situations provide learning opportunities through which steadfast rules evolve into context-based principles. As students progress, instructors take back seat roles, first directing, then coaching, advising, observing, and eventually allowing many student groups to travel on their own. Continued application helps foster the situational judgment needed for independent travel.

**Wilderness Skills** are foundational to the NOLS curriculum. They provide a tangible medium for the entire curriculum and recreational skills that last a lifetime. Significant physical activities provide stimulation, conditioning, and stamina. Coached application and individual goal-setting provide steps toward mastery and independence. While NOLS enjoys a long-standing reputation for the development of technical competence, these skills are directly coupled with a broad education that also includes the development of judgment, environmental ethics, and leadership.

## The Instructor Role in Excellence

Every instructor and staff member at NOLS is expected to help lead our community, both through self-leadership and by taking initiative as a peer leader. While many important changes at NOLS have come from the top down, many pervasive changes have also been made from within our community. Individual leadership has constantly redefined our community.

Our approach to course management encourages all members to take responsibility for leadership, and we encourage instructors to import ideas from other organizations. Leadership is situational and dynamic at NOLS: in our lesson plans, in our instructor teams, and in our offices.

Advances in both technology and teaching strategies happen not because someone at NOLS talks everyone else into trying them; they happen because someone has shown us how they can increase student performance. Excellence isn't something handed down by decree. Rather, it is something that evolves from within an organization. Contributions from all of our staff help shape who we are.

# Chapter Two
# Teaching at NOLS

The NOLS core curriculum defines our courses. It is the primary component of a synergistic educational system that includes personalized education and holistic education. Personalized and holistic education are addressed in the following chapters. The core curriculum is described in depth, with specificity for each course type, in the expected student outcomes, which serve as a three-way contract between the student, instructor, and school. Expected student outcomes can be found in detail on student evaluations and in more generic terms on every course description (find course descriptions at www.nols.edu). The student is expected to work towards accomplishing the stated outcomes. The instructor is expected to help students achieve the outcomes. The school is expected to support courses in ways that help students develop these outcomes.

*"The foundation of the Wind River Wilderness course is to prepare students to: assume leadership roles in their lives through excellent teamwork, communication, and expedition behavior; live and travel in mountain environments while applying the outdoor skills practiced on this course; connect with natural places that enrich their lives and foster a strong environmental ethic; and apply effective decision-making tools to real world problems."*
—WRW course description

## The NOLS Core Curriculum
The NOLS core curriculum has four threads found in every activity—leadership, outdoor skills, risk management, and environmental studies. Each thread has its own progression. When developing a course itinerary and curriculum progression, it is important to do so with the four core curriculum threads in mind and an intentional focus on expected student outcomes.

### Leadership
- Expedition behavior (pitch in, be positive, serve group goals, respect others, work as a team)
- Competence
- Communication
- Judgment and decision-making
- Tolerance for adversity and uncertainty (maintain a good work ethic, step up to challenge, have physical and mental endurance)
- Self-awareness

### Outdoor Skills
- Equipment care and selection
- Ration planning
- Preparing nutritious meals using a camp stove and a fire
- Staying warm and dry
- Route-finding, navigation, map reading, compass use
- Campsite selection
- Sanitation and waste disposal

### Risk Management
- Health and comfort maintenance
- Wilderness injury prevention and treatment
- Judgment: use past experience and knowledge to judge new situations
- Group decision-making
- Identify and mitigate subjective and objective risks
- Emergency procedures

### Environmental Studies
- Leave No Trace camping and resource protection
- Natural history
- Pertinent regional environmental issues
- Function, organization, and local concerns of land management agencies
- Sustainability of ecological, social, and economic systems
- Wilderness ethics and practices for everyday life

## The Instructor Role
NOLS instructors need to be good lecturers, but in general, our role is more like that of a coach: we give students foundational knowledge, then constantly help them progress in applying that knowledge to specific contexts. We teach learning progressions that lead to self-sufficiency. A NOLS course isn't just a test of how well students can use a map or communicate with others; it is a course of instruction with parallel learning progressions, and with instructors who coach students to succeed at progressively higher levels of performance and, eventually, self-sufficiency. As a NOLS instructor, your job is to train students to succeed in all of the expected outcomes listed in the course description and student evaluation.

Effective teachers accomplish high student outcomes through a well-rounded approach to education. Some of the traits shared by effective teachers are that they (adapted from Stronge, 2002):
- Establish and maintain good expedition behavior and a positive learning environment.
- Communicate expectations, organize time, and plan instruction.
- Present curriculum in a way that supports active and engaged learning.
- Educate students via role modeling, guided activities, and lectures.
- Monitor individual student progress, identify student potential, and give students ongoing feedback.
- Relate to students as individuals.
- Provide inspiration.

## Design Your Tests First
The expected student outcomes are the test that will show that the students have mastered your instruction. Students are sometimes expected to simply recite back information, to build an important foundation of rote knowledge, but that isn't enough. At NOLS, the test needs to be a practical application of the material during the expedition. For example, if you are trying to help students develop a working knowledge of the characteristic flora and fauna of the ecosystem, then you should expect them to be able to use the names of key species when discussing related topics like impact concerns, fish habitat, fire building, bear safety, etc. Beyond that, they should be able to identify various ecosystems via those key species, and they should know the types of impact to which that ecosystem is sensitive. The instructor should start with practical applications in mind, then use reverse planning to figure out how the progression will help students achieve the expected student outcomes.

## Course Quality
NOLS conducted a decade-long research project—known as the Course Quality Survey (CQS)—to measure what our students learn, which learning transfers to students lives, and which program factors correlate with greater learning. All NOLS students are asked to complete the CQS at the end of their field courses. In addition to the student outcomes, instructors are expected to support the following twelve indicators of quality education, which can be found on the CQS.

### Course Quality Indicators:
1) Safety was a high priority on this course.
2) My point of view and life experiences were appreciated by others on my course.
3) The NOLS education model was engaging, not boring.
4) I had ample opportunities to reflect on what I was learning during this course.
5) I received a lot of useful feedback from my instructors during this course.
6) I received a lot of useful feedback from my fellow students on this course.
7) There were role models on my course who I respected and admired.
8) I contributed to my group's successes.
9) I had important responsibilities on this course.
10) I made important decisions on this course.
11) Our group worked well together even when instructors were absent.
12) I got along well with everyone on this course.

## Neurobiology—The Science Behind Learning

If we understand the physiology behind learning, we can teach more effectively and efficiently. On the neurological level, learning is changing or enhancing the patterns of connection between the brain cells (neurons) responsible for processing information. This is how all memories, including muscle memories, are formed.

Inter-neural communication is an electrochemical process. Every thought, experience, or sensory input stimulates an electrical impulse. The impulse travels along the dendrite of a neuron to the neuron's nucleus, or cell body. The impulse is carried away from the cell body through the axon. At the terminals of the axon are chemicals called *neurotransmitters* (e.g., acetylcholine, glutamate, and GABA). The neurotransmitters carry the nerve impulse across the space between the axon of the first neuron and the dendrite of the next. This is called the synaptic gap and the connection made between the two neurons is referred to as a synapse. In this way, the nerve impulse travels between cells throughout the nervous system.

It is easier to remember information that is tied to an emotion. When learning is associated with an emotional stimulus (such as listening to a funny story), a flood of neurotransmitters is released in the brain, causing synapses to fire more quickly and effectively and making it easier to commit new information to long-term memory. This helps explain why a student in a challenged and excited state can learn and perform optimally. If the emotion is too strong, however, it may become stressful and a hormone called cortisol will be released into the body. Cortisol has a number of effects that hinder learning; one long-term effect of high cortisol levels in the brain is to physically damage dendrites, reducing the number of synapses.

Some things enhance the transport of information via neurons. One is the flood of neurotransmitters mentioned above. Others have to do with the structure of axons and dendrites. The thicker the axon, the faster the electrical impulse is passed and the less interference is felt from nearby reactions. Well used axons become thickened by developing a fatty sheath called *myelin*. This is one reason why the more you exercise a particular neural pathway, the more efficient it becomes. Practice creates event sequences that become automated, allowing us to perform whole sequences subconsciously without cluttering our working memory with details. Automation is why repetition and patterns are important in learning.

Each neuron is connected, via its axon terminals and its dendrites, to many other neurons. The more connections there are, the more efficiently the neurons communicate. Dendrites physically grow new branches in enriched environments. Enrichment includes both new, challenging, and engaging experiences; and learning from the experiences through interactive feedback.

Providing real experiences coupled with discussions that grant reflection and feedback on those experiences contributes to an enriched learning environment. Discussions that supplement the experience may help provide dual encoding by imprinting the learning in another way and creating yet another channel by which the neural pathways are exercised. We possess both episodic (time, place, emotion, context) and semantic (deep encoding: linked to previous knowledge) encoding abilities: a rich, emotionally charged experience is essential, but actively processing that experience through examination and discussion can add yet another dimension that helps us apply abstract concepts to similar situations in the future, which is what deep learning is all about.

## Creating an Environment for Learning: Maslow's Hierarchy of Needs (Maslow, 1968)

Abraham Maslow turned educational psychology upside down in the 1960s. Rather than studying what was wrong with disturbed people, he focused on studying what was right in the great people of his time. His pyramid displays the fundamental human needs that must be met at any level before a person is motivated to care about the next level up.

In the field, we know that students don't care about learning technical or leadership skills if they are cold or hungry. Tom Myers, MD, explains in great detail how Grand Canyon accidents are often related to basic human needs (Myers, 2001). Few healthy, alert people walk off of cliffs, but a lot of dehydrated, hot, cold, or tired people do. We should use this information not just to teach more carefully and at deeper levels, but also to help our students understand how critical it is that they become self-disciplined in taking good care of their own basic human needs. When Petzoldt commented that some of the world's

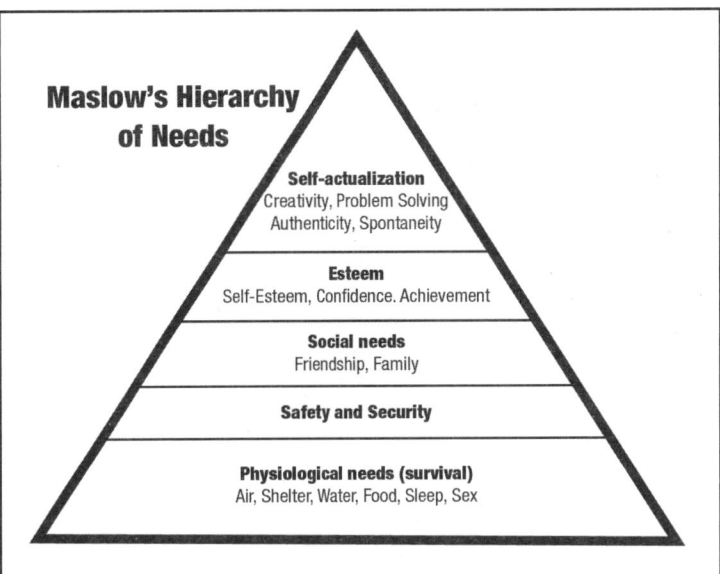

*Maslow's Hierarchy of Needs shows us that in order to perform at our highest potential, we must first address basic human needs. (Maslow, 1968)*

great climbers were not great mountaineers because they didn't know how to camp, he was referring to their ability to take care of themselves, which limited their ability to help a team reach the summit. Competency and self-discipline in this area are transferable for every NOLS graduate. If the first step in creating a powerful learning experience is to attend to students' physiological comfort, then the next step is to create a safe and empowering learning environment.

## Learner Motivation

Connected knowledge is a strength of outdoor education. Connected knowledge is knowledge that is logically connected to other knowledge and to the student's life. Good teachers help students find these connections.

People learn best when they perceive a need to know the information or skill. When camping in cold weather, students will want to know how to stay warm. They'll be more engaged and more likely to apply the cold weather information than if they were taught the same information on a hot course in Baja. NOLS students learn a great deal from real situations and real problems they face, providing *intrinsic motivation*. A need to know can be intrinsic, as in the preceding example, or it can be *extrinsic*—motivated by others.

*"Teachers open the door, but you must enter by yourself."*
-Chinese Proverb

External motivation comes from wanting to please others, like camping carefully because the instructors insist on it. While this beats camping poorly, educationally it pales when compared to camping carefully because you want to minimize your own impact on the wild country that you cherish. As instructors, we foster intrinsic motivation by:

- Choosing course activities and group goals that motivate and challenge students.
- Utilizing teachable moments and teaching classes at appropriate times.
- Inspiring and encouraging inquisitiveness so our students pursue what interests them.
- Helping students to discover their strengths.

We do not need to contrive challenge, difficulty, or especially, risk. While going the exciting way might be appropriate, going that way just because it is difficult models poor decision-making. And, role modeling is an important component of teaching.

Some people call getting cold "direct feedback" and getting scolded because you don't have your mittens on "indirect feedback." Direct feedback from nature builds a respectful relationship between the student and the environment. It connects them. We can let nature give our students the direct feedback that makes experiential education so powerful. The trick is to direct and supervise novices, then move to the next level of student autonomy based on proven student performance rather than basing this progression on time alone.

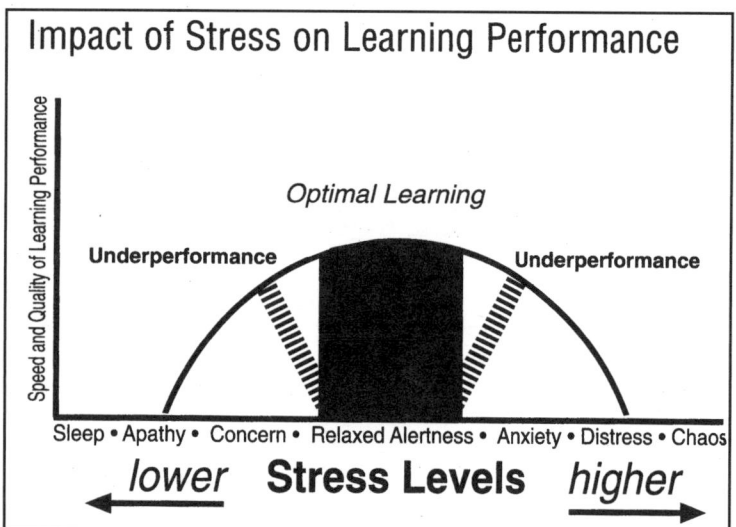

*Optimal learning takes place between no stress environments and high stress environments. The challenge is to identify the appropriate amount of stress necessary to achieve optimal learning. Chart reprinted by permission from "Teaching with the Brain in Mind" by Eric Jensen.*

## Challenge

*Challenge* is an important factor of quality education, but challenge doesn't need to be distressful. Planning enough challenge into a program requires knowledge of what too little or too much stress does to people. It is also important to keep in mind that the amount of challenge a student can tolerate varies from individual to individual. Too little challenge, and people aren't motivated to do their best. Too much challenge, and people get scared. An appropriate amount of challenge can help students engage more fully in their own education. Making challenge feel like a positive event (positive stress is called *eustress*), almost like a thrilling game or a puzzle to be solved—rather than a negative hurdle—can help shape students' attitudes about how they approach future challenges.

Challenges can be physical, psychological, or social, and they are all cumulative. This means that if someone is having a problem with another expedition member, they become less tolerant of difficult hiking or cold weather. Research conducted by NOLS on challenge levels on our expeditions found that social stressors are generally more significant than the physical stressors. This directly supports the notion that expedition behavior is key to the accomplishment of group goals.

## Stress and Learning

Stress affects learning (Jensen, 1998). Chronic stress or intense physical or emotional stress can cause these physiological changes in the body:
- Respiration rate increases
- Pulse rate increases
- Blood Pressure increases
- Muscle tone increases, leading to fatigue
- Strength increases
- Coordination decreases—tight muscles make you awkward
- Balance decreases
- Digestion stops, as blood is shunted to the muscles
- Immunity decreases after 48 hours of chronic stress
- Reactivity increases—you are more jumpy and reactive to physical or emotional stimuli
- Inter-neural communication, coordination between our logical and creative centers, decreases

These stress responses might be bad for learning, but some are exactly what you need in a "fight, flight, or freeze" situation. The stressed student needs to be communicated to directly. Someone frozen with fear on a ledge is incapable of figuring out creative solutions. The more you can help them solve their own problem, the less stressed they will be in similar situations in the future, and the more likely they will be to maintain their calm next time.

An alert brain that is not overly stressed allows better creativity and memory, which need to work hand-in-hand. An example might be if someone badgers you for a simple answer but you can't remember the simple answer you know is stored in your long-term memory. If you get up to go use the bathroom, you often remember the answer halfway to the bathroom when your brain is more relaxed. Another example is if someone gives you a list of double-digit numbers to add. In front of a waiting audience, you would probably need to add them slowly and carefully. In a more relaxed setting, you can find more creative combinations to add those numbers up more quickly and accurately, specifically because your relaxed brain uses creativity and logic in concert with each other.

## Flow

*Adapted with permission from "Finding Flow" by Mihaly Csikszentmihalyi, 1997.*

*Flow* is a state where perceived risk and challenge are balanced with skill, resulting in an optimal arousal zone, with extreme joy and a heightened ability to learn (Csikszentmihalyi, 1990). This is when we get so absorbed by an activity that we lose all track of time. Star athletes exemplify flow in vivid terms. Novices can achieve states of flow as well when they practice in a suitably challenging environment. We help students achieve flow by not only challenging them appropriately, but also by creating a positive learning environment where they can truly relax while they are learning, and by helping them identify and expand their capabilities. Flow is only possible if people are comfortable physically, psychologically, and socially.

Flow is more likely to occur in an activity that has clear goals that require specific actions, activities that give spontaneous feedback, and especially activities that fully challenge a person's skills. The demand on focused mental energy leaves no room for distracting inward thoughts and feelings. As self-consciousness disappears, we feel stronger than usual, we lose all track of time, and we harmonize our mental and physical selves. We don't feel happy while in the moment, because we can't afford the distraction of such introspection. But, we are elated afterwards when we reflect on what we have accomplished. Flow leads to spectacular personal growth, but it takes thorough preparation to perform at this level. To help our students achieve such peak experiences, we have to give them adequate background information, then practice, practice, practice before we expect them to achieve flow during a challenge.

Anxiety and, on the other end of the spectrum, boredom are generally unproductive zones for novices to be in. Some "stress-challenge" programs intentionally put students in the "anxiety zone" to help them learn to deal with stress. This is not a good way to train outdoor leaders. It gives the activity a negative connotation for the novice. We also need to recognize that students have varying comfort zones. Putting everyone on the same climb or ski hill may not be appropriate, challenging only the middle of the bell curve and leaving the others in the anxiety zone.

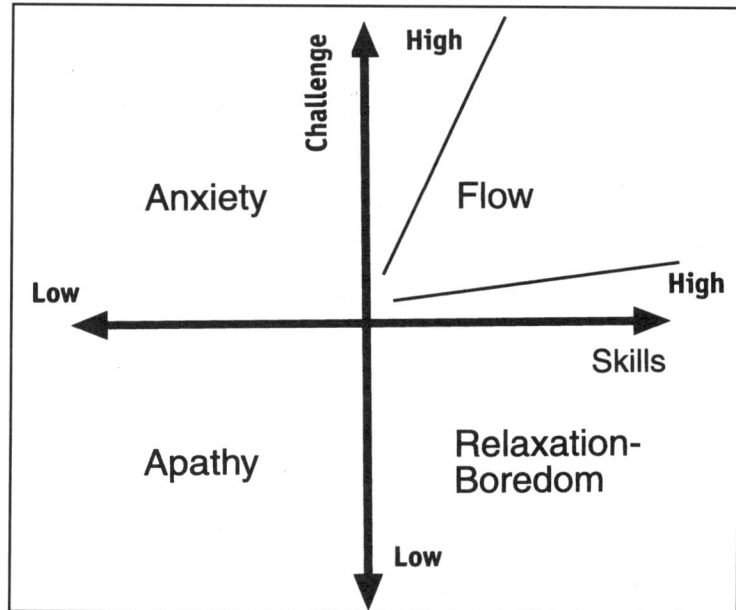

*Similar to optimal learning, flow takes place between high stress and boredom. Having a sense of control throughout a challenge leads to a state of flow. Diagram from Jackson (1999). Used with permission from Mihaly Csikszentmihalyi.*

## Assessment

We need to constantly assess where our students are in their education so that we can decide how much latitude to give them and how much past material needs review or further enhancement. Quizzes and other comprehension assessments are easy ways to check people, but the ultimate test is to observe our students' habits. Their spontaneous reactions to real situations are good predictions of what they'll do as outdoor leaders after their NOLS course. *Formative assessment* is the ongoing assessment we use to coach students. *Evaluative assessment* is our summary of their overall performance at the end of the course, with a focus on their final learned state rather than on their novice performance before your instruction.

## Reflection

John Dewey, the father of progressive education, coined the phrase "Discuss, demonstrate, do, then reflect." He made a clear point, a century ago, that reflection was key not only to retaining material, but also for making the connections that help us apply the information in other settings. Modern neurobiology tells us the same thing. If we want people to remember things, we need to help them develop more neurological connections in their brain so they can relate the new information to varied topics (Jensen, 1998). Reflection can do this, and more.

Reflection can be guided, like when an instructor asks probing questions after an activity to direct the topics of reflection. Reflection can also be unguided, which easily happens during free time or while doing repetitive tasks like hiking or flycasting. Reflection enhances connections in learning and is an important aspect of learning. Like debriefing groups, reflection should be used in ways that people look forward to it and desire more.

Breaking up classes throughout the day gives students time to reflect before moving on to a new topic. Hiking is a fantastic time for unguided reflection. If you need to teach three formal classes in a given day, consider teaching one class after breakfast, meeting for a class (navigation, for example) during the day, and teaching the last class after dinner. Having instructors teach short classes separately to hiking groups during the day provides more class time, more reflection time, and is a great way to break up the day.

Sometimes reflection needs help by creating intentional self-awareness, or mindfulness, during an exercise. Immediately before starting a new activity like climbing or caving, ask folks how they're feeling. When they tell you they have butterflies in their stomachs and are feeling a bit anxious, tell them to remember that feeling, because that's exactly what others (who they might be leading) will probably be feeling in new activities. Then later, after the first rock climb, ask folks to remember the anxiety they felt from the unknown. A good leadership development strategy is to ask the students what they saw the instructors do to lessen student anxiety. As they reflect back on what they saw the instructors do (used a calm reassuring voice tone, demonstrated techniques first, asked about fears, didn't push, etc.), let them know that these are things they can do when leading others. This not only allows them to reflect on what they saw but also helps them see ways to apply the knowledge to future situations.

## The Myth of Sensory-based Learning Styles

Before 2008, NOLS, as well as almost every school in western civilization, promoted the adaptation of teaching styles to sensory-based student learning preferences. Researchers refer to these preferences as *modes of learning*. If a student said they felt they were a "visual learner," then we thought it benefitted that student to use visual teaching for any topic. This approach has been debunked as a myth not supported by research. Teaching styles should adapt to the type of material being taught, like using a diagram to show a complicated haul system. Using a few different modes may help clarify and reinforce material, but it is no longer accepted that students learn better if you use only their preferred senses for education. In 2008, the journal *Psychological Science in the Public Interest* published a special issue entitled "Learning styles: concepts and evidence" that effectively debunked the learning styles approach to education; their challenge for scientists to present data supporting the use of learning styles has so far gone unanswered.

## Teaching Styles

Some teachers like to engineer their instruction, planning out minutia in logical progressions. Others organize their classes around key experiences that connect with peoples' emotions. Some like the speedy delivery of a compact lecture with prepared graphs and drawings. Others like the inquiry method where students are led through the material via questions the students answer. But no matter the teaching style you choose for any one class, we plan classes at NOLS by starting with expected outcomes. Your teaching styles should reflect your strengths. If your students accomplish the expected outcomes in a reasonable time frame and at a high performance level, then the manner in which you got them there can be considered successful no matter what it was. The following teaching styles are all valid ways of presenting the topics on our instructional checklists.

### Role Modeling

Instructors are expected to model the school's values and expectations to their students. Emulation is a powerful method of learning. Students learn by watching us be good campers, safe climbers, effective leaders, positive expedition members, and skilled problem-solvers. But, they can also pick up bad habits from us. It is important, therefore, to keep in mind that you are always being watched, and to be aware of the impact of your actions. An instructor who denounces fishing as cruel influences his students' decisions about picking up a fly rod. Research on what learning transfers to life beyond NOLS has shown that instructor role modeling is an important factor in the learning that transfers. Students who transformed their standards for communication, respect for the earth, risk management, and how to camp in good style have stated that watching their instructors is what gave them a new vision for their own standards.

### Activities

Activities are the "do" aspect of learning. They are at the core of outdoor education. In the wilderness, you can have the students go out and observe the characteristics of trout habitat instead of studying it in a book.

Activities are most effective when they are pertinent. Examples of some you can use to enhance your teaching include natural history games, astro-bivies (sleeping out in a group to stargaze), river crossings, climbing, fishing, solos, accident scenarios, animal tracking, ecology walks, and campsite cleanups. It is also perfectly acceptable to have an activity just for the fun of it, like a course banquet, a costume party, a dance, a poetry recital, a Winter Olympics, or a card game. Fun is not only acceptable on NOLS expeditions, it is vital. Laughter by an entire group is often a sign of a highly functioning team.

Activities are also more effective when they engage the students. This is where giving students choices can help the expedition become more exciting and spirited. But be careful, when you completely hand decisions over to students, who are generally novices, you should expect them to make conservative choices that won't be as exciting. Even on NOLS instructor courses, the more we let students design the course, the less they meet their own expectations for challenges. The lesson here is that we need to give a range of choices but still be free with our own opinions on which opportunities will be more exciting. It is paramount that instructors make sure we have activities that engage the students in our curriculum. Avoid overcrowding a NOLS course, we achieve most of our expected student outcomes through typical wilderness expedition activities.

### Demonstration

Demonstrations should create lasting images of major points. Actually getting on a snow slope and doing a self-arrest is much more effective than describing the technique in a meadow back at camp. However, it is irresponsible to demonstrate what is easy instead of what is important. For instance, consider the implications of someone teaching their students how to lead a sport climb, but then neglecting to demonstrate how to lower off the route. Basic teaching relies on Dewey's discuss-demonstrate-do-reflect formula (explained earlier). A good demonstration helps students excel when it's their turn to do it.

## Teachable Moments

The best instructors have learned to capitalize on the teachable moment. Petzoldt advocated doing this by pointing things out along the trail. He budgeted half his travel time to hiking and the other half to teaching, resting, photography, and attending to personal needs.

Hiking past a creek teeming with fish or through a meadow full of tracks provides great opportunities to learn about animal habitat and behavior. Stopping to brew up a hot drink while on a cold wet hike is a perfect time to get in a discussion on comfort control. But, choosing the right moment is critical. If clouds have socked in the view, you may have to give up trying to teach map reading from what was a perfect ridgetop. Part of the effectiveness of the teachable moment is that it does not feel contrived. Be flexible and seize opportunities as they come up during your course.

If only part of the group was exposed to a teachable moment, they can share what was learned with the rest of the course at the next gathering. This displays that it is normal on an expedition for different people to have different experiences and then share the uniqueness of their personal experiences.

## Problem-based Learning

Problem-based learning helps students learn to apply skills and use their talents in synergy. For instance, you may have a stove that needs repairing; this is a great opportunity to teach stove repair and maintenance to the whole group. A good organizing tool is to have a flowchart showing how certain advanced skills are dependent on prior mastery of other fundamental skills. Problem-based learning helps students develop flexible knowledge, effective problem solving skills, self-directed learning, effective collaboration skills, and intrinsic motivation (Hmelo-Silver, 2004).

The effectiveness of this strategy is directly proportional to the importance of the problem to the students. If the "problem" is some contrivance you've invented (like a "new game"), you could probably only get them to actually follow through solving your problem on a nice day when life is easy and they're having fun. But if the problem is finding their re-ration site, or water in the desert, count on overflowing intrinsic motivation with little tolerance for slackers on the team. NOLS instructors are known for utilizing these naturally significant teaching opportunities to nurture students who go home both competent and self-aware.

Help students transfer this skill of facilitating problem-based learning by asking them how they can use this teaching technique with their friends back home.

## Scenario-based Learning

The scenario-based strategy is especially useful for practicing skills, because it practices both the skills and the context. It taps into the students' existing knowledge, bridging the new skills to more personal memory connections. It easily leads to higher thinking levels (see Bloom's taxonomy of thinking) since students are learning to apply knowledge and evaluate situations rather than just memorizing facts.

Scenario-based learning needs to have challenges that match the students' varied learning needs, and, as always, some students may perform at a much higher level than others: this isn't a caution to design training for your least common denominator, but rather a challenge to differentiate your training and let some students really excel.

In any scenario, remain honest with your students and never deceive them about fake accidents being real: your relationship with your students is more important than the adrenaline they would get from thinking your fake accident was actually real.

## Lectures

Formal lectures can range from a five-minute talk about beaver dams to an involved class on altitude illness. The shorter classes are designed to spark interest or just familiarize people with a topic, while longer lectures provide a more thorough working knowledge of a subject. Formal classes are the fastest way to pass on concentrated information, and it takes hard work to make them really effective. In the early years of NOLS, every instructor developed their own lesson plans, but with the development of the instructor notebook series (beginning with this book in 1990) instructors now take pride in great delivery of lesson plans developed by others.

New teachers can have a tendency to include too much information in their formal classes. Sticking to the basics is essential to success. If you get bogged down in details, you will lose your audience. Follow the saying: "Tell them what you're going to tell them, tell them, then tell them what you told them." The initial outline helps students mentally organize themselves. The conclusion reinforces key points.

Good lecturers engage students by eliciting emotion, giving students choices, connecting new knowledge to students' existing knowledge base, and helping make material relevant to those particular students (Jensen, 1998, p48).

## Inquiry

The inquiry teaching style has students apply their knowledge directly to new situations. For example, follow up your introduction to alpine ecology by having your students look at the tree line and then try to explain why it varies from one slope aspect to another. Or, after students have been introduced to protection placement, have them evaluate several pre-placed anchors and explain any changes they might make. Inquiry empowers students to be better thinkers, learners, and leaders. It hands responsibility over to them, and asks them to apply thinking skills at the next higher level (see Habits of Mind).

Inquiry can add depth to information. Instead of replying to a student question with, "Well, what do you think?" try asking, "What do you think and why?" When a student comes up to you a week into the course and asks you "How tightly should I lace my boots for today's hike?" ask her what she believes is important when lacing boots and if her response is reasonable, suggest she follow her own advice. Be sincere. Ask questions that review what the students have learned. Help them to trust their instincts. When possible, ask students to help answer questions you don't know the answer to—and be clear that you don't know. This can help reduce the suspicion that your questioning is designed around what you know that they don't know. Don't overdo it, since novices initially need quick answers to their basic questions: use inquiry for the next step when you are training them to think for themselves.

The inquiry method is a way of helping students recognize that they have the answers to many of their questions, but it takes time and may cause frustration, particularly when they lack prior experience or confidence. The technique is most effective well into the course after students have had time to accumulate enough knowledge to help find their own solutions. Remember, if you don't ask your students to explain the reasoning behind their answers, you do not challenge them to develop their judgment.

Educators who are black and white thinkers can have difficulty with the inquiry teaching method because of a tendency to focus on the single answer considered to be optimal: this can provide negative reinforcement to beginners. The inquiry method works best if the student is allowed to use any of the reasonable solutions they generate, rather than being expected to always make the choice the instructor thinks is optimal.

Use the inquiry method respectfully. If someone asks you where we are and you respond sharply with "Look at your map" you may be perceived as condescending. The point of the inquiry method is to train students in the mental pathways they need for making decisions. You should view yourself as a coach who helps the student use those pathways enough times that they eventually develop the habit for themselves.

## Briefing

Briefings communicate preparatory information and instructions to teams. In outdoor activities we usually use briefings immediately prior to an activity. Briefings can be used to help minimize stress by taking some of the unknowns out of a situation. During the first few days of your course, demonstrate thorough, open briefings prior to any hikes or activities. Later in the course, when students start hiking on their own, have the student leader brief their team before departing.

## Debriefing

Good judgment develops not just from lots of experience, but also from reflection on that experience. A focused debriefing seeks to identify new learning and reinforce the lessons gleaned from an event or activity experienced by a student or the group. A debriefing by a seasoned professional also adds invaluable mentorship that leverages the experiences. A debrief can also be used to diffuse tensions, raise issues, and encourage students to learn more from their own experiences. The power of an intense learning experience often fades if the students neglect to process their emotions—debriefings are designed to assist in that process.

As the debriefer, do not pass judgment on a student's feelings. Focus the discussion on specific aspects of the experience such as communication, leadership, and decision-making. Use debriefings to enhance the learning process. A good instructor goal is to identify three key points for debriefing activities.

Debriefings should have a purpose. You want students to look forward to debriefings, not dread them. Sometimes it is fine just to have a fun hike and then move on. Don't force feedback if there is nothing to discuss. On the other hand, if deep-seated issues arise, make sure you aren't discussing them when everyone is exhausted. Break for a meal, then reconvene. The NOLS Expedition Behavior (EB) standard is that issues should either be genuinely put behind us, or dealt with, but never left to fester.

One valuable tool you can give your students is a model of how to conduct a debriefing in a casual, sociable manner they can use with their peers back home. A simple model is the "What, so what, now what?" model where the leader asks what happened today, why we care about what happened, and how we can repeat successes and make improvements in the future. Another model is the plus/delta model (see inset). Develop these tools and learn how to apply them with finesse to varied contexts. Check out the *NOLS Leadership Educator Notebook* for more information on debriefing.

---

**Leader of the day debrief template**

1. Own it: apologize for errors you know you made

2. +/∆ Tasks: what went well?
   What can we improve the next time?

3. +/∆ Teamwork: what went well?
   What can we improve the next time?

4. Blue Sky: anything else to discuss?

5. What's next?

6. Thank you

---

*Give students a model for debiefing to help them practice the skill. The plus/delta, or rose and thorn, debriefing template shown here is simple and effective.*

## Story Telling

Brain research says that both telling and listening to stories are very effective learning techniques. Stories are automatically *dual-encoded*, which means they connect different types of synapses in our brain, both reinforcing concepts and applying multiple pathways towards retrieval of the ideas. It is as if through stories we vicariously experience both words and actions.

Students enjoy hearing about an instructor's experiences in moderation, but your stories need to be in good taste. The teller must be aware of the sensitivities of the audience. Stories illustrating a former student's mistakes should be educational, not demeaning, since negative descriptions of former students may make the present group apprehensive about making their own mistakes. Also be careful that your stories don't sound self-aggrandizing. Be sure your stories are clearly about important lessons, not about how great you are.

## Readings

Readings also make a fine addition to anecdotal teaching. The reading can be during the class, or, if you bring a few copies, have tent groups read them aloud at bedtime. Your selections should contain something you want the students to think about. A discussion following the reading can clarify the reason behind your choice of material.

Use of brief quotations can add clarity to an experience, especially if read while the feeling is still fresh. Like any tool, use quotes very carefully to match the situational need and keep the students hungry for more.

## Journals

Personal and group journals record the information, events, and reflections of one's journey through the wilderness. They can also be used as a tool for studying the natural environment. The success of journals depends on how they are presented and how well the instructors follow their progress. Suggested entries include class notes, sketches, species lists, poems, course songs, announcements of social functions, exploration of provocative questions, or natural history observations. It can be valuable to have instructors read journals to see what's on students' minds or to make an assessment. Be clear in advance if you plan to read student journals so students can separate their more private journal entries.

## Guided Discussions

Discussions are a highly transferable teaching skill, since students can do this with their peers at any time. A discussion can be formal and organized like a class, or can be done casually around the campfire about a real issue that needs discussing. A casual discussion can feel more comfortable for students who don't always open up during formal class time, and a casual style is more transferable for students to future social settings.

## Debates

Land management debates are a classic way to help students not only learn facts about specific issues but also learn compassion for both sides of important issues. Issues need to be local and current, and it is helpful to provide packets of information that fairly represent both sides of issues. Come up with a firm plan for how you will manage the debate, or you might never finish the discussion. One aspect of a good debate is getting some people to truly dig into a side they might not agree with, and represent it with passion, so everyone truly learns that side of the issue. Instructors can help students shed new light on the debate topic through questioning using the inquiry method.

## Games

Games can make learning situations fun, memorable, active, and help with group bonding. They can be organized activities, exercises, or explorations of the senses that are used to focus the group on a single concept or idea. A simple approach is to have the game be the primary lesson with a brief follow-up to make sure the students learned the concepts you planned. Games can also be used at the conclusion of a class as a wrap-up activity, but they must never compromise safety, the environment, or the equipment. It's perfectly acceptable to play a game just to have fun, too! A simple, ready-made game for reviewing ecology and land management is the "Wilderness Jeopardy" game described in the *NOLS Environmental Educator Notebook*.

Skill rodeos are good ways for students to practice, and for instructors to assess student competency. A series of stations set up might include: 1) start a stove, 2) tie a knot, 3) draw a simple topo map, 4) identify a plant, 5) identify scat, 6) coil a rope, etc. Make small placards with instructions so the third team gets the same instructions as the first team. Students do each task and rotate every few minutes. Instructors monitor the stations. Some NOLS winter courses have a "Winter Olympics" event with ski races, transceiver location races, and ski dancing competitions. Other winter courses have "better domes and gardens" contests based on snow shelter and kitchen construction. Transceiver orienteering is a game played in non-avalanche terrain where students leave a transceiver in the woods, mark an X on the map, then trade maps with another team, trying to locate each other's hidden transceiver. This uses both map reading and transceiver location skills.

# Teaching Tips

The following teaching tips come from a variety of sources, including senior NOLS instructors and professionals in the field of education. They represent proven methods for taking your classes from good to great.

## Themes and NOLS Priorities

Instructional themes provide a lattice that can be applied to a variety of discussions, activities, or instructional settings. When you mention the NOLS field priorities—safety of the individual, safety of the environment, and care of the equipment—in both your basic stove class and your "staying warm and dry" discussion, you are teaching with themes. Themes can be used to bring out similarities between subjects and to unify seemingly unrelated topics. Don't let yourself be intimidated by the 65 topics on the instructional checklist; look for themes to help present them in manageable chunks. Everything from low-impact camping to safety, judgment, and ecological concepts lends itself to this approach.

Themes can also be used to integrate information, emotion, and a variety of teaching techniques into a powerful educational experience. An astro-bivy provides a great opportunity to marvel at the immensity of the universe while sharing an experience that helps a student group bond. Combining first aid instruction with emergency procedures during a simulated accident gets students thinking on their feet and prepares them for traveling on their own. Including the importance of hydration and proper nutrition in a class on how to stay warm and dry helps reinforce critical themes. The use of themes helps students learn abstract concepts they can apply in their lives beyond NOLS.

## Signature Style

Petzoldt recommended using a factual, dignified manner coupled with a sense of humor when addressing a group of students, but you need to develop a style with which you are comfortable. A dramatic voice and vibrant presence may catch the students' attention but, if this isn't you, they will know. People are more likely to listen to a person being herself than they are to an uncomfortable mimic. This is called the *voice of authentic authority*. This is especially true for adult learners. Our actions and words as the teacher need to enhance trust with these learners. Have fun and make the learning fun, but be yourself.

Transfer your enthusiasm to the audience by using a calm, alert, and natural tone. If you don't feel calm, breathe deeply and see if you get calmer. Sitting like a sack of potatoes, fidgeting, or lecturing with your hands in your pockets conveys nervousness or disinterest. Avoid verbal and physical tics. Speaking in front of a group becomes more comfortable with practice. Educators typically adjust their teaching style depending on the cultural norms of the population they are addressing.

## Carpe Diem—Seize the Day

Don't forget to do the things most of us go to the wilderness to do, even if they are for pure enjoyment rather than to demonstrate some educational point. Excellent instruction supports those experiences at a higher level. Some defining experiences can be planned for, but others you need to be ready to take advantage of when opportunity knocks. Changing the plan to sit and enjoy a spectacular sunset, guiding your group up a 3rd class ascent on a beautiful day, or stopping the boats to sunbathe on a beautiful beach, are all things we dream of doing in the wilderness. Change your schedule occasionally to make these dreams into reality.

## Preparation

Do your homework. Expanding our knowledge base allows us to connect topics and explain key points. A teacher generally needs to know 5-10 times as much detail as is taught to be considered proficient enough to teach a topic. A professional is up-to-date and knows where to refer a student with questions she cannot answer. Many instructors choose one or two topics to research between courses, just to stay informed. New instructors should choose classes to teach in which they have extensive experience, then broaden their repertoire slowly and carefully. Borrow successful elements of classes from co-instructors. Old hands find that by the time they run out of new topics on the NOLS instructional checklist, they can find plenty of new information on the topics they researched in the past. Then, the most important notes you take are the field notes, reminding yourself of what worked well and what didn't.

*"To study the phenomena of disease without books is to sail an uncharted sea, while to study books without patients is not to go to sea at all."*
-William Osler, MD

## Accuracy

The material we teach to our students needs to be well referenced. We need to challenge each other on questionable information, and trade sources to routinely debunk myths. An example is watermelon snow. Many outdoorspeople think it is as poisonous as toxic mushrooms—some mushrooms can kill you in hours. In a quick Internet search, a strong reference can be found that addresses this question and debunks this myth. In reality, if consumed in extremely large quantities, some of the 60 species of watermelon snow can cause diarrhea (Duval, 2000). Big deal. This is a clear case where an interesting factoid slowly became elevated to an important issue. This pattern of teaching interesting trivia, then having that information get mistakenly reprioritized as important is common. Interesting factoids may help us engage our students, but we should be careful about clarifying their significance.

The creation of student handouts on topics of interest can help our staff not only trade notes on interesting topics, but also offer better opportunities for peer review and advance our collective state of knowledge. When creating handouts, please add your name and the date, and cite some references for folks who either want to dig deeper or clarify some points. A simple reference style is to cite books (Petzoldt, 1975, p42) with or without page numbers, right in your text, then at the end in a list by author, title, and year.

## Classroom Setting

Constant evaluation of your classroom is essential in the outdoors. Be aware of conditions that may jeopardize safety and comfort. Ask yourself, "Can I manage my students in this environment safely?" If the answer is "no" or "maybe not" then modify the activity or change the location. By explaining your decision, you can further your students' education. In addition, an instructor must assess whether the students' physical comfort is affecting their ability to learn. Difficult weather, loud noise, other people, intense sunlight, wind, and exposure are distracting and should be minimized in order to maximize your audience's comprehension.

## Learning Progressions

The conscious sequencing of instruction is a learned art. For example, when teaching how to build a Tyrolean traverse, students are best able to focus when they have been instructed about pulleys, rope throwing, and basic anchor techniques beforehand. Students need careful progressions with mastery of each step along the way to truly master skills and achieve a state of flow in an activity.

In order to develop an effective teaching progression, ask yourself these questions: "What do the students need to know next in order to face the challenges ahead? How will I assess competence at each stage, before moving to the next step? Do I have enough time planned for mastery or will this just be an exposure with no expectation of competence?" Choosing activities and instruction that match the abilities and interests of your group can be challenging, but your students will learn more quickly and with less stress if you do not overwhelm them with information too early in the course. You can learn a great deal about when and where to teach different topics by watching other instructors who excel at education.

## Instructional Scaffolding

Scaffolding is a broad instructional strategy based on Lev Vygotsky's *Zone of Proximal Development*. The ZPD is the edge between the student's current expertise and the next higher thing they can do with good coaching from an expert. You start with giving people all of the support (the scaffold) they need to do a basic task, then as they develop you provide less and less direction, pulling away the scaffolding. After they hone their expertise at that level through repetition, you provide new scaffolding to help them perform at even higher levels. A simple example is pack-packing: on day one we tend to model exactly what we want and direct students to do things exactly as we tell them to. The first time they pack a pack they just want to be told what to do. Later, after they have packed their pack a few times, and they have the challenge of packing the new food ration in their pack, we usually ask them to apply general concepts to pack-packing rather than telling them specifics like where to pack the cheese. The point is to keep raising higher levels of scaffolding. This is especially important on semester-long programs.

## Brevity

Paul Petzoldt advocated brevity and exactness for effective outdoor teaching. Keep this in mind when preparing your lectures. Formal classes work best when they are an appropriate length and to the point. Time saved with precise instruction can be put towards activities, socializing, or enjoying the wilderness—all important components of a NOLS education. Brevity takes more work, skill, and practice than loquaciousness. Experienced instructors tend to whittle down and refine their classes over time, looking for ways to better emphasize the take away points.

## Keep it Simple

The expression, "Keep it simple, silly" (KISS) reminds us that effective instruction usually does not require complex explanations or fancy demonstrations.

## Visual Aids

Visual aids can be drawn on a sand bar, your body, a small whiteboard, or a sleeping pad. They can also be a natural feature such as an alpine cirque that helps to illustrate a glaciology class. A good visual aid leaves a strong image and reinforces the topic of discussion. A bad one is boring, distracting, messy, or too noisy. In order to ensure that your prop enhances rather than detracts from your class, make sure it is visible to everyone, and use simple, precise illustrations. Artistic ability helps, but it is not as important as clarity. If your presentation lacks substance, even the best visual aid is not going to save it.

Some examples of effective visual aids include using blowup globes to teach weather patterns, using a climbing rope to illustrate a geologic timeline, or drawing bones and tendons on your knee. Use colors for greater impact. A 25-point outline written on your sleeping pad is probably not going to have the same kind of impact that flashier graphics will. Detailed notes are best passed to students as handouts. If you want to give a strong presentation, try to weave the visuals in with the rest of the material rather than give out all the eye-catching props at once.

## Handouts

Give students outlines of important information so they aren't distracted by having to take notes. Handouts also guarantee the accuracy and completeness of students' notes. This allows them to participate in more discussions that apply the material. You can also use reprints of articles (one per tent group) to be read the evening before your presentation.

Handouts like the pamphlet "Leadership At NOLS" work best if you train people to use them by referring back to them when debriefing leader of the day activities. Novices crave basic information, and handouts help them master the basics sooner so they can advance to higher thinking levels more quickly. Handouts also provoke dialogue among colleagues about what content to include.

## Guest Speakers

Have an outside expert talk to your course. In the backcountry, this is often a backcountry ranger or a horsepacker. For a virtual guest, use a costumed instructor. Ask the guest to speak on a subject of interest to the students and pertinent to the course. Most students appreciate hearing a new perspective. They also tend to enjoy hearing about other outdoor professions, local history, and land management issues. If the speaker is unfamiliar with NOLS, prepare them by explaining who we are and what the course has been doing.

## Variety is Important

One trap for educators is always doing the same thing, employing the same "best" method, for every topic. We need to develop a variety of teaching styles to create enjoyable learning experiences that keep students hungry for more. We used to think that specific students each learned better if we employed that student's preferred sensory-based teaching style, but that strategy has been debunked. Certain teaching styles definitely align with certain types of information, but research does not support that some people are kinesthetic learners and some are auditory learners. In general, teach music with auditory; teach physical education with kinesthetic; teach cooking with taste and smell. Mix it up to make it interesting as long as you apply common sense—avoid trying to use music to teach cooking skills.

## Be Creative

Creativity in teaching can be helpful. But creativity is not inherently good. Creative development of a new method for teaching a topic is risky. Sometimes this leads to exceptional advances, but it may also be less effective for your

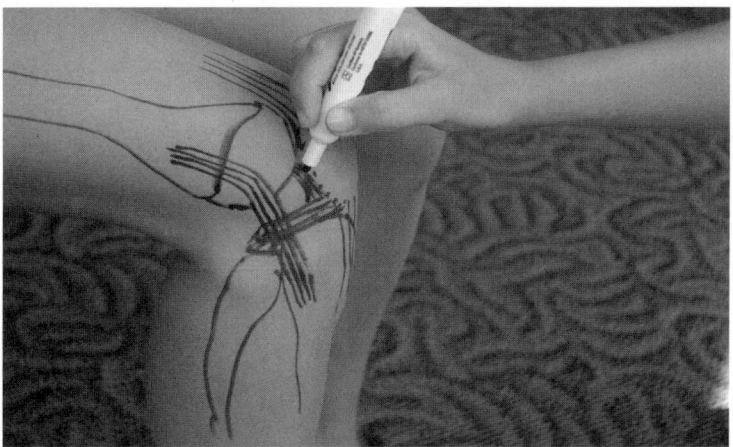

*Drawing a meniscus, ligaments, and tendons on a live model is a great example of how a visual aid can help students understand how to avoid athletic injuries via careful trail techniques.*

students compared to taking a tried and true method and creatively adapting it to the specific situation and, most importantly, to those specific students. An excellent "bad" example of creative teaching is miming a first aid topic that then needs to be re-taught. An excellent "good" example is whoever first drew color-coded muscles, bones, ligaments, and tendons on their knee to support the teaching of prevention, assessment, and diagnosis of athletic injuries.

## Feedback

Feedback is a gift. Constructive feedback enables people to acknowledge their accomplishments and make improvements. Feedback is essential to the learning process and is most effective when it is immediate, specific, growth-oriented, tactful, and shows a cause-and-effect relationship (See the *NOLS Leadership Educator Notebook* for more details on feedback).

## Teaching Chapter Summary

Competency, discipline, and positive energy in our teaching are essential for developing the fundamental skills, knowledge, and attitudes our students need to excel at the activities on NOLS expeditions, and to transfer that learning to their lives after NOLS. Excellence in our teaching habits sets the stage for quality education for each individual, as described in the next chapter.

## Chapter Two References

- Csikszentmihalyi, Mihaly (1990) Flow: the psychology of optimal experience. Harper & Row.
- Dewey, John (1983) Experience and Education. Collier Books.
- Gardner, Howard (1991) "The tensions between education and development". Journal Of Moral Education, 20 (2).
- Hmelo-Silver, Cindy E. (2004) "Problem-Based Learning: What and How Do Students Learn?". Educational Psychology Review 16 (3): 235.
- Jackon Susan & Csikszentmihalyi Mihaly (1999) Flow In Sports. Human Kinetics Press.
- Jensen, Eric (1998) Teaching With The Brain In Mind. ASCD.
- Kinsley, Carol & McPherson, Kate (1995) Enriching Curriculum Through Service Learning. ASCD.
- Knapp, Clifford (1993) Lasting Lessons: a teacher's guide to reflecting on experience. ERIC.
- Markova, Dawna PhD (1996) The Open Mind: exploring the six patterns of natural intelligence. Conari.
- Maslow, Abraham (1968) Toward a Psychology of Being. D. Van Nostrand Company.
- Myers, Thomas, MD (2001) Over The Edge: Death in the Grand Canyon. Puma Press
- Sibthorp, J., Collins, R., Rathunde, K., Paisley, K., Pohja, M., Gookin, J., & Baynes, S. (2014) Fostering Experiential Self-Regulation Through Outdoor Adventure Education. Journal of Experiential Education.
- Stronge, James (2002) Qualities Of Effective Teachers. ASCD.

# Chapter Three
# Personalizing Education

Excellent education includes the teaching of a technical core curriculum, personalized education that addresses each individual, and holistic education that addresses non-academic aspects of education. These educational processes are meant to work synergistically. Personalized education strategies work hand in hand with technical education and holistic education strategies.

## Excellent Education is Personalized

Each student constructs their own meaning out of any experience. This personalized meaning is based on their own existing knowledge, past experiences, and even genetics. This "constructive" approach to education means two things for educators:

1) If you need every student to perform specific skills (like Leave No Trace camping skills), it will take a variety of teaching strategies combined with plenty of reinforcement to help different folks develop the same skills, knowledge, and attitudes (values) you want them to acquire.
2) There are important lessons being learned that go well beyond the technical core of the course, but these invaluable lessons are different for each person. Look for opportunities to help students see what they've learned in the bigger picture of their own education. This can help improve their aptitude or learning skills.

## Developmental Psychology

We should generally expect our students to act their ages. It helps educators to understand the general patterns of human development over the lifespan, so we don't look at our students as being "broken" when they might just be acting their age.

There are several models for human development; Erikson's *Stages of Psychosocial Development* provides a solid foundation. Another developmental system that is specifically relevant to teaching situational judgment is the problem solving stages described by Kitchener and King (1990). Two other models are the stages of moral development and Vigotsky's *Zone of Proximal Development*.

### Erikson's Stages of Psychosocial Development

Erik Erikson (1982) developed a system that describes a general pattern of human development from birth to death. The stages are rough estimates because people develop differently. Each stage has a dilemma where tension develops between the old and new norms: failure to follow a developmental norm is sometimes problematic and sometimes leads down a different path.

Use this model carefully because all of these developmental models are generalizations about what "normal" development is. Our intent in providing these models is to help educators determine the developmentally appropriate needs of their students.

**Elementary school years** (~ages 5-12): This is when children start to develop competence. They develop special talents that help define them as unique individuals. Eventually, they learn to apply space and time concepts in practical ways. They develop morals and may rebel against authority. They are typically concerned about fitting in socially.

**Adolescence** (~ages 13-19): Development is now intrinsic rather than from extrinsic forces, that is, they are more self-actualized. They are concerned with appearance to others. They become devoted to causes and friends. They tinker with trying different roles, and this identity crisis helps develop a stronger identity. There is tension between societal expectations and self-actualization. They develop a sexual identity during this stage.

**Young Adulthood** (~ages 20-39): This is when people typically transition from schooling under the care of their parents to independent living and careers. Many young adults begin long-term intimate relationships, while others remain independent.

**Middle Adulthood** (~ages 40-64): This is a period of generativity—they do things to make the world a better place. Some middle adults have a new identity crisis, perhaps after their kids grow up or after reflecting on their careers, and rethink what they want to do with their lives (see Mezirow, 2000).

**Late Adulthood** (~age 65-death): There is retrospection on the value of their life that leads to fulfillment or despair.

## Signature Style: Part of the NOLS Leadership Education Model

NOLS teaches leadership using a model of four leadership roles, seven leadership skills, and the one signature style that each individual develops to be an effective leader. Helping students find their personal style is a critical part of this education. Command of this signature style is just as important for NOLS course leaders as it is for NOLS students. Helping students to discover and make the most of their own signature style is a simple example of personalizing education to meet the specific needs of each student (See the *NOLS Leadership Educator Notebook* for more information about the NOLS leadership model).

## Teaching to the Material

Educational theorists promote teaching styles that match the topics being taught. They discovered this when teachers were randomly assigned specific teaching styles for topics being taught to groups of students with different preferred learning styles—they found that no sub-group of students benefitted more than the others from any single style, but certain styles showed greater comprehension in everyone depending on what topic was being taught. Use numbers and logic to teach math. Use poetry to teach English literature. Use role playing to teach debate tactics. If you want someone to develop muscle memory they can perform in a crisis, forget using a rap to teach it. Instead practice, practice, practice.

## Advancement and Enrichment

We should be just as careful to adapt to the needs of our gifted students as we are to students with other special needs. Advancement and enrichment are two teaching strategies enjoyed by a spectrum of students.

**Advancement** refers to teaching the same curriculum but letting the more advanced students move ahead more quickly than the other students. A simple example is teaching climbing on an instructor course, where the experienced lead climbers move through the typical climbing progression but at a faster rate. We need to be careful to assess performance just as carefully as with other students before allowing these more experienced students to advance to higher levels. This is called *objective based performance* because the students need to meet a specific performance standard before progressing to the next step. We also still need to provide careful coaching for advanced students or they will assume that our silence is affirmation of what they are doing.

**Enrichment** refers to the addition of higher thinking levels to the same curriculum. A simple example of enrichment is helping students understand the principles of LNT, rather than them just obeying our initial rules as we camp and travel. This enriches the curriculum for all of our students by teaching the overlying concepts. A student who learns to critique the telemark turn of other skiers is learning an enriched curriculum, especially if they are melding those talents with the social skills to give feedback to peers in an unobtrusive manner.

If you offer an enriched curriculum to some students, it doesn't have to be a formal process where others might feel left out. It can take the form of casual discussions where you talk about course activities at higher thinking levels.

The habits of mind information in this book offers a simple framework for enriching curriculum. A more thorough model for enriching curriculum is called "Bloom's Taxonomy of Educational Objectives" (See next page) (Davis & Rimm, 1989). This takes the same general objective and dials the level of competency up or down based on what the students can handle.

## Reaching Adolescent Learners

Adolescence, roughly defined as the stage of life that begins with puberty and ends with adulthood, is a period of profound change. This age heralds a major shift in thought process and the discovery and acceptance of the defining characteristics of the self. Adolescents learn differently from adults. We routinely deal with adolescents on Adventure courses and Wilderness courses. Adventure courses have the reputation of being both the most difficult and the most rewarding courses that NOLS offers. Recognition of the different needs of adolescent learners can open the door to success with both Adventure and young Wilderness students.

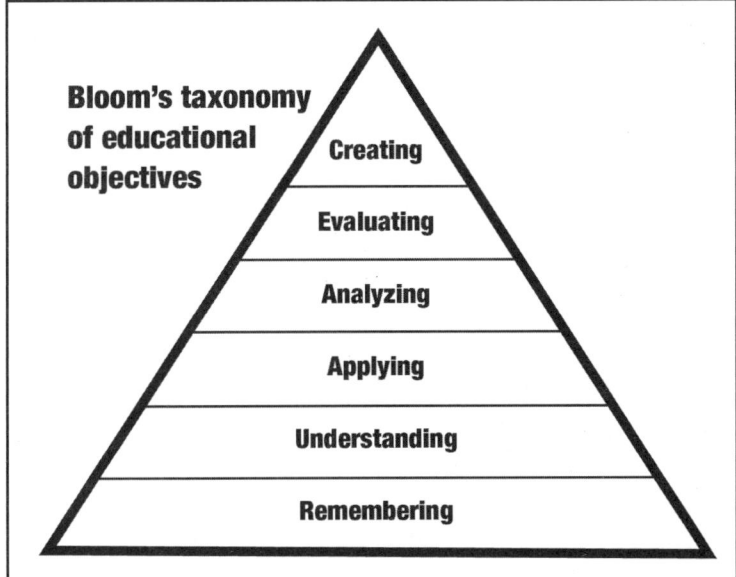

*To attain higher levels of learning our students must first master the prerequisite skills and knowledge.*

Some instructors get frustrated because they want adolescent students to act like adults. It is important to let adolescents be themselves. They can be as zany and juvenile as they want. They are likely to talk about movies or video games, which is perfectly acceptable as long as it falls within a positive learning environment. Don't let it bother you that they're acting like teenagers—they are teenagers.

### Physiological Changes

Between the ages of twelve and seventeen, humans can grow more than five inches in one year. Much of this growth occurs in "spurts" during which adolescent bodies receive massive infusions of hormones. The tremendous adolescent growth rate prompts students to eat a disproportionate amount of food for their weight. Excess hormones and nutritional sugars manifest themselves in the infamous short attention span of teenagers as well as in their seemingly endless stores of energy, wild mood swings, aggressive behavior, and a tendency toward low self esteem.

Deemphasizing physical and athletic issues can help reduce stress and decrease negative self-esteem. Reinforcing the power of positive attitudes, resiliency, and tolerance for adversity can aid in the development of a healthy sense of self. Instructors should strive to build rapport and make connections with students, complete with plenty of positive reinforcement. Teaching nutrition and talking about how to fuel your body with field rations can help with students' concerns about body image and problematic relationships with food. Students are often capable of more than they expect. Keep them happy and well fed and they will exceed expectations—yours and their own.

### Basic Needs (Maslow, 1976)

Most adolescents have had their basic needs fulfilled by others to this point. A NOLS course is likely to be the first time that they are responsible for providing for their own food, water, and shelter. This can create anxiety. It is critical for our students to feel safe and secure with these basic needs so they can move forward to take care of their next layer of needs, which include physical comfort and hygiene. Physical comfort and hygiene can be a lower priority than basic physiological needs in the minds of adolescent students. Food stress runs rampant on Adventure courses, as do sleepless nights due to fears of collapsing shelters. It is important to discuss the difference between fear and danger.

Instructor teams can counteract this stress and anxiety by making the basics a priority. Each tent group should be able to cook a tasty meal safely, erect a stormproof shelter, and sleep warm within the first few days of the course. Some instructors use sleepovers during the first two or three nights of the course to comfort students who are anxious and to ensure that students can reliably perform basic tasks on their own. Group kitchens, where instructors can provide hands-on coaching and mentoring, are strongly encouraged on these courses.

### Need for Structure

Adolescent students often come from an environment where every minute is planned for them. The typical American secondary school is based on heavily structured institutional learning models. Students are accustomed to learning in a structured environment. They are used to a lot of rules and few guidelines. They expect structure and need it in order to succeed. A typical NOLS course is incredibly loose in comparison to middle school. This lack of certainty can cause anxiety in adolescents that may hinder learning.

Many of our teenage students are black and white thinkers who have simplistic views of their worlds. Biologically, they are more comfortable in a simpler and more structured world.

Emphasis on timeliness, focus, and behavior can provide the structure that adolescent students prefer. You want the students to be on time. When they are in a class or activity, you want them focused. Classes should be of appropriate length, to the point, and active. Establish a positive learning environment early on in order to prioritize emotional safety. Make your behavioral expectations abundantly clear, and allow the students to express their own expectations. When students violate established behavioral expectations, your responses should be swift and feel more like natural consequences than retribution. Help them to see that the natural consequence of any transgression is less free time and less privilege (See bullying in Chapter Thirteen for more details).

A full schedule usually works best with these students. Three to four day small group expeditions with instructors have proven helpful in providing structure at the beginning of the course. Instructor sleepovers occasionally get used the first night when a student is scared of camping outside. Visual representations of the course progression help students understand the steps toward independence. As students become more comfortable with fulfilling their basic needs (cooking, staying warm and comfortable) they will have more success with planning and self-direction. You can almost build your course progression directly off of Maslow's hierarchy of needs (See Chapter Two).

Excessive free time can be detrimental to student success on adolescent courses. Activity is essential. Structure does not imply students sitting and listening to class after class, but rather spontaneous top-roping, fishing, peak ascents, and early morning elk stalks. Providing structure and parameters to free time is helpful for students: "Right now you have one hour of free time during which you can choose to do the following…" It is critical that we do the fun stuff with young people; it is also critical that we build connections and establish positive rapport early on.

### Cognitive Transition (Piaget, 1995)

Cognitively, adolescent students are moving away from the *concrete operational* stage (late childhood), where students learn best by using hands-on activities and role playing in order to comprehend abstract or hypothetical ideas. Fourteen and fifteen year old students move sporadically in and out of the next *formal operational* stage of development. Students in this stage are beginning to develop the capacity for self-reflection and hypothetical thought.

Instructors often report vast differences in individual cognitive ability within a student group because of this transition. By combining one on one coaching and hands-on teaching techniques with reflective exercises, instructors can take advantage of the shift in thought process. Games and initiatives can have a greater impact in the leadership curriculum than sit-down classes and discussions. Students should be encouraged to reflect often and in a variety of ways. Debriefs, self and peer evaluations, journaling, and frequent check-ins can help students progress to a greater self understanding and allow them to exercise their newly acquired reflective abilities. Reflecting will help them start to find their own identity, and learning the importance of reflection and how to do it will help them continue down the path to greater lifelong self-awareness.

Most students this age are used to receiving non-specific feedback. Instructors who make conscious use of specific feedback, both specific positive and specific constructive, can have a greater impact on their students' reflective processes and identity formation. As with any student, giving plenty of positive feedback builds the rapport necessary to convey constructive feedback.

Adolescents search for boundaries because they have a new and untried perception of what is possible. Firm structure and honest, timely feedback can help these students to stay grounded and maintain focus.

### Adolescent Identity Crisis (Erikson, 1970)

One of the defining characteristics of the teen experience is the search for a personal identity. Students are making a conscious attempt to understand who they are and who they should be. The search for identity involves trying new behaviors and activities that may have been unimaginable to the student a year before.

A NOLS course offers students a panoply of new experiences. This is perhaps the school's greatest value to adolescent students. Technical skills and environmental studies classes should be a general sampling of many topics so that students can experience a myriad of new activities that have the potential to become passions, and so influence the formation of their identity. If students show a strong interest in an area, allow them the individual freedom to explore it further. They might even need staff encouragement to feel they have permission to excel at some aspects of NOLS more than others. In light of the adolescent's search for personal identity, a focus within the leadership curriculum of an Adventure course toward self-awareness can produce significant positive changes in the individual.

It can be very difficult for an adolescent to gain perspective on larger social issues because they are so focused on themselves. Instructors can help adolescent students having a hard time within the social group by providing both copious positive feedback and an unconditional positive regard (Evans, 1975). An instructor exhibits unconditional positive regard toward her students simply by being aware of each student's value and letting the students know that she recognizes and appreciates this value. She is truthful about student shortcomings without being negative. This attitude can bolster the learner's esteem while providing the critical feedback crucial to accurate self-perception.

## Education in the Stages of Adulthood

Educator Malcolm Knowles (Knowles, 1970) used Piaget's and Erikson's work to study the unique needs of adult learners. Adults have life experience sufficient to make their whole personal foundation more solid and more individualized. They bring this experience with them on a course and construct new meaning around it. They also add their experience to any learning community they join (See Chapter Four for more detail).

As individuals mature into adulthood:
- They need to be less dependent on others.
- Their experience base gives more meaning and context to what they learn.
- They become more concerned with social roles.
- They want to apply new knowledge immediately.
- Rather than just learning information, they want to learn how to use that information to solve problems.

A critical factor for educators who work with adults is the concept of trust. Trust is important with all students, but adult students don't inherently trust their teachers like younger students often do. We must ensure that our actions, words, and classes develop and bolster our students' trust in us as educators. This includes making their education relevant. More independent students like responsibility, but adults are wary of doing menial tasks that are labeled "leadership." We support their independence and their experience base when we connect our curriculum to them as individuals. In addition, we support all people better by treating them as individuals first, rather than strictly adhering to a teaching guide. Adults like to be involved in decision-making and group planning, such as discussing the pace of the course. In more technical situations, many adults prefer 1:1 coaching. They often enjoy structure, but they also like to be able to explore new activities and experiences freely.

Just because they are independent people doesn't necessarily mean they like to be alone. Many adults actually prefer to spend time in groups, whether socially or at work. This makes cooperative and collaborative education popular with this crowd, making it easier to create a highly functioning learning community with adults. But don't waste their time by asking them to use "teamwork" to do a task more easily done by one person.

Social roles are established through formal and informal development of social structure within the course. We need to be bold when we describe what expedition behavior (EB) means at NOLS and what our expectations are; these pro-social values are a key part of who we are at NOLS. Our concerns for a positive learning environment are just as valid on a course with adults as with adolescents. Adults are generally discrete about establishing pecking orders and other social rankings on conscious or subconscious levels. Be certain that everyone feels validated. Make sure that every leader of the day is respected as a person and as the group's leader while in that designated role. Esteem is preserved carefully by adults by taking fewer risks, whether it is on a top-rope or cooking a meal. Capitalize on this reticence by helping students see how mastering preparatory skills will help them in their new roles as leader of the day.

The best way to help people envision how to apply knowledge to future problems is to start asking them regularly how they may use the course information in the future. This visioning process is an important part of transfer of learning. Adults typically come to NOLS with some specific goals; help them develop an action plan to reach those goals during the course.

### Bodies Get Old

Generally, the older people are, the less physically conditioned they are. Their cartilage erodes so they are less resilient. Eventually, some body functions are harder to control. They may need more rests, or slower paces. They may need to spend more time staying clean and will need information on bathing and washing socks, as well as t-shirts and the time to do it. The good news is that they won't let you drag them along faster than their optimal speed.

## Working with Students from Backgrounds Underrepresented at NOLS

Remember your first few days in a new organization or with a new group on an expedition? How often were you bewildered because you didn't understand the context from which people spoke or acted? To an extent, all of our students are entering a new culture: the NOLS expedition culture. But for our students from underserved communities whose culture, ethnic and racial identity, and socioeconomic status are underrepresented at NOLS, NOLS can feel like the moon, and for some, like Mars. It is for these students that providing a positive learning environment can be the most challenging and is the most essential.

If you have ever experienced gender dissonance (i.e., you think you are not understood by the opposite gender or don't hold a similar value and way of doing something), then multiply that feeling many times more and you begin to understand what someone from a nondominant culture can feel when stepping into a NOLS course. Our personalities play a huge role in how we view newness, and it matters greatly whether or not a person has a lot of inter-cultural experience. It can be exhilarating or it can be alienating. Usually, it is a complex mixture of both. The beginning is the most challenging.

In a multicultural situation, you may agree whole-heartedly with the other culture's way of seeing the world, or you may be forced to assimilate in order to survive. This usually creates tensions. More likely, and hopefully, when you understand another's context and they understand yours, you begin to feel the immense power and creativity of cross-cultural teams and relationships. In the end, truly successful groups create a common context—a new shared culture that incorporates the strengths of all its members. To do this, everyone changes in some way to meet the common goal while also maintaining their individuality.

### Signs of Cultural Dissonance
- Feelings of isolation due to culture, language, or stories told by other students.
- Frustration from feelings of not being understood.
- Frustration surrounding relationship with wilderness and the outdoors being different from others.
- Boredom and discomfort with upper middle class & white North American youth conversation.
- Discomfort with other students' wealth or lack of it.
- Perceptions by other students of getting a "free ride" scholarship.
- Perceiving other students from more affluent backgrounds as spoiled or uninformed.
- Tension due to attitudes and discussions that relate to socially disadvantaged people.
- Perceptions of any culture that deviates from the norm of the course as a personality flaw.
- Socially ill at ease or inappropriate when trying to fit in.
- Not understanding NOLS' positive learning expectations right away.
- Hesitant to engage with others.
- When any mistakes are made, getting embarrassed, then withdrawing.
- Large stress load from being in a new culture, a minority, and in the wilderness.

**Tools for Student Success**

Keep in mind two goals for all students:
1) The ability to function well on their NOLS course.
2) The ability to transfer what they learned to their home community.

Approach students as individuals, not as representatives of their cultural group. Be aware that some students may have to make more of a cultural leap than others do into our NOLS world. Try to personally greet students when they first arrive. An early one-to-one connection eases folks into a new environment. Do what you can beforehand to learn about each student's home area, culture, or organization. Even a little knowledge can spark a connection and give a warm welcome.

Make expectations clear with examples of, "and this is what that looks like…" Our number one request from students from underserved communities underrepresented at NOLS is: "Help me know what is expected of me here. Tell me more than once if necessary".

In the beginning, beware of asking students to define course expectations themselves (stating "This is your course" too early). This style of education can be empowering, but it can also be profoundly alien and alienating for students who have no idea of the parameters.

Early on, explain that you all come from different backgrounds and that you will work together to form a strong expedition culture that will be unique. Get each student's input on what this should look like. It helps brand new campers to hear that even though there may be large differences in outdoor experience, that is fine and the gaps will close. It is also helpful to discuss what brand new campers bring to a group—wonderment, a different perspective. From a student:

*"I didn't feel separate because I was African American—it was because I had never done anything in the outdoors before and they all had."*

In the first week of your course, pay particular attention for signs of loneliness in your students from diverse cultures. From one student:

*"I really just wanted someone to talk to who understood where I was coming from."*

Some students have expressed later that they wanted to leave the course during this time—but were glad they stayed on.

Small talk isn't small. It's a vital way to build rapport, loyalty, and trust in a group. In the beginning of a course, try to avoid getting in a pattern of all business and task. Make time to speak informally with each student, and find out what they like to talk about. Notice with whom your students from non-dominant cultures interact early on. Support naturally forming bonds and relationships. In the first ration period, consider putting students from the same culture or sponsoring organization together in a larger cook group. Afterward, as they feel more comfortable within the course community, splitting them up may help make the group more cohesive.

If dominant culture consistently pervades the student discussions (e.g., TV shows, music, travel, pop culture etc.) and appears to be unfamiliar to some students, broaden the discussion. Foster a climate that values all differences and similarities. Do "cultural nuggets" where each student talks about their home area, way of life, and environment (without putting students "on the spot"). Role-model a desire to learn from others.

If you haven't already, broaden your scope on all courses to include multiculturalism. Include cultural curriculum on the people who inhabit(ed) the course area, consider tweaking curriculum such as the Leave No Trace principles to be more culturally relevant, use both feet and meters in describing distances when individuals from outside the USA are present, use leadership examples from many different ethnic groups, read stories from a variety of cultures, etc.

We encourage you to create a mentor program for all students. A mentor is essential for a student making a large cultural leap. Maintain high standards for all students, but realize that some students are dealing with many new situations, not just the wilderness. For those having difficulty, give extra help and coaching. As with all students, use positive reinforcement liberally and give focused, behavior-specific feedback. From a student regarding an instructor:

*"He did something for me that made the trip everything it was. He set such a high standard to be reached. I was never made to feel that I couldn't compete to be good at this."*

Check in early on real and perceived risks: "Because the wilderness was new to me it was very important that I felt safe and knew I could stay healthy."

Don't worry about making mistakes or saying the wrong thing or making a cultural faux pas—warm, well-intended effort works! Good teachers reach students across cultures because they care about the students.

**If Issues Arise**

Multiculturalism on courses is a wonderful opportunity for everyone. It may not always be easy or straightforward, but neither are many valuable educational experiences. Encourage individuals to talk about their companions' backgrounds rather than treating it as taboo subject.

Cultural issues may arise. Deal with any clear-cut case of inappropriate behavior (e.g., a blatant racist comment, gay bashing, or religious bashing) directly and swiftly. The 80/20 rule states that you can assume that 20% or less of the problem is personal (the result of what individuals consciously intended to say to one another) and 80% is rooted in the cross-cultural gap (values, interpretation, lack of understanding of expectations, etc.). We rarely deal with blatant cultural bias, but we routinely deal with slights we refer to as microaggressions.

Don't assume: "It wasn't racism," "It wasn't sexism," "It wasn't homophobia," etc. You are not in that person's shoes. They are "experts" of their own history and experiences and you have much to learn from that. That doesn't mean you can't also have them explore alternative ways of viewing a situation if you think that is appropriate.

If a problem does arise, first get the facts and stories. Listen non-judgmentally. Consider asking the participants some form of these questions:
- How does this incident relate to other experiences you have had either in this group or with others?
- What cultural differences and values surface as a result of this issue?
- What are possible alternative interpretations (of what she/he said, did, or what you meant, etc.)
- How would you like that person (or the group) to respond to you?
- What do they need to know about you or your experience that may help improve the situation?

Even if something is a cultural norm elsewhere (e.g., swearing), that doesn't mean it has to be part of the expedition culture. Give reminders early on to help move all students towards the expedition culture. The avoidance of certain language can also be framed as being part of leadership school. It is a skill that needs practice. Leaders are in the business of appealing to a broad audience. People judge them by their words. Remember that a leader can't just speak one way in front of the group, and another while "off-duty." It will be noticed.

# English Language Learners (ELL)

### Signs of Language Barriers
- Lack of information because of not understanding directions; you or they may think they understand when they don't.
- Made fun of because of English pronunciation or needing a translation.
- May be perceived as lazy or uninvolved as a result of not understanding directions or needing more time to process directions.
- Personality differences perceived when really it is lack of language.
- Stressed from not understanding.
- Subtleties of language missed (i.e., only able to express "I'm mad at you" without being able to explain why), idioms.
- May come across as very direct or rude due to lack of language ability.
- May need to have directions or information repeated.

### Tools for Student Success

Each branch decides what level of a language (English, Spanish, Hindi, Swahili, etc.) a student needs to enroll on a particular course. There are written guidelines for English competency standards for instructor courses.

Acknowledge that understanding directions, discussions, and complex classes will be more demanding for ELL students. The group as a whole can help. Have someone sit beside the ELL student to help coach them to understanding. Coaches should sit and/or talk in a way so as not to distract others. During formal classes, an instructor is a better choice for a coach/translator. Informally and during group activities, students are great coaches. Remember that it is this surrogate translator's course too. If the coaching position is rotated, this support technique is often quite a bonding experience for the group.

Take more than one dictionary on the course. The ELL student should have one and everyone else can share.

Write directions down. Illustrate. Bring a little whiteboard.

Work with the student to make a list of often-used words, especially technical terms that they may not have encountered elsewhere.

Avoid the use of North American-centric jargon. Also avoid sarcasm or explain it when you are employing sarcasm, as it is often interpreted literally by ELL students.

Do not punish students for using their native language when English is not expressly required. While consistently talking in another language in front of others can be exclusionary, understand that their heads will be hurting after a whole day of English. Let it be okay for them to converse in their language when it won't negatively affect learning or the group.

Remember that all students like to be in on decision-making. Be sure that the ELL student understands the issues at hand and has a chance to participate in decisions as much as other students.

Help other students communicate better with folks who speak English as a second language. Point out when they talk too quickly, give too much information, and use jargon, acronyms or slang. Set everyone up for success early in the course by showing how speaking a little slower than normal (not louder) can really help comprehension. Beware—we tend to be inconsistent and often harder evaluators of people with heavy accents, especially those we have a hard time understanding. Humor is also different around the world. Pre-test humor. If someone is offended (or you are offended) approach it as a learning experience. Expect delayed reactions. Expect occasional miscommunications, and more when people are tired. Develop the habit of having them paraphrase key messages. You don't have to learn an entire language to show respect: routine use of a couple common greetings, humility about your own lack of command of their language, and clearly expressing appreciation of their English abilities may be enough. As with students from nondominant cultures, it helps to have someone in the first tent group who shares the same first language with the ELL student. After the first tent group experience, splitting up same language speakers may foster greater integration.

## Chapter Three References

- Brooks, Jacqueline & Martin (1999). In Search Of Understanding: The Case For Constructivist Classrooms. ASCD.
- Davis, Gary & Rimm, Sylvia (1989). Education Of The Gifted And Talented (2nd ed.). Prentice-Hall.
- Erikson, E. H. (1970). Childhood and Society., 2nd ed. Norton.
- Erikson, E. (1982). The Life Cycle Completed. NY: Norton.
- Evans, R. (1975). Carl Rogers: the man and his ideas. Clark/Irwin.
- Gookin, John & Leach, Shari (2004). NOLS Leadership Educator Notebook. NOLS.
- Kitchener, K., & King, P. (1990). The reflective judgment model: Ten years of research. In M. L. Commons, et al.
- Knowles, Malcolm (1970). The Modern Practice of Adult Education. Cambridge.
- Maslow, A. (1976). Motivation And Personality, 3rd ed. Addison-Wesley.
- Mezirow, Jack et al (2000). *Learning as Transformation*. San Francisco, CA: Jossey-Bass.
- Piaget, J. (1995). The Essential Piaget. Gruber, H. E. and Voneche, J. J. (eds.). London.

# Chapter Four Holistic Education

*"The greatest discovery of my generation is that a human being can alter his life by altering his attitude"*
-William James

*Holistic education* refers to teaching to the whole person, which includes the student's character, their maturity, their intelligence, their resiliency, their attitudes, their physical abilities, and other non-cognitive aspects of who they are and how they function as a person in society and in nature. Some of this fits in our leadership and our environmental studies curricula, but most of it is beyond what we can measure in a student. For instance, while we don't measure how mature our students are, we can help them grow in the area of human development.

Holistic education also refers to connecting education across the curriculum, where we take the technical core of education and personalized education (described in Chapters Two and Three respectively), and help the student apply the concepts to their life. This is almost innate on NOLS expeditions, because every major aspect of our curriculum is relevant in most course activities. Educators can excel in this area by helping students become more mindful of how the many topics on our instructional checklist work together.

## Non-cognitive Skills

There is a skillset being taught in some schools that pertains to learning how to learn rather than merely measuring what knowledge (cognitive information) is learned. These non-cognitive skills include study habits, metacognitive (knowing about knowing) strategies, self-regulated learning, time management, and goal-setting. Collectively, these are often called aptitudes or learning strategies. NOLS student outcomes in this area include "take responsibility for their own education" and "the ability to set and attain goals."

A recent meta-study (a study of studies on this topic) at the University of Chicago showed that development of non-cognitive skills in a school is dependent on a positive school culture, which aligns with our emphasis on a safe learning environment for all students and our values related to inclusion that expect us to respect all persons.

Recent research (Sibthorp, 2014) shows that NOLS semester students are better at self-regulation in the college environment after NOLS than they were before NOLS. Furthermore, the head of the Archer School for Girls states that she sent every Archer girl to NOLS three times during their high school education mainly because they learn these non-cognitive skills. The engaging educational environment and positive culture at NOLS supports development of non-cognitive skills. We can do this better if staff are more metacognitive, or mindful, about development of non-cognitive skills.

## Human Development

Human development refers to our normal maturation as human beings, and is an important lens for outdoor education effectiveness. Primarily, it is important to note that different students are at very different places in their development, so they have different needs. With this in mind, instructors may need to vary their roles as educators to suit the different developmental needs of the student group. On a course with students ranging from 16 to 25 years old, instructors may see a wide range of stages of human development.

Normal maturation happens over a lifetime, so any change in maturity over a month is likely to be small, but this knowledge should not dissuade instructors from positively influencing students in a way that supports growth. Quality programming generally supports human development, though development can be difficult to measure.

One aspect of human development that is relevant to both our leadership and environmental studies curriculum threads is moral development. Kohlberg listed six stages of moral development through which people move:
1) Obedience to avoid punishment.
2) Obedience for greater personal benefits.
3) Interpersonal conformity to social norms.
4) Law and order mentality—do the right thing for social order.
5) Social contract—what goes around comes around.
6) Universal ethical principles and self-actualization—do it because it is right.

Ideally, our students come to NOLS at a high stage of moral development: we can see this if we explain an ecological reason for an LNT practice and they practice that behavior routinely because it is the right thing to do. But some students are not at that stage of moral development and they might only practice that behavior if they think they need to in order to not get in trouble. Rarely, an instructor may need to threaten a student with severe consequences if they don't respect the landscape in a way that is sustainable for NOLS to bring thousands of people into the wilderness each year: this usually feels like the least objectionable alternative, rather than being a choice we like.

### Identity Formation

Another aspect of human development relates to the idea that people sometimes "find themselves" while in the wilderness. That is to say, they achieve some sort of self-realization of their own personal identity. James Marcia describes four categories for identity formation (Tanner, 2006). Like most developmental stages, people tend to only move up in these stages and rarely move backwards. Marcia refers to these stages as *statuses*, as measured by the Marcia Identity Status Interview. The status names are simplified here.
1) *Mimic*—the person mimics the identity of a parent or other adult figure.
2) *Amorphous*—the person doesn't really care about their identity. This carefree state is low anxiety.
3) *Exploration*—the person is actively exploring identity options, trying on various personalities, sometimes leading to anxiety.
4) *Identity Achievement*—the person has typically been through an identity crisis of some sorts, explored some identities, and made a commitment regarding who they want to be. It is important that they feel they have an internal locus of self-definition and aren't being coerced by others to display this identity.

## Training, Teaching, and Educating

*Training* means getting somebody to exhibit a certain behavior. It implies rote and drill to get people to do some action desired by the trainer. For instance, you can train your dog to fetch sticks. Fido clearly doesn't know why retrieving is so important; he just likes affection and dog bones, and dislikes scolding. A well-trained person can tie a good knot, recite your class outline back to you, or is obedient when you ask them to stay at least a body-length away from the edge. Training is an important part of teaching.

*Teaching* means giving people knowledge that then directs them toward some desired behavior. They start doing that desired behavior because they understand its importance. A well-taught person can tell you why certain behaviors are important and may feel like an expert on the topic. They will understand why tying a good knot is important. Striving to teach a minimum level of understanding whereby students can explain at least one reason why a certain behavior is important helps them grasp the logic behind an action. This understanding is key to the eventual development of judgment. Teaching is an important part of educating.

*Educating* means discovery of latent abilities. It implies motivating the student to develop her own thoughts to figure out what the right behavior is. Educated students are able to apply previously learned skills to new situations. Our theme of developing judgment exemplifies our commitment to education. Well-educated people can creatively apply information and will see themselves as students of that discipline.

*If you ask a master educator what they do for a living, the classic response is "I am a student of education."*

A pitfall of this triad is that some educators skip the fundamentals of training in their educational package. This fosters students who are "free spirits" but who may lack the basic habits of self-discipline required for true mastery. Effective schooling balances training, teaching, and educating in a way that is developmentally appropriate for each student.

Our goal at NOLS is clearly to educate, yet sometimes students look for simpler avenues to knowledge and skills that require less personal responsibility on their part. Early in a course, we often have to help motivate these students to take more responsibility for their own education. For these students, discovering a newfound motivation for education could end up being their single greatest accomplishment during their course. People often come to NOLS for training; they get very good training, but we also give them first-rate teaching and education.

## Educational Scaffolding

Scaffolding is a strategy for education based on Vygotsky's "zone of proximal development." This approach suggests providing more direct guidance to students who have more basic developmental needs (e.g., novices and beginners), and later withdrawing support as students mature as learners. As the student develops knowledge and skills, the teacher steps back and lets the student direct themselves at a higher level. This strategy is exemplified by the approach NOLS uses for preparing students for independent travel.

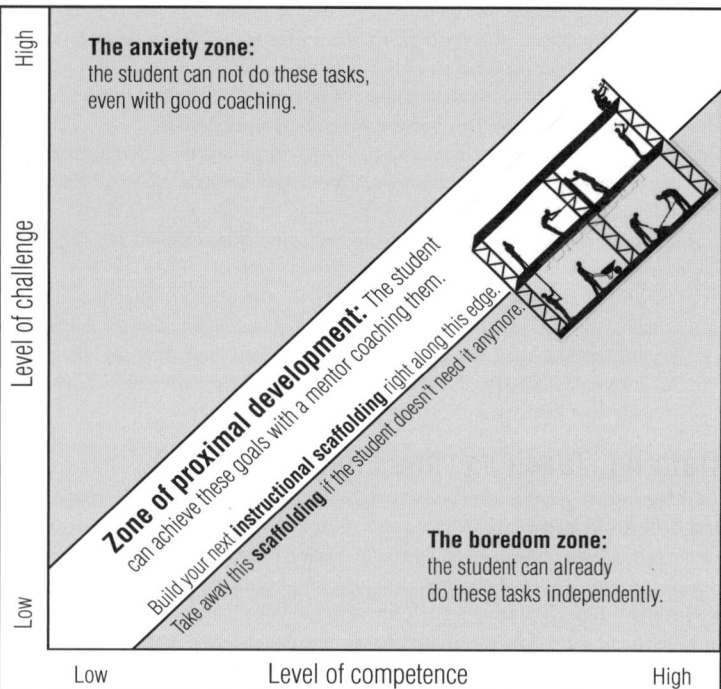

*Vygotsky's Zone of Proximal Development provides an educational scaffolding that is based on students' needs.*

## Standards-based Education at NOLS

Structure of the core teachings at NOLS is critical not only to maintain our identity on every course, but also to make sure our evolution as a school is both intentional and universal within NOLS. Expected student outcomes, written by our own field staff, have provided structure for NOLS students, instructors, and administrators. Instructor Notebooks provide a foundation of curriculum for any course at NOLS.

While we specify the desired outcomes of our technical core of education, it is important that we do not specify teaching methods. If we dictate quality programming and teaching, we help all teachers and students. However, if we dictate methodology, we constrain our best teachers. NOLS intentionally resists a high level of control and inflexibility in teaching methodology. We will always need clarity in our more technical student outcomes, but we need to leave room in our outcomes for educating the whole student and running the spirited (high energy) expeditions for which NOLS is famous.

We have to balance technical education with holistic education. Some experiential education programs are run as personal pep rallies where students feel good about what they talk about, but without excelling in specific skill sets or doing tangible activities. This type of education can feel hollow. Psychologists refer to this as counterfeit self-esteem, rather than authentic self-esteem, and it may do more harm than good (Henderson, 2002). NOLS' strong suit in the field of experiential education is that our students develop a deeply seated confidence based on their own technical competence in our core of leadership, outdoor skills, travel, risk management, and environmental studies.

## Objective Evaluation versus Personal Growth

Some students come to NOLS for holistic education, but solely get evaluated and graded on our core curriculum, and are disappointed. This happens a lot on 25 and over courses and adventure courses. We can mitigate this trap.

We need to be clear about what students will be graded on—letter grades represent how well students perform the core curriculum of NOLS. Tell your students in advance that this is what they are graded on. If students want their more personal lessons counted towards their grade, they will need to convince you that the lesson is connected to our core curriculum. This can be done creatively in leadership categories, or other ways, as long as you maintain the integrity of consistent grading for all students on each course.

If students want their more personal lessons as part of their written evaluation, they have two choices:

1) They can coach you, explaining through a self-evaluation what they learned. Then on their evaluation you can write something like "Fred said he learned a lot about relationships with other men of his age that he didn't realize before." This is a great service to the student, but their personal gains typically aren't going to impact their NOLS grades.

2) They can write a self-evaluation, which you will staple to their original evaluation. If they do this, you need to be clear whether you will read it and use it to help you write the summaries on their Instructor-of-Student evaluation.

If a student doesn't want to see their evaluation, staff still need to write it so NOLS Admissions can use it to make decisions for future enrollment, or for use if the student asks NOLS for a reference.

## Habits of Mind—Four Levels of Education

Habits of mind include intelligent behaviors that help us deal with information. We teach these mental habits by modeling them, by asking people to do them, and especially by reflecting on their successful application. There are four levels of education that culminate with the Habits of Mind.

### 1) Facts and Activities

Teachers often present information to students, then test them on how well they remember the information. Easy examples are the wording of the NOLS leadership skills or the LNT principles. Novice students like to learn simplified rules to guide them. Novice teachers like to teach simplified rules that are easy to measure. Facts and simple rules are especially important at the start of a NOLS course. Being guided through an activity, just for the sake of doing it, is just as valuable as learning facts. Foundations in facts and activities are essential for beginners, and are the building blocks for higher-level education.

### 2) Concepts

It is considered a higher level of education to help students learn the concepts behind the information or activity. The general principles, once understood, help students creatively deduce new information, which helps them apply the knowledge to new circumstances. This is exactly why the LNT principles are better than an LNT list of rules.

### 3) Processes

Learning processes help students develop patterns for discovering new information about topics given to them by the teacher. Teaching students to measure their own environmental impact, check the local regulations, and to look for related books, are all ways that students learn to learn by themselves. Helping students become more self-directed learners includes both showing them where to find things and helping them develop the self-image necessary to seek knowledge for themselves.

### 4) Habits of Mind

The highest level of education is to help students develop habits of mind that help them both collect knowledge and figure out how to act on it. The average NOLS grad has certain states of mind regarding things like EB and LNT—you can expect them to have an attitude that puts group goals ahead of their own; they display choices that show respect for the land; they have a *can-do* attitude about conflict resolution. This isn't stuff you learn in a lecture, but it frames everything we choose to do. Helping people organize a state of mind is considered to be three levels higher than just teaching basic facts.

### The Habits of Mind (Costa, 2000)
1) Persisting
2) Managing impulsivity
3) Listening with understanding and empathy
4) Thinking flexibly
5) Thinking about thinking
6) Striving for accuracy
7) Questioning and posing problems
8) Applying past knowledge to new situations
9) Thinking and communicating with clarity and precision
10) Gathering data through all the senses
11) Creating, imagining, innovating
12) Responding with wonderment and awe
13) Taking reasonable risks
14) Finding humor
15) Thinking independently
16) Remaining open to continuous learning

## Maslow's Hierarchy Expanded

Maslow did more than develop his hierarchy of needs (see Chapter Two). He had specific recommendations for educators so they might minimize how stifling traditional education can be and maximize how personally fulfilling education can be. Maslow said that the goal of education should be to help people:

- Be authentic
- Transcend their cultural conditioning and become world citizens
- Find their vocation
- Know that life is precious
- Be good and joyous in all kinds of situations
- Transcend trifling problems
- Learn from their inner nature
- Appreciate beauty
- Understand that controls are good, and complete abandon is bad
- Grapple with serious problems
- Be good choosers

Maslow's simple list of the basic goals of education is probably of greatest utility to wilderness educators in seeing how a wilderness education fits in a person's overall education—to look at the end goal and work backward. Some of our students arrive having already mastered these concepts. Others come with serious lessons to learn. While some of these more needy students may take more of our time than other, honed students, helping students appreciate what they've learned in respect to these higher-level goals can create life-changing experiences.

## Resiliency Education (AKA Tolerance for Adversity, or Grit)

Resilience is almost identical to what NOLS calls tolerance for adversity, or what some people colloquially call grit, but most educators call it resilience. Resiliency education started by studying the high frequency (50-70%) of kids from at-risk settings who seemed not only to survive, but thrive. Out of that research has grown an educational strategy that helps all students be more resilient. The strategy focuses on the process of developing resiliency; it is about how you treat the students and how you guide the social activities within your learning community. What you end up with are students who are better engaged with other people, better engaged with their own education, and better engaged with their own lives.

What does resiliency look like? (adapted from Benard, 1991)
- Social competence (responsiveness, cultural flexibility, empathy, caring, communication skills, and a sense of humor)
- Problem-solving abilities (planning, help-seeking, critical and creative thinking)
- Autonomy (sense of identity, self-efficacy, self-awareness, task-mastery, and adaptive distancing from negative messages and conditions)
- A sense of purpose (goal direction, educational aspirations)
- Belief in a bright future (optimism, faith, and spiritual connectedness)

Ways we can nurture resiliency (adapted from Henderson, 2002)
- Provide care and support: Give the message that we care about this person, we respect them as a person, and we will support their educational development.
- Set, communicate, and support high expectations: Help students use their own styles to perform to high standards.
- Provide opportunities for meaningful participation in activities.
- Increase social bonding: Use collaborative learning, involve everyone, maintain a mutually respectful atmosphere, and have social events.
- Set clear consistent boundaries: Make sure consequences are clear and logical and are then enforced fairly and consistently.
- Teach life skills: Let students make real decisions. Help students learn strategies for resolving conflict. Model the attitudes you want your students to mimic.

Nan Henderson at www.resiliency.com addresses resiliency education in pragmatic ways. Her attitude of *positive psychology* focuses on the empowerment and potential of these skills rather than on the adversity that bred them. She asks students to identify good traits in other people and to use positive imagery as an avenue to help students identify who they want to become as people. This teaching technique is commonly used with leadership traits on many NOLS expeditions, but is just as easily done with a more specific field like resiliency. Early in a NOLS course, we should be careful to nurture resiliency using the strategies listed above. Near the end of a NOLS course, it might be appropriate to discuss this educational strategy for when our students move on and lead others.

This topic supports the NOLS leadership skill "tolerance for adversity and uncertainty," which has lesson plans in the *NOLS Leadership Educator Notebook*. An excellent book that integrates resiliency education with many of the educational strategies in this chapter is *Building Resilient Students: Integrating Resiliency* into what you already know and do (Thomsen, 2002.) Nan Henderson also has a simple self-test for the conditions and attitudes that breed resiliency: http://www.resiliency.com/htm/resiliencyquiz.htm

This quiz, or part of it, could be an excellent tool for NOLS semester students to dig deeper into "tolerance for adversity and uncertainty." You can either print it right off of the website or put it into expedition terms for better context.

## Awakening Genius

Exploring the natural world is an excellent medium for nurturing the natural sense of wonder in people. This innate curiosity, the joy of being in beautiful places, and doing exciting things in a well-developed community can not only provide life-changing wilderness experiences, but can also help awaken the genius in any student. Wonder, curiosity, and joy are three of the twelve aspects of genius described by educator Thomas Armstrong (1998). He says we all have the qualities of genius, which include playfulness, imagination, creativity, wisdom, inventiveness, vitality, sensitivity, flexibility, and humor. All of these qualities can be integrated into education at NOLS. While they aren't specific enough for us to assess and measure on NOLS courses, we can still intentionally foster them. When we notice these qualities in our students, we should reinforce them: tell them how important they are and make note in their written evaluation since this type of success isn't always self-evident. Help people play to their strengths, which they can only do if they are cognizant of what their strengths actually are.

## Piaget's Developmental Theory

Piaget postulated that there are four things that contribute to mental maturation:
- Physical maturation
- Experiences that involve concrete objects
- Social interactions with peers
- Events that involve the development of all three of the above factors to constantly redefine our mental abilities and self-perception

At NOLS, we emphasize concrete experiences you can feel with your hands and social interactions with peers. This is no license to drop all classwork, however. Students need rote learning for reinforcement of key knowledge and spatial learning (connections to other knowledge) for context clues. It takes a balanced educational approach to reach all students.

Parents who tell us that their child "grew up" at NOLS noticed the significant mental development and the individualism that grew out of the real events that involved the above factors. Most of these students have an intuitive feel of their own identity before they come to NOLS; it is a concrete experience that sends them back home with conviction about this personal identity. While we can't give students feedback that they "grew up" at NOLS, we can give them tools for making mature decisions, for behaving as self-directed individuals, and for filling a specific niche that ultimately helps their expedition team.

For example, NOLS researcher Dr. Betsy Lindley studied wilderness values in 108 WRW students, finding that they all scored the maximum value on a pre-course test that was normalized for the general population, indicating maximum wilderness values for every single student. This meant they had nothing to learn at NOLS in this area. However, her post-course interviews showed that these students became much more aware of these values while at NOLS; they gained important tools for sharing these values with others in their home community, and they went home with much more conviction about using these values in their lives.

## Emotional Intelligence

The basic thesis of emotional intelligence is that success in our world is dependent not only on our intellectual skills, reflected in our IQ scores, but also on our emotional skills—our emotional intelligence. In many ways, this is something we all know: the person we want to be with on a serious mountain isn't necessarily the person with the best technical skills. Rather, it's the person who brings the strongest combination of technical and interpersonal (EB and leadership) skills. In fact, emotional intelligence has significant overlap with NOLS' leadership skills.

What is emotional intelligence? It is that set of skills that makes the average performer in the academic world excel as a business person; or that set of skills that explains why the less-gifted athlete, nonetheless, consistently outperforms the athlete with so much physical promise; or that set of skills that differentiates two people with similar technical/rational skills and establishes one as a clear leader. Emotional intelligence is a broad set of skills falling into five main domains:
1) Self-awareness
2) Managing emotions so that one can deal with the vicissitudes of life
3) Motivating oneself, including delaying gratification and stifling impulsiveness
4) Recognizing emotions in others, or empathy
5) Handling relationships, which involves managing emotions in others

The classic book *Emotional Intelligence* (Goleman, 1995) sets forth the scientific and psychological research that explains why interpersonal skills are so significant. *Working With Emotional Intelligence* (Goleman, 2000) discusses how to use it in small teams more specifically.

## Cooperative Learning

Cooperative learning refers to people working as a team to solve a common problem. A simple example is setting up a shelter as a tent group. The factors that make cooperative learning work (adapted from Johnson, 1994) are:
- They know that their success depends on each individual pitching in.
- Students know they all sink or swim together.
- Students hold themselves and each other accountable for their contributions.
- They are working in plain view of each other so they see what everyone does, they help each other succeed, and they give each other feedback.
- They are taught the social skills to communicate at a high level and to solve conflicts. They are expected to use these skills to accomplish group goals.

We support cooperative learning when we coach students in the skills they need to make tent groups function at a higher level. We start by modeling our own instructor tent group teamwork. Next, we have to be around student camps enough to assess the level at which they are working, give them pointers, and be ready to use the waterline model (explained in the *NOLS Leadership Educator Notebook*) to help them improve their teamwork. Consider asking tent groups how functional their tent group or hiking group is, but don't expect them to know what a good tent group looks like without you both providing a model and telling them what a good student tent group looks like.

An excellent course activity on about the third day is to have a discussion of what a good tent group looks like. On day one, they haven't seen enough situations, but by day three, a NOLS course usually has enough collective wisdom to come up with a lot of great ideas on this subject. A good way to close this discussion is by asking students what other tools they need from the instructors to keep becoming better tent groups. Be ready with a menu of instructional topics. Later, you can ask students what a good hiking group looks like using the above educational guidelines for cooperative learning. This approach is called *appreciative inquiry* and is detailed in the *NOLS Leadership Educator Notebook*.

*Collaborative education* is like cooperative learning, but now the instructor has joined the team of learners. An easy example is when we are in the desert, looking for water, and the instructor genuinely has no idea where the water is. Maybe the biggest instructor contribution is that they know generally where to look. Some students are hard to convince that the instructor doesn't know every answer, but as soon as they realize that the instructor is indeed clueless, students take their share of the responsibility much more seriously.

Fundamental issues like finding water, locating the re-ration site, and finding a decent river crossing are excellent mediums for collaboration. Collaborative education is part of becoming a learning community.

## Building Community

A community is a group of people with common goals and values. There are four things we can do to help our expedition become more of a community (adapted from Schaps, 2003):
1) Foster respectful relationships among students and staff
2) Emphasize group goals
3) Engineer opportunities for collaboration and service to the group
4) Provide opportunities for group input and autonomy

When we help students set both personal and group goals, and coach them to accomplish these goals, we help our expedition become more of a community. When we discuss values, we usually find a lot of commonality, which helps us mature as a community.

People need to feel like they belong to the group to feel like part of a community. Behaviors that make some people feel physically or emotionally unsafe can impair our development into a community. A positive learning environment is essential to becoming a community.

People need to be functional team members, on the expedition scale, to feel like part of a community. Friendship makes for a much better community, but isn't essential.

We need to be sure these strategies are implemented in a developmentally appropriate way, that is, individualized according to Chapter Three of this book. An easy error to make on NOLS instructor courses is to let students make too many choices: we get a happier community of people, but they make the conservative decisions you would expect of students. These students are usually happy they got to make decisions for themselves but unhappy about how unchallenging their course was. It is more developmentally appropriate to give them narrower choices to make so they still feel empowered by making real decisions, yet still have an exciting course that pushes their horizons.

The biggest thing we have going for us as a course develops is common experience. People who have accomplished significant challenges together, endured hardships together, or just had fun together feel like a tighter community. Discussing these things after they happen can help our students become more cognizant of these patterns, so they can be more proactive outdoor leaders after their NOLS course.

Read more about building community in Mona Hajjar's book *Belonging: Creating Community in the Classroom* (Hajjar, 2000).

## The Learning Community

A learning community is a community as defined above, but with the added element of being on an educational quest. You count on each other for information. A good learning community is synergistic, learning much more together than they could have learned on their own. If you can point out to your students how they do this, they'll probably make it happen more often (Wald, 2000). A discussion about what constitutes a good learning community can increase awareness of its importance and foster implementation of the concept.

NOLS expeditions can become excellent learning communities because we are a very good size for a "think tank." Put folks in a group of less than about eight people, and you don't get enough diversity in viewpoints to challenge each other enough for rich conversation. Put more than fifteen people together, and you can no longer expect to have your voice heard very often. Groups that have more than fifteen expedition members ought to consider breaking the group in half for important brainstorm sessions, then reconvening and sharing the best ideas.

## Service Learning

Service learning is volunteerism with an added educational component directly based on the context of the task (Allen, 2003). Picking up trash is volunteerism; it becomes service learning if you also do things like:

- Discuss the differences between trash, historically significant artifacts, and archeologically significant artifacts.
- Discuss the overwhelming scale of the ongoing trash problem, come up with reasonable strategies for dealing with it, and brainstorm other environmental projects that warrant such pragmatic approaches.
- Look at trashy and cleaned up sites and discuss what looks different about them, why that might matter to some people, and why it might not matter to others.

Service learning has been touted in traditional schools because it anecdotally shows that it helps students meet higher standards for reducing, reusing, and recycling (Billig, 2000). One of the primary goals of service learning is to help students learn more skills for becoming engaged in civic life. The four increasing levels of civic participation are: uninvolved, responsible, participatory, and social reformer. Service learning gives people experience being involved in civics at a higher level on this scale. It can also help students develop personally and it exposes them to potential career opportunities.

Service projects at NOLS—like picking up trash, helping maintain a trail, or pulling exotic weeds—are tangible ways for students to be citizens and stewards that serve their communities. Service is a great educational tool and can be integrated into any NOLS expedition. Our high standard for expedition behavior means that serving group goals is often a higher priority than personal goals. Service learning goes beyond group goals and provides altruistic service that serves the earth or society. Research has shown that service projects benefit the participant as much as they benefit the resource.

Service projects can help teach students about sense of place. By spending a day doing trail maintenance under the guidance of a local ranger or volunteer, students can learn more about the history, lore, and people of the area through the eyes of a non-NOLS-affiliated teacher. If students are given the chance to help manage the land, they are given one more way by which they may connect with the environment.

Service projects can help our students feel like they "own" public lands. An indicator of the appropriate level of ownership is when students stop referring to lands as "the" public lands and start referring to them as "our" public lands or even "our" Earth. While this may sound like mere semantics, it provides a clear subtext that the person feels they own the land, in the same sense of the word that we can "own" our feelings. Ownership is an essential step towards stewardship.

Projects are a valuable way to give back to the areas and communities that NOLS utilizes for our courses. We need to not only give back to our local communities, but also model this altruism at a level high enough that it provides leadership within our community. We should view our community as an association or partnership that we are part of. A discussion with our group of who else is in our community can help provide reflection that can help students transfer the concept of community to other settings.

Reflection can help students practice using critical thinking skills and see their efforts in a bigger picture, although sometimes a powerful experience like reclaiming a fire ring in a beautiful location speaks for itself. There is a crisp message in doing a job just because it needs doing rather than for self-serving reasons. But in general, mental preparation for, and reflection after, any service project can help the actions reinforce specific learner outcomes.

Finally, students who participate in environmental conservation or activism first hand are that much more likely to pursue such forms of environmental consciousness on their own. A student who is guided through the process of giving back to the community via a service project will be less daunted by the details, logistics, and potentially intimidating unknowns of getting involved in the future.

## Teaching for Transfer

Good education is the teaching of abstract concepts such that they can be applied to future situations. Many educators mistakenly think that learned facts and technical skills are automatically transferred to life back home. What transfers most universally are the learning experiences, which affect all future learning experiences. Reality-based experiential learning teaches powerful lessons that bolster self-confidence and reinforce basic principles, including the synergy of cooperation, the simple reliability of self-sufficiency, and the importance of self-awareness and individual skills mastery. These principles transfer easily whether students are aware of them or not. You can see this in NOLS groups that are issuing, and comparing them to sister courses that are de-issuing. The de-issuing students are noticeably more productive, efficient, and having a lot more fun.

One of the most important things we do for transfer of learning is to teach principles instead of rules. This helps people directly apply the information in more settings, and it helps students develop habits of mind. The fact that we do actually use rules in some situations is another lesson about when rules fit better than principles.

There are many things we can do to help our students transfer their lessons to life after NOLS. The most important one is to constantly give them images of using their NOLS skills back home. For instance, when we are doing our third camp inspection in a row, we can ask students how they'll deal with their peers' messy camps if they are out backpacking with friends next summer. This type of visioning has a subtext that you expect them to use these leadership skills on future endeavors. This slowly sinks in to students who might not have predicted that they'd be taking a leadership role back home. If students say they don't plan to be a leader back home, let them know that they'll become a de facto leader when they have knowledge to share with others.

Another valuable strategy for transfer of learning is to have students write action plans, where they choose a target group back home, and plan for how they can influence that group. Be sure to have them keep this plan simple to increase the chances of them doing it.

Remember that transfer of learning will be different for each student because they are all applying the principles they learned at NOLS to different settings. With our guidance, they can all go home as more confident citizens, leaders, and stewards.

## Nurturing Spirituality

Spirituality includes an insightful relationship with yourself and others, a strong personal value system, and meaningful purpose in your life. Character traits associated with spiritual well-being include self-esteem, self-efficacy, self-comfort, and self-reliance. A spiritually strong person feels empowered to influence the universe and can think and act in a calmer state of mind. People sometimes confuse religiosity with spirituality, because they seem like the same thing: we can use our cultural competency skills to easily support their spirituality without agreeing with their religious beliefs.

NOLS expeditions provide a setting for spiritually uplifting experiences without spirituality being an overt part of our program. NOLS' strengths are that we immerse people in the grandeur of nature, provide real leadership lessons, insist on a high level of self-discipline, run expeditions that are long enough to accomplish great things, provide time for reflection, and provide good coaching. We create an environment where people feel like part of some things that are bigger than themselves—the natural community, the expedition team. It is not an academic explanation of the human experience that provides spiritual growth; it is the deep human experience that provides spiritual growth.

Dr. Judith Neal (Neal, 1997) has great advice for teachers who want to provide more spiritual opportunities for students. She says not to worry about how to teach spirituality as a topic, but to work at practicing it while teaching. She says to teachers: know thyself, act with authenticity and congruency, respect and honor the beliefs of others, be as trusting as you can be, and maintain your own spiritual practice.

She says, "The most frequently mentioned spiritual practice is spending time in nature. I find that when I faithfully commit to my particular spiritual practice, I am calmer, more creative, more in tune with students, and more compassionate. When I let the multiple demands of a teaching job interfere with my practice, I feel more stressed out and off-center, I get involved in more conflict, and I feel less effective in the classroom." Dr. Neal accommodates individual religious practices in her viewpoint but doesn't present an individual practice as an integral part of spirituality. She lets every individual find what makes spiritual life meaningful for them.

NOLS instructor John Abel is convinced that physical tasks are a critical part of the spiritual experience. Others agree that hands-on work toward a goal is key. John Taylor Gatto defines an approach to spiritual development (Gatto, 1999). The tasks that help develop the spiritual person are:
- Purposeful work to achieve self-knowledge and self-respect
- Genuine independent decisions where you have to choose right from wrong
- Tasks where you have to practice self-discipline
- Practicing tasks meaningful to society where you develop a sense of duty

## Chapter Four References

- Allen, Rick (2003) "The Democratic Aims Of Service Learning" in Educational Leadership V60N6, March, 2003, ASCD.
- Armstrong, Thomas (1998) Awakening Genius In The Classroom. ASCD.
- Benard, Bonnie (1991) Fostering Resiliency in Kids: Protective Factors in the Family, School, and Community. Portland, OR: Western Center for Drug-Free Schools and Communities. US Dept. of Education.
- Billig, SH (2000) "The Effects Of Service Learning." www.asa.org/publications/sa/2000_08/billig.htm
- Csikszentmihaly, Mihaly (1997) Finding Flow. Basic Books.
- Costa & Kallick (2000) Activating & Engaging Habits Of Mind. ASCD. (see also 3 more titles in this series)
- Cumes, David, MD (1998) Inner Passages, Outer Journeys. Llewellyn Publications.
- Dewey, John (1983) Experience and Education. Collier Book.
- Elmore, Richard (2000) Building A New Structure For School Leadership. The Albert Shanker Institute.
- Gatto, John (1999) "Education and The Western Spiritual Tradition" in Steven Glazer's book The Heart Of Learning. Putnam.
- Goleman, Daniel (2000) Working With Emotional Intelligence. Bantam.
- Hajjar, Mona (2000) Belonging: creating community in the classroom. ASCD.
- Henderson, Nan & Milstein, M. (2000) Resiliency In Schools: Making It Happen for Students and Educators. Corwin Press.
- Henderson, Nan (2002) "The Resiliency Route to Authentic Self-Esteem and Life Success" www.resiliency.com
- Jackson, Susan & Csikszentmihaly, Mihaly (1999) Flow In Sports. Human Kinetics.
- Johnson, David, et al (1994) Cooperative Learning In The Classroom. ASCD.
- Kellert, Stephen. (1998) "A National Study Of Outdoor Wilderness Experience". Yale School Of Forestry.
- Kessler, Racheal (2000) The Soul Of Education. ASCD.
- Kinsley, Carol & McPherson, Kate (1995) Enriching Curriculum Through Service Learning. ASCD.
- Maslow, Abraham PhD (1968) Toward a Psychology of Being. D. Van Nostrand Company.
- Miles, John PhD (1990) Adventure Education. Venture Publishing, PA.
- Schaps, Eric (2003) "Creating A School Community" in Educational Leadership V60 N6, Mar 2003. ASCD.
- Tanner, J. (2006) Emerging adults in America. APA.
- Thomsen, Kate (2002) Building Resilient Students: integrating resiliency into what you already know and do. Corwin Press.
- Torp, Linda & Sage, Sara (2002) Problems As Possibilities: problem-based learning for K-16 education, 2nd ed ASCD.
- Wald, Penelope & Castleberry, Michael (2000) Educators As Learners: Creating a Professional Learning Community in Your School. ASCD.

Summaries of many of the ASCD (Association for Supervision & Curriculum Development) books are available in searchable format at www.ascd.org

# Chapter Five
# Empowering and Engaging Students

## Empowering NOLS Students
Empowerment is the act of giving people the authority or power to do something; making them stronger or more confident, especially in controlling their lives and claiming their rights. A universal factor that affects what students learn at NOLS is a category called student empowerment. For example, a student who agrees with the following statements has been empowered on the course:
- I contributed to my group's successes.
- I had important responsibilities on this course.
- I made important decisions on this course.

Generally, the students who agree with these statements have also achieved more of the outcomes that define a NOLS education. This positive correlation (i.e., when one factor increases, so does the other) is strong in every sub-category of our curriculum (Sibthorp, 2006). The more we empower students on NOLS courses, the more they learn.

However, this study by Jim Sipthorp was done within the confines of our current practices where we treat student empowerment very carefully. The study has shown correlation but not causation, meaning that we know that empowerment has helped our students achieve more outcomes, but we don't know exactly why. Furthermore, we don't know what aspect of empowerment is so important to our students. So, we need to be careful not to assume that increasing empowerment beyond the NOLS norms will have an increased positive effect. Otherwise this logic would encourage us to simply cut students loose when the bus drops them off and meet them briefly at each re-ration to "maximize" empowerment, which clearly wouldn't be wise.

We are very careful about helping our students develop necessary skills before cutting them loose to make independent decisions. This practice has worked well, and we should continue to strive to empower students within our current practices. We can't work harder; we need to work smarter.

*"There's a fine line between experiential education and instructor laziness."*
-Joe Nold

## Ways We Empower NOLS Students
This sampler of how we empower students is cursory. Look elsewhere in this book for more details on some of these topics.

### Pre-course Information
The NOLS catalog and each online course description note what the instructors will teach, but what the students ultimately learn will depend on what the students practice. This puts some of the burden for education, and ownership, on the students' shoulders.

### Course Orientation
*Language of ownership*—when we routinely refer to the expedition as "our" expedition, we are helping each student feel like an integral part of the expedition. The ideal is to achieve a sense of oneness, where all students view themselves as critical members of the team.

*Group goals*—leadership at NOLS is defined by setting and attaining group goals. Group goals create the need for leadership. Creating a list of group goals for your course, in a style that engages students and motivates them, helps the group focus on some specifics. The list of goals can also empower the students when the goals are directly connected to your expectations of them. It is important for the students to understand that in order for the group to accomplish those goals, each individual must participate as fully as possible in the expedition. Goal setting is more empowering when the students take personal ownership of the goals.

*Social contract*—our expectations for a positive learning environment, expedition behavior, and harassment should help people feel emotionally safe on the course. It should be clear to students that their opinions and differences will be respected, which ought to help them open up sooner on the expedition. This empowers students to join the group with fewer social fears.

*Expectations for student contributions*—classes, nature nuggets, etc., are great ways to involve students. It is important that you explain to students what you expect from them and why. These expectations should leave them feeling like they have some responsibility to contribute to both the content and character of the expedition.

*Grading explanation*—students who are used to short-term memorization of knowledge as a means to high grades may be easily disappointed at NOLS. Make it clear that A's are earned at NOLS by applying the course material to the student outcomes listed on the student evaluation. Some students are obsessed with their grades, but they may have trouble adjusting to the NOLS grading system. Remind them that the NOLS grading system is performance based, and that simply reciting the material is not sufficient to earn high marks—they must apply the material. Be clear that ours is a more subjective grading system than they are likely used to. Helping them understand our grading system and what we expect from them helps them see their own choices as the deciding factors in their performance. Grading is another form of feedback to increase self-awareness—when students understand that their choices and performance directly determine their grade, they are empowered.

### Leader of the Day
LOD exercises direct responsibility to a specific student. The exercise also dictates followership responsibilities for the other students in that group. Depending on the LOD, followership needs may vary. Establishing precise expectations of leaders and followers helps all of the students in the group. Revisit these expectations as the expedition matures. Their level of ownership with leadership expectations is often directly coupled with their motivation to excel at them. Instructors can set students up for greater success in these roles by being clear with expectations.

### Student Classes
Reading an appropriate quote at a meeting, presenting a nature nugget, delivering a formal class, or being an assistant to an instructor's class are all ways that students can contribute to NOLS expeditions. For these student-led activities to succeed at high levels, staff usually need to coach students. For example, a botched class can be a bad experience that can negatively affect a student's confidence, but is usually avoidable with instructor oversight. Some students need more coaching than others, and it is up to the instructor to assess this factor before the student class. Many students have never taught before, and, as with technical skills, novice teachers should be heavily coached in giving classes early on in the course, then given more latitude as their teaching prowess increases.

### Student Jobs
Titles such as "beach boss" (a student in charge of establishing camp on river, sea kayaking (jefe de la playa), and sailing courses) and "rock camp CEO" (a student in charge of organizing climbing gear) are jobs that offer students chances to organize things for their whole course. Semester planning teams between sections offer additional student responsibilities. The trick with all of these jobs is balancing clear expectations while leaving enough room for student initiative. Coaching, especially the first few times the jobs are done, is paramount to success. Base camps are an area that generally offer fewer student options (than expeditions do) for leadership, so establishing some jobs for student management offers more leadership roles. Make sure to frame student jobs appropriately, so that jobs are empowering to students and not simply a chore. Or, if they are just a chore (e.g., capping the groover) that must get done, be clear about that to students and don't frame it as a leadership opportunity.

### On the Job Training
OJT is when one student assists the current job holder (e.g., beach boss or rock camp CEO) as an intern, then the next day they take the helm as the new job holder. A written job description can help the leader to do the job and to train their replacement.

### Independent Student Group Travel

ISGT is one of our most powerful empowerment tools, and has a strong positive correlation with student outcomes. This correlation is strong for both the total number of hours students are on their own and whether or not they have a multi-day student expedition. NOLS has a very specific system to set students up for success in this activity, and research shows that this system is very effective at increasing student learning.

## Styles that Empower NOLS Students

### Coaching
Our Course Descriptions explain that instructors will act as coaches, helping students perform at higher levels. This is an important image for students because it puts more of the motivational needs on student shoulders. This coach/athlete style relationship is an important part of the NOLS style of education specifically because it empowers students to perform our expected outcomes rather than just mimicking what their instructors said in classes. Coaching is what helps students take the information we teach them and apply it to the expected outcomes.

### Inquiry
Instead of teaching students facts, rules, and unbending methodologies for course activities, try to get them to think for themselves through inquiry. Guide students through the learning process by asking carefully crafted questions about the activity. This process may be time consuming or even frustrating, but if done well, students find their own solutions to problems, increasing their ability to solve such problems on their own in the future. Inquiry is about the learning process, rather than the final product.

Teachers who are good at the inquiry method usually do it in a way that helps the student feel more empowered rather than feeling like an idiot. Frontloading this style can also help deflect negative reactions and help students understand the method. Consider watching and picking up cues from a co-instructor who is well versed in the inquiry method before trying it yourself for the first time.

### Problem Solving Approaches
Individuals and groups of students inevitably bring problems to the instructors. If we hand them a quick solution we get the problem solved more quickly, but we miss the opportunity to empower students by helping them to solve the problem. In some cases we can teach students systems for dealing with problems instead. The more we can help the student own the solution, the more we empower them to solve future problems on their own. Like the inquiry method, this only works if it actually helps the student solve the problem at hand and requires more staff time and energy than just handing them a quick solution.

### Allowing Direct Feedback
Direct feedback is when a student hangs out with a bare head and they get cold. Indirect feedback is when the bare-headed student catches grief from an instructor for not having a hat on. The "Love & Logic" series of books (Klein & Fay) encourages us to help the student see the connection between the bare head and being cold but also to let them get cold so they really feel the direct feedback. There are obviously many levels to this and we need to balance managing risk with letting our students learn from direct experience.

## Engaging NOLS Students

Engaging students is one of the most important factors in predicting student success in classroom-based education (Danielson, 2004). Engaging isn't simply keeping students busy, it is getting them emotionally attached to the curriculum. In the field, it is much easier to engage students because our curriculum is so easily connected to student needs during a NOLS expedition. There are three primary ways we engage students in education: personal needs, choice, and fun (Danielson, 2004).

### Students' Personal Needs
We help students develop a hunger for the course information when we tell them why this information will be important during our expedition. The more direct and immediate, like finding water in the desert at the end of a hot day, the easier it is to help students understand why they need to know this information. The less direct and immediate, the more we need to help students understand why they need to know this information.

Try starting a first aid class with a personal story of mastering, or even botching, a first aid response. Sometimes we have case studies that fit the topic. Telling stories like these in a way that helps the students really want to be the person who handles these situations well (not the person who botches it) engages students in the class. If you don't have a personal story, tell a story about someone else. The goal of these stories is to help them use visioning to set a goal for their own mastery of the topic. Have them practice envisioning themselves on their student expedition or post-NOLS when they won't have their peers backing them up. This should be done before you begin downloading information to them. It's helpful to wrap up your class with a reminder.

You can engage students by seeking out their personal needs in orientation and informal chats. Find out why they came to NOLS. This makes it easier to match students' leadership roles with specific student needs.

### Student Choice
When people get to choose between alternatives, they "own" their choices more. Ownership means they have more personal responsibility for making that choice work for them. A simple example is tent-groups. On most courses, we allow students to choose the new tent-groups. This makes the students much more responsible for making those tent-groups work than if the instructors arranged the tent-groups.

"Challenge by Choice" is a term used to describe student empowerment in situations that include risk and that evoke fears. Ultimately, students make the choice to participate or not in an activity. Ensuring students feel comfortable voicing their feelings is essential in respecting a positive learning environment. "No" is a very powerful word, potentially holding as much power as "yes". Honoring "no" is essential in PLE.

Student level of challenge:
- Giving students language to differentiate between "learning zone" and "panic zone"
- Set "challenge goals" with them – for example, in rock climbing, have them pick their own top of the climb (which may be above the granite shelf 2/3 of the way of the climb).

### The Fun Factor
Fun has inherent educational value because it helps bond groups and engage students. It helps lighten the atmosphere, which reduces stress. John Dewey warned teachers about making school into drudgery (Dewey, 1938). Great NOLS courses typically have a high fun factor.

Some course activities are inherently exhilarating, like surfing kayaks, heavy weather daysailing, multi-pitch climbing, vertical caving, heavy weather sea kayak recovery, paddling big water, extreme self-arrest class and snow gully descents. It sometimes only takes participating in these activities once to get students to raise the bar for their own performance standards.

Social activities help bond groups. Playing cards, singing songs, telling stories, dancing, baking cookies, sipping cocoa, knitting, juggling, or doing any of the things we might do while hanging out with our best friends are informal and easy ways to bond with students and to help them bond with each other. Other fun activities like costume parties, poetry contests, a Winter Olympics, better domes and gardens contests (in winter), bake-offs, bad hair day contests, and other zany social events are more contrived, but still effective.

Fun can also be used to lighten up some activities that may be potentially uncomfortable. Crossing an icy cold river is an excellent medium for practicing tolerance for adversity. A sense of humor helps. Appropriate use of humor is something that students tend to learn from instructors by osmosis.

## Intrinsic Motivation

When we do things because we truly want to, we are intrinsically motivated. Extrinsic motivation, on the other hand, often causes people to do things for rewards from others or out of fear of negative consequences. When our students are intrinsically motivated, they are self-directed learners—they are into learning because that's what they want to do. When we encourage intrinsic motivation in our students they are more likely to stay engaged in their courses, increasing their chances of achieving student outcomes and having a positive experience.

While we have little to no impact on why students choose to enroll in a NOLS course, we can have a significant impact on students' motivation and desire to learn while on a course. The following are some ways, according to Deci (1995), that we can encourage intrinsic motivation.

### Personal Goals
Goals that come from within students, rather than those imposed by parents or instructors, are intrinsic motivators that drive students to achieve through participation. Help your students set specific and realistic goals for their experiences. Create time for a structured goal-setting talk that gives them parameters for setting goals. Discussing goals in small groups might help students feel more comfortable speaking up. Revisit goals during check-ins to gauge progress and to revise goals if necessary.

### Choice
Choice fosters feelings of freedom and buy-in. It lets people decide what works best for them, which caters to their intrinsic motivation. Choice also creates responsibility and ownership for decisions. Discuss student expectations by giving them the chance to tell you why those particular expectations are important and what they should look like. Storm-proofing is a great example. If students see that they should storm-proof for their own comfort and safety (not because their instructor is insistent), they are more likely to meet a higher standard for storm-proofing. Start a course with choices that students have the skills and the knowledge to make. Monitor their decisions and over time give them as much responsibility for the course as they can handle.

### Competence
If our students know what they are doing well, they are more likely to stay engaged. Help your students see their competencies during course check-ins and during other opportunities to give feedback. Give students specific feedback that highlights what they are doing well. A well-placed compliment can leave a surprisingly long lasting impression on the receiver and those overhearing. Give your students ownership over their skills by acknowledging what they are doing well. Make sure there is ample time to practice skills so that students can develop competence.

### Autonomy Support
To be autonomous, in a nutshell, means being true to yourself, feeling free, and being willing and fully committed to doing whatever it is you are doing. Provide autonomy support by encouraging (not pressuring or threatening) self-initiation, experimentation, and responsibility. Autonomy support requires one person to take the other's perspective and work from there. Say, "I know it feels really nice to stay in your warm bag in the morning instead of getting up for breakfast, but we need to be respectful of everyone's time while we are out here," rather than, "Good NOLS students should get out of bed on time." This supports students' feelings and autonomy while also sending an important message.

## Self-efficacy
Efficacy is the ability to produce a desired or intended result. Self-efficacy is a person's ability to organize and execute courses of action required to manage prospective situations. Perceived self-efficacy refers to people's beliefs about their own capabilities to produce effects. (Bandura, 1997)

Students' perceived self-efficacy comes from their beliefs about their abilities. Students who believe in their abilities to succeed will stay engaged, will be self-motivated, and will be equipped to have a positive NOLS experience. We already do many things to increase students' self-efficacy on NOLS courses, but we might not always know why they work. The following are some examples using Bandura's (1997) four main sources of self-efficacy.

Perceived self-efficacy is good when it is based on realistic experiences, but it is bad when it is a false self-confidence based on shallow successes that had no real options for failure. This is why it is so important that our experiential education model includes optimal challenges for our students that include options for failure, within sensible boundaries.

### Mastery Experience
Mastery experiences are our past successes that give us the tools we need to tackle new problems. Take paddling, for example. We can set our students up for mastery experience by making sure they have the skills they need to paddle the next rapid so that they do it successfully. If we challenge our students before they have the skills, equipment, and the comfort level they need, we crush the opportunity for mastery experience. Start out slow and give students a progression that is more challenging as the course continues. Progression allows students to build on past successes without being overly challenged too early. Over-challenge can lead to fear and anxiety. Coach your students as they use what they have learned, and make sure they are practicing skills correctly so that those skills will be useful to them in the future. In general, structure situations where students can succeed and avoid situations where students are likely to fail.

### Vicarious Experience
Where mastery experiences are personal, vicarious experiences come from listening to and watching other people. The most consistent source for vicarious experience on a NOLS course is the instructor team. Students will always look to you as an example, so be sure you are modeling what you want them to see. Students also look to each other for vicarious experience. Rappelling is a great example. You can be certain everyone will be watching as the first student commits over the ledge; if they make it look easy, it will be easier for the students who watched them. When students set good examples, be sure to debrief those experiences and highlight what they did well using language that everyone understands. This gives students the opportunity to learn from others' experience for their own success.

### Verbal Persuasion
All competent wilderness educators know how to give feedback. Verbal persuasion is the feedback and encouragement we give our students. Provide feedback that attributes successes to the efforts of the student rather than to external circumstances. For example, "The work you put into navigating really helped you today" rather than "The terrain was easy to navigate today." This will help students see that it was their skills, not easy terrain, that led to their success. Use specific language such as, "You are really good at keeping your brake hand on the rope," rather than just saying, "Your belaying is awesome" to reinforce good skill practice. Measure a student's success by self-improvement, and give feedback to individual performance, not performance as compared to others.

### Physical & Emotional States
NOLS courses should be fun. When positive feelings and emotions such as happiness are tied to experiences, students are more likely to stay engaged and recall those experiences in the future. Create positive learning environments (PLE) where students feel comfortable, trusted, trusting, and safe. Give your students the option to create their own PLE by defining the elements of a PLE that are valuable to them, then re-visit the PLE talk to be sure it still works for your course. As members of the group, instructors can also contribute basic expectations.

## Chapter Five References
- Bandura, A. (1997) Self-Efficacy: The Exercise Of Control. W. H. Freeman and Company.
- Danielson, Charlotte (2004) Engaging Students In Learning: The Core Of The Framework For Teaching. ASCD audio.
- Deci, E. L. (1995) Why We Do What We Do. Penguin Books.
- Dewey, John (1997) Experience & Education. Free Press.
- Fay, Jim & Funk, David (1998) Teaching With Love And Logic: Taking Control Of The Classroom. The Love And Logic Press.
- Klein, Foster & Fay, Jim (2006) Parenting With Love And Logic: Teaching Children Responsibility. Pinon Press.
- Sibthorp, Jim, Paisley, K. & Gookin, J. (2006) Exploring participant development through adventure-based programming: a model from the National Outdoor Leadership School. Accepted by Leisure Sciences.

# Chapter Six
# Teaching Basic Outdoor Living Skills

Being comfortable in the outdoors is paramount to a successful expedition. Mastery of the basic outdoor skills presented in this chapter is important for all course types at NOLS. These basic outdoor skills form a base of foundational knowledge that every well-rounded outdoor educator should know, regardless of the type of expedition they are leading.

Our students must be able to stay hydrated, well fed, and warm regardless of the conditions. As outdoor leaders, they are expected to return home and supervise the safety and ethics of their peers. This means they not only need to have stellar habits, but also an understanding of the rationale behind those habits. Instructor Patrick Clark says he tries to get all students to the "one-why" level of understanding—meaning that they all know at least one good reason why they do the things they do.

*Many branches have specific regional practices related to local laws and regulations and to local environmental concerns. They supersede the general principles in this book.*

## Leave No Trace

Leave No Trace (LNT) is both a systematic way of implementing an environmental ethic and an international environmental advocacy organization. LNT has a long and enduring history with NOLS and its core concepts are taught on every NOLS expedition. The overarching themes of LNT are universal and can be woven into curriculum every day of a NOLS course.

### Learning Objectives
- Understand the importance of an environmental ethic based on the history of outdoor recreation in the U.S.
- Develop a life-long environmental ethic.
- Develop creative ways to integrate LNT into the expedition and life.
- Attain an LNT Trainer or Master Educator certification.

### History of LNT
In the decades after World War II, the United States saw a boom in outdoor recreation—people were turning to the outdoors to seek solace, breathe fresh air, and get exercise. Veterans of the 10th Mountain Division would popularize downhill skiing, and aircraft manufacturer Grumman would use aluminum stockpiles left over from the war to produce sturdy, budget-friendly canoes. In the 1960's technological breakthroughs in fabrics and other materials led to lighter pack weights making the wilderness more accessible. As a consequence of increased traffic in America's wildlands, land managers at the U.S. Forest Service (USFS) struggled to counteract the growing environmental impact left behind by recreationists. Attempts to increase regulations on federal lands had little success, leading to a realization that an educational program was necessary. Out of fear that Americans were "loving their parks to death," early concepts of the Leave No Trace principles, such as Wilderness Ethics and No-Trace Camping, were created.

In 1964 the Wilderness Act was signed into law, highlighting a growing concern for wildland protection. Among the pundits in support of the bill was NOLS founder Paul Petzoldt. Through the 1970's and early 1980's federal land management agencies occasionally worked together to build some semblance of a national minimum-impact education system, but struggled due to a lack of funding. In 1987 the USFS, National Park Service (NPS), and Bureau of Land Management (BLM) coordinated to produce the Leave No Trace Land Ethics pamphlet, and in 1988 NOLS published its first book, *Soft Paths* (Hampton and Cole) on the subject of minimum-impact camping. By the time the U.S. Forest Service partnered with NOLS for a national minimum-impact program in 1991, the name Leave No Trace had stuck. As stipulated by the official *Memorandum of Understanding* signed by NOLS and the USFS, NOLS took the lead role in developing LNT ethics and the educational component of the program. The first Master Educators course was run by NOLS in the Wind River Mountains of Wyoming in 1991. Soon thereafter, the other federal land management agencies—the BLM, NPS, and the Fish & Wildlife Service—joined the partnership.

In 1994, in an effort to gain greater recognition, financial backing, and outdoor industry support, LNT was incorporated as an independent non-profit organization. Now known as the Leave No Trace Center for Outdoor Ethics (LNTCOE), the organization is located in Boulder, Colorado and has grown to include 18 staff and over 25,000 active members. In addition to NOLS, LNT-COE is partnered with nearly 400 other organizations including equipment manufacturers, scouting troops, clubs, and even the automaker Subaru.

By supporting LNT through membership fees and donations, NOLS students can be part of this ever growing and increasingly visible national program.

### LNT Certification
When students graduate from a NOLS course, they should know how to use the LNT principles both for making their own minimum-impact camping decisions and as a way to teach their friends Leave No Trace principles, regardless of whether or not they obtained an LNT certification. They should feel comfortable figuring out where to hike, how to camp, and what to bring based on the principles they learned no matter where future trips take them. Our students should leave their course feeling they are part of the LNT movement.

Some NOLS courses certify successful students as official LNT Trainers or LNT Master Educators. On courses where LNT certification is an option, refer to the LNT Trainer/Master Educator paperwork that accompanies these courses for more information on the certification process.

### The Leave No Trace Principles
Minimum-impact practices have been boiled down to seven easy-to-remember principles that are applicable to almost any ecosystem and outdoor activity.

### 1) Plan Ahead and Prepare
Unnecessary impact in backcountry areas can be avoided by preparing for your trip. Impact concerns are secondary to visitor safety, but preparation can help ensure that the trade-offs between the two are minimal. Before you hit the trail, know the area and what to expect. Ask local land managers what to expect in terms of popularity, terrain, weather and trail conditions, regulations, and wildlife concerns. This information helps you plan your route, clothing, equipment, food, and fuel.

### 2) Travel and Camp on Durable Surfaces
Minimum-impact practices differ according to whether you visit popular or remote areas. Making this distinction helps determine the practices appropriate for each site. Wherever you hike and camp, it is best to confine your use to surfaces that are resistant to impact. Such surfaces include established trails, designated campsites, rock slabs, snow, sand, pine needles, or resilient plants such as dry grass.

In popular areas, concentrate use. Well-established campsites and trails are usually hardened—they've lost their vegetation—and continued use causes little additional impact. You must stay on a trail or in the site to avoid enlarging it. Traveling outside the main tread to avoid rocks, mud, or snow tramples vegetation and contributes to the formation of wide or multiple paths. Camping outside the barren core of an established site compacts soil, kills plants, and expands the size of the impacted area.

Take rest breaks well off the trail on durable surfaces such as rock or bare ground. Camp away from trails and water. Since the distances required by local regulations may vary, make it a practice to camp at least 200 feet from these features. For most adults this means 70 to 80 steps.

In remote areas, spread use and camp on durable surfaces such as rock or snow. Don't follow single file in each other's footsteps when hiking off-trail. Pick your own path and spread out so you don't create trails. Remote areas are typically seldom visited and show little sign of human use. Visit such places only if you are committed to and knowledgeable of Leave No Trace techniques.

Avoid places where impact is just beginning. It doesn't take long until a threshold is reached where the regenerative power of the vegetation cannot keep pace with the trampling it receives. The threshold for a particular site is affected by many variables, including vegetation type, soil fertility, and length of growing season.

### 3) Dispose of Waste Properly
Pack it in, pack it out. Trash and garbage have no place in the backcountry. Trash is nonfood waste which should be carried out. Garbage is food waste

leftover from cooking. Reduce garbage by planning and preparing your meals carefully so you have minimal waste. All food scraps should be packed out. Burning food is not recommended because campfires are usually not hot enough to consume the material completely. Likewise, burying food is an inappropriate disposal method because it is often dug up by curious animals.

Practice good sanitation. As visitors to the backcountry, we create certain types of waste that cannot be packed out. These include human waste and waste water from cooking and washing. The three guiding principles behind the LNT sanitation practices are:
- Avoid polluting water sources
- Eliminate human, animal, and insect contact
- Maximize decomposition

Catholes are the most widely accepted means of waste disposal. For more details on disposing of human waste, see the Waste Disposal section.

Although most NOLS courses don't use toilet paper, LNT discusses its use and proper disposal. It is important for our students to understand how to use toilet paper in the backcountry, because many of their friends and family will refuse to go without. The LNT guidelines encourage sparing use of undyed, non-perfumed toilet paper. The best disposal method is to pack the toilet paper out in a plastic bag. Burning toilet paper is not recommended because of the potential for the fire to get out of control. Burial is better than leaving toilet paper on the surface, but in the arid West, it decomposes slowly and can be dug up and strewn about by animals.

Waste water from cooking also can't be packed out. Such water should be scattered away from camp and water sources. Completely remove all food particles from the water before disposing of it, and pack them out with excess food or other litter. Strainers make it easy to do this, so bring them along.

In bear country, bury strained waste water in a small cathole or deposit it into fast moving, high-volume rivers (but never into small, clear rivers or creeks). These practices minimize food odors that attract animals but may cause some resource impact, so they're not recommended if you are not in bear country.

### 4) Leave What You Find
People come to wildlands to enjoy them in their natural state and experience an environment that produces surprises and challenges. We all share the responsibility to preserve these resources for future generations. Allow others a sense of solitude and discovery by leaving wildlife, plants, rocks, archaeological artifacts, and other objects of interest undisturbed. On many public lands, it is illegal to remove artifacts or natural objects.

### 5) Minimize Campfire Impacts
The majority of the recreating public enjoys some sort of fire in the outdoors, so it's critical that NOLS students understand Leave No Trace fire building techniques. LNT boils fire building down to the following basic guidelines: consider alternatives such as camp stoves, know regulations and weather conditions, determine the suitability of the site, use only dead and downed wood, and clean your fire site so you leave no trace. For more detailed information on minimizing campfire impact and how to build LNT fires, see the section on Fire Building in this chapter.

### 6) Respect Wildlife
Outdoor recreation can cause a variety of impacts to wildlife: habitat alteration, disturbance, harassment, and behavior modification. Such impact may diminish animal health, increase mortality, or alter population structure or composition. For example, wildlife that avoids human visitors are displaced from their preferred habitats and may lose access to essential food or cover. Alternately, wildlife fed intentionally or unintentionally by visitors become unnaturally attracted to areas of visitor use. In either case, wildlife may experience greater competition for food and cover, suffer nutritionally, and become more vulnerable to predation.

### 7) Be Considerate of Other Visitors
Increasing backcountry use can cause visitor crowding, conflicts, and noise. These impacts threaten the quality of recreational experiences for many visitors. To minimize your social impacts, respect the privacy of other campers by camping away from trails and out of sight. Keep your voices down and let nature's sounds prevail. If you bring a pet, keep it under control. Avoid popular destinations or visit them in the off-season when crowds are small.

### Teaching Considerations
The LNT Principles can be used to provide students with a framework for making decisions about impact concerns. Repeat the guidelines whenever you discuss minimum-impact skills so they become a part of your students' vocabulary.

There are LNT Skills and Ethics Booklets for the following areas: North America, Rocky Mountains, Southeastern States, Backcountry Horse Use, Northeast Mountains, Alaska Tundra, Rock Climbing, Western River Corridors, Temperate Coastal Zones, Desert and Canyon Country, Pacific Northwest, Sierra Nevada, Caving, Mountain Biking, Lake Regions, and Tropical Rainforests (Spanish and English). Bring some booklets for the area you are traveling in on your course. It might also be fun to bring a couple for areas where your students are from—say the Southeast. That way they can look at the suggested techniques for an environment they are familiar with and explore the variables that go into deciding how to minimize your impact in different ecosystems.

### Transfer of Learning
If every successful student puts their education and ethics into action by accepting the challenge of "each one, teach one," NOLS can change the way America and the world enjoys the outdoors.

Challenge students to think about how they will implement their environmental ethics beyond their course. An LNT action plan can help with this process.

## Pack Packing
For the first week of a course, your students' enjoyment of their NOLS experience may be directly related to how their packs feel during hiking days. They need to know how to load 55 pounds of gear into their pack so it is balanced and comfortable.

### Learning Objectives
- Proficiency at packing and organizing equipment.
- Taking off and putting on a pack safely and efficiently.
- Give ideas on ways to adjust packs for different terrain.
- Emphasis on staying organized both in and away from camp.
- Awareness that leaving lost gear in the backcountry is leaving a trace.

### Parts of a Backpack
Understanding how backpacks are designed can help your students use them with comfort. Every pack has a frame that provides structure and transfers weight onto the hips. Modern expedition packs have internal stays that bend to conform to your body. The shoulder straps, waist belt, and sternum strap comprise the pack's suspension system. Some packs have additional straps for pulling weight forward. These straps can be adjusted as you hike to shift the weight from one muscle group to another for maximum comfort.

### Care of a Backpack
Broken packs are difficult to repair in the field and uncomfortable to carry—basic care prolongs pack life. Thoroughly inspect your pack before leaving for the field. Check for wear points, particularly where the materials are stressed, such as shoulder strap attachments, stitching, buckles, and the bottom of the pack. Fix any problems, however minor, in town lest they become exacerbated on the trail. Pack extra buckles that match those on your pack and strong string in your repair kit.

In the field, store your pack away from salt-starved animals that may chew waistbands or shoulder straps. For the same reason, avoid leaving food in an unattended pack. Never drop your pack or throw it roughly to the ground.

### Pack Packing
Many NOLS instructors teach pack packing in town as a logical progression toward basic field competence, while others teach it on the first morning in the field with a short hiking day already under their belts, so that students can feel the difference in comfort between a properly packed and poorly packed backpack. One format that is commonly used to teach this concept is the ABCs of pack packing.

**A**ccessibility—Think about what you are going to need during the day. Food, water, an extra layer, rain gear, sun protection, maps, and a first aid kit should be easily accessible while extra clothes, shelters, sleeping bags, and gear you won't need until camp can be packed deep inside in the pack.

**B**alance—Weight distribution is critical to comfort and ease of travel. Pack heavier items high and towards the frame (your back) to help with balance while traveling on trail. For terrain that involves boulder walking, bushwhacking, or lots of twisting, ducking, and large steps, pack the heavy items lower, down around the kidneys.

**C**ompression—Fill up all the voids in your pack. Air pockets are a waste of valuable space and can lead to an unbalanced pack. Cram loose items like tent flies around solid items like pots to fill up air pockets. Removing sleeping bag compartment dividers to create one giant space can aid in compression and reduce air pockets. Fill empty cook pots and helmets with food or equipment to prevent wasted space. Frybakes make for excellent tortilla storage.

**D**ry—For many NOLS courses, keeping personal gear dry is a big risk management concern. Traditional pack covers don't cut it for NOLS expeditions because they only protect from light rain and not inundation from river crossings and complete deluges. To mitigate those concerns, line the inside of the pack with a sturdy contractor trash bag and store all gear inside of it. Twist the top of the trash bag and tuck it into the side of the pack to close it off—no knot required. Consider sending in extra contractor trash bags at re-rations in case of tears during the expedition.

**E**verything inside—Avoid having items dangling off your pack—competence in the backcountry starts with a streamlined, professional looking pack. Anything that must go on the outside, e.g., the bear fence or ice axes, should be attached tightly to the outside. Don't settle for droopy "brains" and carabiner clad crazy creeks. A well-packed backpack is closed and tight before traveling.

**F**uel under food—Avoid contamination by packing your fuel upright and away from food. Put fuel bottles upright at the bottom of your pack between the liner trash bag and the side of the pack, or in vertical side pockets. Check fuel bottle cap O-rings for leaks before packing the bottles.

### Putting On and Taking Off a Pack

Demonstrate good techniques for getting a pack on. Encourage your students to limber up before they load up. Make it socially acceptable to ask others for help—the "pack assist."

To lift the pack by yourself, first loosen up the shoulder straps and waist belt. With a straight back, raise the pack onto your thigh. Lift the shoulder straps using primarily your legs to minimize strain on your arms and back.

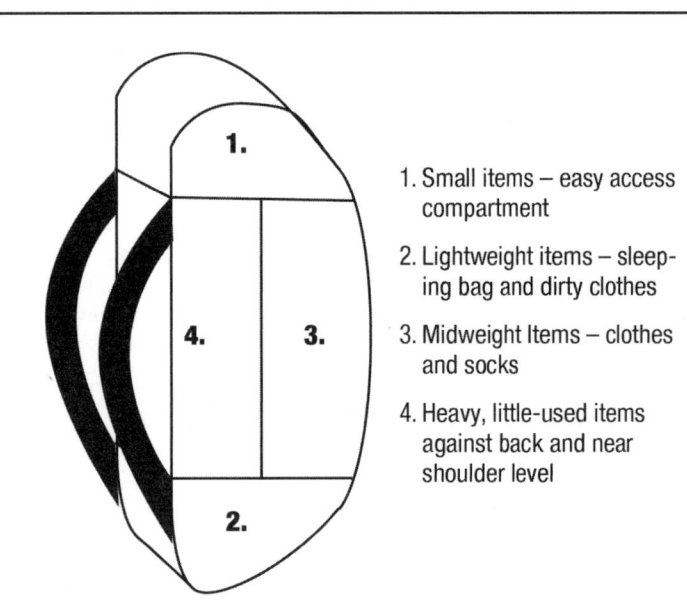

1. Small items – easy access compartment
2. Lightweight items – sleeping bag and dirty clothes
3. Midweight Items – clothes and socks
4. Heavy, little-used items against back and near shoulder level

*A well-packed pack is more comfortable than a poorly packed pack and additionally helps to keep gear organized.*

Once the pack is on your thigh, slip one shoulder into the strap, and swing the pack around onto your back. Slip your other shoulder in and fasten the waist belt. Tighten the straps so the majority of the weight rides on your hips.

To remove your pack, reverse the process. Packs should never be dropped, as this can cause ruptured food bags or worse. During rest breaks, look around for logs or rocks where you can park your pack in an upright seated or standing position and get in and out of it without lifting.

### Teaching Considerations

Thorough gear checks ensure that everyone has everything they need for the course and that they are not bringing excessive personal items. On issue days make your packing class concise and to the point. Issue day can be overwhelming and much of what you say may not sink in. Give them essential information to get started. You can reiterate points and expand on them in the field.

Themes such as accessibility, balance, and organization are easier for students to remember than specific packing locations for individual items. Pack packing is the perfect time to introduce the concept of competence and the importance of personal organization in the wilderness. Make it clear that we expect them to keep track of their gear at all times. Let students know that not everyone's pack weight is going to be the same.

### Transfer of Learning

Pack packing is a good time to start encouraging organization, teamwork, and openness to questions. Your attitude and flexibility during the packing and loading process can set a tone that will last throughout the course. This tone can indicate whether you are asking students to be obedient clones to get through the immediate situation quickly or whether you expect them to interact with you and learn the information. The demeanor of your responses to their questions can either ward off or welcome future questions.

## Campsite Selection

Campsites concentrate impact. Our students should learn to consider safety and impact when choosing a site to spend the night. Remember the Leave No Trace principle: Camp and Travel on Durable Surfaces. Use these guidelines to help students develop their understanding of how to select an appropriate site.

### Learning Objectives

- Students should be able to choose a campsite that is safe, durable, out-of-the-way, and comfortable.
- In heavily traveled areas, students will be able to choose an established, or hardened, site.
- In pristine areas, students will be able to identify durable vs. fragile surfaces. They should recognize how vegetation, terrain, previous use, and duration of stay must be considered every time they stop for the night.
- Students should develop habits that show that good campsites are found, not made. Remember, however, that in some areas the law requires groups to camp in a pristine spot that is a legal distance from water, even though there are obvious impacted sites closer to a river or lake.

### Risk Management Concerns

Before settling on a campsite for the night be sure to check for the safety concerns listed below. It may be difficult to look for and identify these hidden threats after a long, challenging day on the trail, so make sure that everyone on the expedition is aware of the consequences they entail and the importance of reminding tent groups to check for them.
- Dead trees or widow-makers that could fall in wind
- Thick woods with low branches that can poke you in the eye at night
- Avalanche paths or areas of rock and ice fall
- Potential lightning targets and exposed terrain
- Flash flood paths
- Animal trails

### Durability

Identify the difference between a fragile and a resilient site in your operating area. Avoid camping on delicate, woody, or moist broad-leaved plants that will not recover quickly. Try to find spots with bare soil or thick duff. Dry meadows are also quite resilient. Find a large slab of rock or spot of gravel for your kitchen. In heavily traveled areas, use established sites rather than create additional impact by camping in a pristine place. Again, the law may dictate that you camp 200-300 feet away from water. If you choose an impacted site under the legal distance, you may still be fined even though you are practicing good LNT skills. Know and follow the local regulations.

### Limiting Impact
Try not to camp in a site that shows early signs of prior use. Left alone, such sites are likely to regenerate; used again, they can become sacrifice spots. In heavily traveled areas, stick to developed trails; in pristine areas, spread out. Alter the way you travel to your kitchen or to visit other tent groups so you don't create social trails. Try to stay out of view of other backcountry users. When you leave, replace any rocks or branches you may have moved to disguise the site and minimize the chance it will be used again. Leave established campsites in better condition than when you found them.

### Comfort
Look for a site that is sheltered from the wind and has water nearby. Try to find a flat location for sleeping. Avoid low spots, like drainage bottoms, where cold air collects at night. In hot weather, look for shade. In cold weather, southeastern exposures offer solar heat in the morning when you need it most. A view never hurts, either.

### Teaching Considerations
Try teaching campsite selection on your first night. The sooner students are aware of what goes into selecting a good spot to camp, the sooner they will be able to exercise their own judgment. Introduce the Leave No Trace principle Travel and Camp on Durable Surfaces, and explain the local laws on camping including required distances from water or trails.

Use camp checks to enhance your students' grasp of site selection. If you come upon a poorly selected site, give your students a chance to explain their reasoning. Discuss their thought process, review the key points of site selection, and have them choose a better location. Encourage your students to take time to find a good spot. Have them leave their packs, put on extra layers, and explore the area for a location that is durable, safe, comfortable, and, when possible, aesthetic.

### Leadership Opportunities
After presenting this topic, students should feel comfortable selecting a campsite and being open to both defending and listening to feedback on that choice. Watch people's tones as they discuss their decisions, and give them feedback on what emotional message you hear, so they can learn to monitor their tone in future conversations. A key goal of this openness is to create an atmosphere of mutual respect early in the course.

## Tent and Fly Pitching
Know the parts of your shelter. Develop the habit of conducting a careful inventory every time you pack up. Tent stakes are a classic disappearing item, particularly in snow or tall grasses.

### Learning Objectives
- Students will learn how to erect their shelters efficiently and securely with minimal assistance.
- As the course's experience broadens, so must the students' ability to make a safe and organized camp in exposed terrain and foul weather.
- Students will recognize that taking good care of their equipment is not only a matter of personal responsibility, but also a question of risk management.

### Setting Up a Tent or Fly
After you choose a location, demonstrate setting up a shelter. Show your students how to tie a slippery taut-line or trucker's hitch (start with just one knot; they can learn other knots later). Discuss the attributes of a well-pitched shelter: tight guy lines, good knots, and a roof pitch that will shed rain or snow if you anticipate inclement weather. The long axis of the shelter should be facing into the wind. The corners and ridge line should be pulled so the shelter is smooth and secure. Nylon fabric may abrade or puncture when in contact with another object, so watch for branches or rocks rubbing the shelter. Flies should be low and have a steep roof when they need to be storm-proof. They should be high and flat when you want more air to move under them.

### Camp Organization
Food, climbing gear, fishing equipment, and packs do not need to be in the shelter. Items that must be kept dry, such as clothing, books, and binoculars can be brought in. Everything left out must be secured against wind. Keep drying laundry nearby and tie it to branches or guy lines, and put rocks on your butt pad and over your pots. Avoiding lost gear is important to both minimize your impact and for your safety. Encourage students to stay organized by keeping their gear either in their pack, on their person, or in their shelter. There is a lot of NOLS trash in the Winds—telltale plastic bags, p-cord, and tea bags—don't add to the mess. Encourage your students to take pride in minimizing their own impact, and, if they are motivated, packing out trash left by others.

### Cooking in Shelters
Stoves and lanterns produce toxic fumes, which in a poorly ventilated space can, at best, give you a headache and, at worst, be fatal. Cooking inside a tent is unwise. Stoves can flare up unexpectedly and burn both you and your shelter. Spilled boiling water can be catastrophic. Cooking in the front door of a tent or at the edge of a fly is convenient in foul weather but is still risky.

### Tent Care
Care of equipment is a high priority at NOLS because it parallels our concerns for safety and ethics. Zippers are often the weakest part of your tent. Open and close them carefully by holding the tent as you zip. Assemble your poles methodically. Do not force or twist the sections in and out of joints. Do not use excessive force when putting stakes into the ground. Look for another placement rather than trying to penetrate underlying rocks or hard ground by pounding harder—force only breaks stakes. If possible, dry your tent out before packing. Definitely dry it before storing. Make any necessary shelter repairs before returning from the field to ease the stress of de-issue day and to set up future NOLS courses for success.

### Teaching Considerations
The first day's instruction typically includes setting up tents or flies. If you are pressed for time, stick to the must-know information. All you need to do is make sure your students are warm and dry. Alternate techniques and situational judgment can be introduced later.

Students rarely master knot tying the first day, but be sure everyone can tie the knot successfully when coached. Use camp visits to give feedback on specific fly or tent pitching skills, to monitor campsite impact, and to offer suggestions on ways to improve your students' outdoor living skills.

### Leadership Opportunities
Setting up shelters can turn into the guys' job on NOLS courses while the women end up in the kitchen. A well-rounded leader is competent with all skills and gives others the opportunity to achieve the same level of expertise. If your students actively decide to take on individual roles in their tent groups, that is their decision, but make sure everyone becomes competent with the basics, and don't let gender bias inadvertently shift behavior.

## Waste Disposal
Many people give little thought to human waste disposal, which usually disappears with a flush of a toilet. For many students, disposing of waste on their NOLS course is a dramatic change from their habits at home. Improperly disposed human waste can contaminate water and infect humans with protozoans such as giardia, bacteria such as campylobacter, and viruses such as hepatitis. Health concerns aside, waste that has been dealt with improperly can have a negative impact on the experience of other backcountry visitors and on the environment. Seeing and smelling unburied feces and toilet paper is offensive and, unfortunately, not uncommon.

### Learning Objectives
- On the first day in the field, students should be taught how to dispose of human waste in the wilderness and have an understanding of how decomposition works.
- As the course progresses, students must demonstrate the skills and judgment to manage human and kitchen wastes in all environments encountered.

### Urination
There aren't any significant health issues with urine. Be discreet and respect other people's privacy when urinating around camp or on the trail.

### Defecation
Catholes are the recommended technique for feces disposal. Choose a site that is at least 200 feet from water and areas of human activity, such as campsites, trails, or climbing routes. Take care to avoid places that collect or drain water

after a storm. Dig a hole six to eight inches deep and six inches wide to serve as a personal latrine. After defecating, use a small stick to mix your feces with soil, then fill in the hole, and disguise the spot thoroughly. Spread catholes over a wide area away from camp. Don't let urgency dictate location. Wash your hands after defecating (see hygiene section).

Other methods of waste disposal include portable toilets (groovers) often used on river trips, wag bags (leak-proof bags) or other methods for packing waste out of the wilderness (these may be required in some locations), a latrine dug in snow, or if camped on a glacier using a narrow crevasse for a latrine. When available, use outhouses.

### Natural Toilet Paper
At NOLS, we have employed natural toilet paper for years and we advocate its use in most situations. When done correctly, this method is as sanitary as regular toilet paper and does not present the challenge of disposing regular toilet paper. Popular types of natural toilet paper include smooth stones, spruce cones, sticks, and snow. Warn students that some vegetation can be irritating, so use caution.

Some instructors choose to carry a roll of toilet paper to help students ease into the idea of natural toilet paper and having a roll per course can be useful if someone contracts diarrhea. Burying or burning toilet paper is not an acceptable NOLS practice, so provide students a sanitary means to pack it out, such as providing a resealable plastic bag and a stuff sack to carry it in. Wet wipes or moist towelettes must also be packed out.

In addition, consider the backcountry bidet technique of cleaning after defecating. Bring soap and a liter of water to your cathole site. After defecating, wipe with natural toilet paper and cover the hole as usual, then wash your inner buttocks and anus by pouring a little water into a cupped hand. Wash your hands with soap and water (not hand sanitizer) afterwards. Be careful to avoid contaminating your water bottle.

### Decomposition
Organic material is decomposed by bacteria and UV radiation from sunlight. Bacteria in humus soil can break down feces if there is adequate oxygen, moisture, and heat. However, in most of the environments NOLS travels through, decomposition is very slow. Nonetheless, burying feces is the best way to avoid accidental contamination and an unsightly mess. Direct UV radiation can penetrate the soil and speeds up the decomposition process, so if possible and appropriate for dispersal reasons, position catholes where they will receive direct sunlight for at least part of the day.

### Feminine Hygiene Products
Tampons and other feminine hygiene products should be packed out in a sealed container in the same fashion as used toilet paper. Research has shown that bears and other predators are not attracted to menstruation; however, used feminine hygiene products may have an odor and should be kept with other odorous items in the kitchen area while traveling in bear country.

An alternative to tampons and pads are re-usable silicone "cups" such as the Diva cup. These are inserted like a tampon, but rather than being solid and absorbing menstrual fluid, they are hollow and catch menstrual blood. Instead of changing a tampon or pad, women stop, dig a small hole, empty the cup, rinse with water, and re-insert. There is no waste to pack out. Women should be familiar with the use of these products prior to going into the field and consider bring some tampons or pads as backup.

### Waste Water
Leftover food and wastewater need to be disposed of properly to avoid contaminating water sources and feeding wildlife. Animals that habitually eat human food scraps often become nuisances or even hazards. Pack out solid food scraps. Scatter dishwater away from camps, lakes, or streams.

If you choose to bathe with soap and/or shampoo, do so with a biodegradable soap at least 200 feet from water sources. This procedure allows biodegradable soap to filter through the soil and break down before reaching any body of water.

### Teaching Considerations
To put apprehensive students at ease, you should use a relaxed, matter-of-fact tone and sense of humor when teaching this material. Show them a sample disposal site, dig a model cat hole, and exhibit samples of readily available natural toilet paper. Make yourself available to address concerns after the class for students who may feel uncomfortable asking questions about this sensitive topic in front of the whole group. This instruction needs to take place on the first day in the field.

Encourage students to wash their hands after they defecate. Teach students to keep the hand soap handy while in camp and on the trail.

Explain that changes in bowel movement regularity and stool characteristics are normal and expected because of the NOLS diet, physical activity, and hydration. Encourage students to heed nature's call and not hold it in. Humorous demonstrations and illuminating anecdotes may help relax first time users of a wilderness toilet, but profanity and graphic explanations may offend.

### Transfer of Learning
Defecating in the backcountry is a unique way to become part of natural ecological processes. On the first day in the field when sanitation is introduced, you usually only have time for a few quick comments. When there is more time, however, make an effort to open the topic for a discussion on personal responsibility, choice, good citizenship, transfer of learning, and how our actions affect the environment. Talk about biological decomposition and provide our students with guidelines based on science and the land management rules we abide by as good stewards of the wilderness. Sanitation is one place to plant this seed. See the *NOLS Environmental Educator Notebook* for more ideas on how to tie biology into your waste disposal class.

## Water Disinfection and Hygiene
Staying healthy is vital to having a successful wilderness expedition. The most common illnesses at NOLS are diarrhea (29%) and flu-like and upper respiratory infections (15%). Diarrhea and flu-like illness are spread from person-to-person and one of the main transmission vectors is hand to mouth contact. Diarrhea can also be spread from drinking contaminated water, and although recent studies have indicated that poor hygiene habits—particularly poor hand hygiene—are a more important factor in contracting diarrheal illness than drinking contaminated water, the risk from waterborne pathogens is significant.

Diarrhea, flu-like illness, and respiratory infections in addition to skin infections (which account for 15% of all NOLS injuries), can be controlled with proper hygiene and water disinfection practices.

### Learning Objectives
- Understand the importance of water disinfection and personal hygiene to prevent illness.
- Learn and practice proper techniques for disinfecting water.
- Establish habits for maintaining appropriate personal hygiene.

### Water Disinfection
Water, for obvious reasons, is vital to wilderness living. We need it to cook and clean, and we need to drink it to maintain our bodies' hydration for optimal performance. However, contaminated water can lead to illness.

### Waterborne Illnesses
Without specialized equipment, it is impossible to tell whether or not a surface water source contains waterborne pathogens. Wilderness water sources may appear to be pristine, yet they may be host to microscopic contaminants left by humans and animals. Waterborne pathogens include viruses, bacteria, protozoa, and parasites. The risk of becoming sick from waterborne pathogens depends on the number of organisms consumed, virulence of the organism, efficacy of water treatment system, and your body's defenses. The concentrations of pathogens in wilderness surface water can change drastically due to various influences on the water source such as rain storms, snow melt runoff, wind, currents, and human and animal activity. While some scientific studies have indicated that the risk of contamination of wilderness water is overstated, there is no way to know for certain and it is prudent that wilderness travelers disinfect surface water before consuming it.

*Giardia*—a microscopic protozoan that causes gastrointestinal distress in humans—is one of the more commonly known waterborne pathogens. There are many species of giardia, but the one that affects humans (*Giardia duodenalis*) is hosted by mammals, birds, and reptiles and is introduced to the environment by infected feces from these animals. However, giardia's role in causing diarrheal illness seems to have been overstated. Some studies have shown that giardia is not prevalent, or that concentrations can be quite variable, and that bacteria are the pathogens we should be most concerned with.

## Methods of Disinfection

*Boiling* is a very effective way to disinfect water as it kills bacteria, viruses, and protozoa. When water is brought to a rolling boil it is disinfected. It doesn't matter what altitude you're camped at, and doesn't need to be boiled for any period of time.

*Chemical disinfection* of water using halogens (iodine and chlorine) or chlorine dioxide is effective. Done correctly, halogens kill nearly all waterborne pathogens with the exception of cryptosporidium. Chlorine dioxide is effective against cryptosporidium, but requires four-hour contact time in ideal conditions. Chlorine dioxide is widely used at NOLS. Keep in mind that cold, cloudy, or silty water generally requires more treatment or contact time than warm clear water. Do not add any sort of drink mix to the water until the disinfection period is over.

*Filters* and *portable UV* purifiers are commonly used backcountry disinfection methods, but are seldom brought on NOLS expeditions. Both are effective at eliminating nearly all waterborne pathogens, some even claim to remove cryptosporidium. Filters may not be effective on viruses and can be bulky and may clog up in less-than-clear water.

## Hygiene

Students need to be taught about hygiene on the first day and reminded often to wash their hands. We need to teach, coach, supervise, and role model to our students so they understand their responsibility to practice good hygiene as a habit. Students should be held accountable in some appropriate manner if they are not practicing good hygiene. Do not let hygiene succumb to complacency. There is no doubt that it can be challenging to maintain reasonable hygiene while in the backcountry, but the challenge shouldn't be viewed as an excuse.

## Hand Hygiene

Wash your hands thoroughly after defecating and prior to food preparation to avoid the spread of disease. Handrubbing with alcohol-based hand sanitizer immediately after defecating is effective and people are more likely to do it than hand washing with soap and water each time. However, hand sanitizer does not remove dirt, fecal matter, and grease residue so proper hand hygiene needs to include regular hand washing with soap and water. Ideally, wash your hands once or twice a day. When washing hands with soap, wash for at least 30 seconds—that's actually longer than you might think. Soap and alcohol-based hand sanitizer should be kept handy while in camp and on the trail. Also keep your fingernails trimmed and clean out the dirt that accumulates under them. Open wounds on your hands should be covered.

## Kitchen Hygiene

Wash your hands prior to preparing food to avoid the spread of germs. Hygienic cooking habits need to be enforced, such as not using personal spoons to taste out of the cook pot.

Wash your dishes after each meal. NOLS has long had the tradition of not using soap to wash dishes out of concern for the environment and causing diarrhea (believing we can't adequately rinse away the soap). There is no factual evidence to support the latter claim and at least one scientific study found that washing dishes and utensils with soap and water reduced diarrhea illness. This study found that rinsing in cold water had no effect on the removal of bacteria. However, in lieu of dish soap rinsing dishes and utensils with boiling water and periodically dipping them into boiling water is likely an effective substitute. Leaving visible food residue and grease on cooking and eating utensils is unacceptable.

Consuming left over cooked food should be done cautiously. Cold temperatures may slow the growth of bacteria, but leftovers should be thoroughly heated prior to consuming.

## Trail Hygiene

Good hygiene also applies when on the trail. Don't share water bottles or hydration tubes with others. Don't scoop trail food out of a common bag with your hands. Make up personal trail food bags or pour it from a bag into your hands.

## Bathing

Take advantage of or create opportunities to bathe periodically—instructors should factor this into activity schedules. This could be a dip in a lake or flowing stream or a backcountry shower with a few pots or dromedary bags of water and a bar of soap. You can warm the water in the sun, or if you have the luxury of plenty of fuel, you can warm the water on the stove. Follow LNT practices for bathing (biodegradable soap and rinse off 200 feet from water sources) and note that LNT practices do not discourage bathing—there are just ways to do it to minimize impact.

Women and men should not neglect their personal hygiene and wash their genitalia regularly to avoid urinary tract, yeast, and skin infections. Women (or people with female genitalia) should pay specific attention to this. It is a good idea to use a "pee rag" (a bandana dedicated to this purpose) to wipe off excess urine to avoid acidic build up that can lead to infection. Urine is mostly sterile and doesn't smell if you are well hydrated. Keep your pee rag on the outside of your backpack so that throughout the day it receives UV radiation that will neutralize any odor and bacteria. Every other day the pee rag should be cleaned with water. No soap is necessary and this can be done in a river or large stream.

Another good habit to get into is cleaning your genitalia once a day with a damp cloth and water. Once every three days, or when taking a backcountry shower, the judicious use of soap is a good idea.

## Transfer of Learning

Good self-care in every team member is essential to the success of the expedition. Make sure students are aware that practicing good hygiene and taking care of their own physiological needs matters not only to the individual, but to everyone. The concept that one person's seemingly trivial actions have the potential to affect the outcomes of the whole group is critical in developing a sense of greater responsibility.

# Stove Use and Care

The ability to use a stove safely and efficiently is a skill every expedition member must master. Mastery of this skill prevents burns from spilled hot water, stoves, and hot frying pans.

### Learning Objectives
- Students must know immediately how to operate a stove safely and properly.
- As the course progresses, they need to learn how to troubleshoot and to perform basic maintenance procedures.
- Advanced stove repair can be taught before student group expeditions.

### Stove Operation

Start cooking each meal with a mostly full fuel bottle. Leave some air space in the bottle to aid with pressurization. Fill fuel bottles away from food and allow any spilled fuel to evaporate before lighting the stove.

Choose a flat, protected area to operate your stove. Avoid sites near combustible material like dry grass, duff, nylon tents, or low branches. Make sure all valves are closed and pump the stove to build pressure in the fuel tank. Do not over-pressurize. On an average, pump a Whisperlite™ 15-20 times.

After the stove is pumped, open the fuel valve and release enough fuel to wet the generator and fill the spirit cup. Turn the stove off and light the liquid fuel. Make sure you turn your face away from the flame. When the fuel is burned down, turn the stove on and relight. The stove should burn with a steady blue flame. Protect stoves from rain and snow when not in use.

### The "Tweener"

The dreaded tweener occurs when attempting to relight a stove that has been off for a few minutes, but is still hot and when the valve is opened intermittently spurts liquid white gas and gas vapor. This is a dangerous situation due to the substantial fireball that oftentimes results when relighting a stove in this condition. Mitigate this hazard by either waiting until the stove has completely cooled, or by opening the pump valve until the spirit cup slowly fills, then closing the pump valve and blowing away excess gas vapor before relighting the spirit cup. As always, keep your head away from the stove when lighting it.

### Troubleshooting and Maintenance

To prevent problems with your stove, keep it clean and dry, oil the pump cup, clean the jet occasionally using the shaker, and pack it properly. When problems do occur, check simple things first. If fuel is not coming out, you may have a clogged fuel line, or lack of pressure in the tank. Low tank pressure can stem from a bad o-ring, a dry rotted pump cup, or a bad one-way valve in the pump mechanism.

A poorly running stove can be caused by dirt or water in the fuel, by an offset flame spreader, or by a partial obstruction in the fuel system. You may also have a pressure leak, or the stove may have been over- or under-pressurized, or over- or under-primed. Instructors need to be competent at disassembling and repairing common issues with the stoves we use.

### Safety

If you get a fuel fire, let it burn out. Carefully set the lid on any burning fuel container. Choose a good, nonflammable spot for cooking to prevent wildfires. Handle hot food and equipment with care. Don't pass boiling water over humans and do not lean over a stove when lighting it. Watch loose hair or clothes around flames. Smother flaming body parts immediately. STOP, DROP, and ROLL! Apply cold water to burns instantly or the hot skin will burn even deeper.

### Fuel Efficiency

Bring the right amount of fuel for your course. Most summer wilderness courses bring 0.3 liters of white gas per cook group per day. Conserving fuel saves weight. Furthermore, it is an integral part of our minimum-impact philosophy. Save gas by cooking when all members of your tent group are around to eat or drink. Cook out of the wind using a wind screen and reflector. Keep your stove well-maintained and at peak performance. Turn off the stove when food is finished or when water reaches a rolling boil. Don't "cook air" or let water boil for minutes on end.

### Stoves versus Fires

Stoves help minimize our impact in the backcountry because they allow us more freedom in selecting campsites and require no wood gathering. Stoves are faster than fires in wet weather and allow us to camp above treeline. When used properly, they lessen the chance of accidental wildfires. Stoves cause less local air pollution and are legal in places where fires are not. But stoves burn fossil fuel that is pumped out of the ground in places like Alaska or Iraq, while wood fires burn a local and renewable fuel. A discussion of stoves versus fires needs to include the oil exploration, recovery, refining, and transportation needed to support the stove.

### Teaching Considerations

Start with a simple class on lighting, operating, and refueling stoves. Address troubleshooting and repair in a later class. Let folks know that to be truly self-sufficient, they need to know how to maintain and repair any of their gear, including stoves.

Model impeccable stove use to establish good habits in your students. Stoves are potentially dangerous. Be familiar with the course's specific stove type prior to going into the field. The issue room staff can help train you to be an expert stove mechanic.

## Basic Cooking and Food Identification

Good cooking has a positive effect on health, safety, and enjoyment of the wilderness. Being able to prepare an edible and nutritious meal allows students to keep pace with the mental and physical challenges of an extended wilderness expedition.

### Learning Objectives

- Provide cooking instruction early on so that students can make tasty and nutritious meals quickly and efficiently.
- All students must be able to prepare simple meals by themselves by the end of the first ration period.
- Later in the course, your instruction can address baking and more involved meal preparation.

### Organization

An organized kitchen simplifies cooking and makes preparing a meal enjoyable. Place the ingredients, utensils, and cooking equipment you will need within reach. Put them away when you're done. Clean up as soon as meals end. Having everything out and in front of you beforehand will ultimately save fuel because less time is spent searching through food bags for ingredients while the lit stove is needlessly burning white gas.

### Hygiene

Good hygiene helps prevent food borne illness. Washing your hands before handling food is critical. Do not share personal utensils or allow them to come into contact with communal foods. Utensils should be sterilized routinely with boiling water. Pour snacks out of snack bags instead of reaching into them with your hands.

Clean pots and dishes after every meal to eliminate foodborne illnesses. Bacteria and their toxic by-products grow quickly on food residue. Scrub the pot with hot water and a natural abrasive like sand or pine needles. Starches dissolve best in cold water. Strain wash water away from camp and pack any remnants from the strainer into a garbage bag. Rinse with hot water. Do not scrub Teflon coated fry pans with sand or gravel. These items can be cleaned by scraping the pan with a spatula and using hot water to cut the grease. Let clean pots dry in the sun; a blast of UV helps keep viral and bacterial populations down.

### Food Identification

Basic food identification classes include preparation guidelines for all the items in our food bags. Most of our dinner and breakfast foods are simply boiled, but students may need help determining proportions, water amounts, and cooking times.

Food identification classes are a great opportunity to introduce concepts of basic nutrition (see nutrition class). While introducing the items in the food bags, categorize them as carbohydrates, proteins, and fats. Tell students that the greater the number of ingredients they use in a meal, the greater its nutritional value.

Cheese and margarine enhance the taste, texture, and caloric value of a meal. Both items must be stored in the shade to slow down spoilage. To avoid bacterial contamination, do not touch cheese with your hands.

White powders are the most confusing item found in our food bags. Show your students how to tell the difference between them: milk squeaks, cheese cake has two different grain sizes, flour is quiet and smooth, baking powder is fizzy to the tongue, and potato pearls are yellowish and granular. The bulk of the other powders found in our ration are drink mixes or desserts.

Soup bases are concentrated and salty. They can be used to flavor sauces, make a broth, and provide flavoring. Spicing is personal: respect the tastes of others. Conserve spices by cooking them into the food. Dried vegetables add flavor, color, and vitamins to food. They need to be soaked in boiling water prior to cooking to re-hydrate. Save trail foods for the trail when it is not practical to stop and cook.

### Group Kitchens and Cooking with Students for the First Meal

Attempting to create a meal in an unfamiliar setting, with strange equipment and curious ingredients, can be daunting to students new to backcountry cooking. Appease student's nerves by cooking with them during their first meal, emphasizing the joy of cooking, and explaining the process.

Maintaining group kitchens throughout the expedition increases instructor-student rapport, helps maintain a high level of EB, and provides a space for students to voice culinary questions.

### Helpful Hints for New Cooks

- Keep heat low and make sure there's plenty of grease or water in the pot to avoid burning food.
- Make sure you start cooking pasta in boiling water. Rice can be thrown into cold water that is heating up.
- Add milk products after food is cooked and stir constantly to prevent burning.
- Mix powders with liquids separately to avoid lumps.
- Melt cheese by adding a few drops of water and covering the pan to create steam.

### Knife Wounds

Knife cuts are a common camp injury. Cuts to the fingers and hands often take a long time to heal and are difficult to keep clean during an active course. Demonstrate and model cutting away from the body, and not towards or against body parts.

### Teaching Considerations

Introduce a relaxed attitude toward food on the first day of the course to minimize the potential for food stress. Encourage all students to try their hand in the kitchen. Instructor eating preferences should be kept to oneself.

Cooking and food identification can be taught to the whole course or to smaller groups. If you decide to work with individual tent groups, get the instructors together and agree on key points before splitting up, or gather together as a group after the meal and have everyone share tricks they learned about outdoor cooking. Inviting tent groups over to the instructors' kitchen or having an instructor eat out are other ways to provide cooking tutorials.

Emphasize fuel conservation and hygiene throughout the course. Course banquets are enjoyable when everyone is committed to preparing food hygienically, but they have a reputation for sending food-borne illnesses raging through camp. Wait until students have demonstrated good habits before introducing the idea of a banquet. Use the *NOLS Cookery*. Most courses issue one *Cookery* per tent group.

### Leadership Opportunities
Promote teamwork in the kitchen and encourage students to be open about what they want. Sometimes good teamwork is leaving the cook alone, other times it means fetching water or cutting cheese. The critical leadership point is that the cook needs to tell people if they do or do not want help, and the entire tentgroup should be willing to pitch in and do their share around the kitchen.

### Transfer of Learning
Many alumni remark on how they learned to cook at NOLS, and in doing so, developed a passion for cooking that endures well beyond their NOLS course. Emphasize that the basic tenets of cooking learned at NOLS apply to the kitchen at home. Cooking serves a basic human need and is a great area to practice creativity.

## Baking
Baking provides creative and nutritious alternatives to cheesy fried pasta. This skill allows our students to buy cheap staples such as flour and live like kings; plus, it can earn them social points when they return home and camp with their friends.

### Learning Objectives
- Learn basic baking principles that can be reproduced without further instruction or a cookbook.
- Students will be able to efficiently produce biscuits, scones, pizzas, and calzones.
- Good hygiene must be an integral part of the baking experience.

### Basic Baking
Start with a simple, quick-rising dough (See the *NOLS Cookery*). Explain the difference between yeast and baking powder, and point out different properties of whole wheat flour, white flour, corn meal, and baking mix. Make sure you have both clean utensils and clean hands. Demonstrate how to mix a basic dough. Explain how moisture determines the bread type: pancake batter pours easily, cake batter is thicker but still pours, cookie dough falls in wet glops from a spoon, and bread dough is dry and can be handled without sticking. Pie and pastry crusts have margarine cut into the flour first, then a trace of water is added.

Yeast baking includes some further considerations. You will get the best results on a warm, sunny day when the dough can sit outside to rise, but when it is cloudy, you can use a sleeping bag or warm belly to provide heat. Often it is helpful to activate your yeast separately from the dry ingredients to make sure it is alive and producing carbon dioxide. The yeast is working when it foams after being placed in warm sugar water. Once your dough is made, grease and flour the frying pan to avoid sticking.

### The Outdoor Oven—Specialized Baking Techniques
Baking requires low, even heat on all sides. In the wilderness, you can create such an oven using your stove. The following methods can be done in conjunction with each other or individually.

To achieve a low simmer on MSR Whisperlite® stoves, you must *depressurize* the fuel bottle. First light the stove as you normally would in order to heat up the generator, then turn off the stove and blow out the flame. Next, with the fuel bottle upright, unscrew the pump slightly to release the pressure. Retighten the pump and set the fuel bottle back down. Open the valve, relight the stove, and you have a low flame for baking. You may need to pump the pump once or twice to maintain the flame.

The *Tower of Power* is another method for reducing the heat on the fry pan that helps with even baking. Form the windscreen into a small circle just bigger than the diameter of your stove and fold the ends securely together so they don't come apart. Using the pot grips, lightly bend the top of the windscreen in toward the stove at 45 degree angles all the way around the windscreen, each notch about an inch apart. Now you have an elevated platform to cook on away from direct flame.

The *rotation method* requires you to turn the pan every few minutes to ensure even heat. Find a sturdy rock that is equal in height to your stove and set it right beside the stove. Balance the fry pan partially on the stove and partially on the rock. Baking will be most controlled if your rotations are systematic.

The *flip method* refers to carefully flipping the fry pan over so that your bread lands on the lid and is finished upside-down. Be careful not to burn your hands handling the hot fry pan, and be sure to grease the bottom side of the lid before flipping.

The *twiggy fire* achieves even baking by lighting a small fire on the frying pan lid to provide heat from above. Burn pencil-sized sticks. Ignite the twiggy fire by piling twigs on top of a forked stick and holding it over the flames of the stove. Once the baked good is finished, let the twig fire burn down to ash and cool before you spread the remains. Twiggy fires are messy, leaving the lid charred and difficult to clean. Do not use twiggy fires if there is a fire ban in effect in your operating area.

A more efficient alternative to the twiggy fire is the Pot Parka, a commercially available flame-resistant insulating cover that is placed over top of the pan and stove while cooking. Pot parkas are essential pieces of equipment on winter courses and research has shown that they greatly increase fuel efficiency in any cooking environment.

### Cooking on Camp Fires
The principles of baking are the same with a campfire, but you use coals as your heat source. Build a fire and let the wood burn down to hot coals. Spread a layer of coals off to one side of the main flame, and place your frying pan on top. With a shovel or pot lid, pile more coals on the frying pan lid. If your coals are even, you do not need to rotate using this method. Check to make sure your dough is not burning. If it gets too hot, cool the pan in snow or a shallow puddle. If you are cooking many dishes on one fire, have a coal generation fire on one side and a cooking area on the other.

### Teaching Considerations
Get students baking as soon as they show a basic aptitude for cooking. For some, the idea of baking is intimidating. Ease natural fears by showing them how to create tasty items with a minimum of fuss. Model impeccable hygiene throughout your demonstration to establish better habits in your students.

The instructional area needs to be uncramped and durable. Allow plenty of time for preparation and cleanup. Consider presenting other topics or having a discussion to fill in the slow times in the baking process.

### Leadership Opportunities
If you do a bake-along, this gives you the opportunity to show a flexible, coaching style of leadership and to demonstrate comfort with chaos. Chaos can be critical to the development of leadership in individuals. Tolerate it when you have the time for it.

## Nutrition
The NOLS ration is designed to satisfy our nutritional needs, provide adequate caloric intake, pack easily, and be inexpensive. Using the limited items in our food bags, we must learn to keep ourselves energized and nourished for the duration of the course. It is beyond the scope of our instruction to dictate a strict dietary regime for our students; instead, you should show them how basic nutrition can affect their performance in the wilderness. Good nutrition provides energy to perform physical activities and to produce heat so we can work, play, and sleep warmly in a cold environment. In addition, good nutrition facilitates the repair of body tissues and provides building blocks for our immune system.

### Learning Objectives
- Nutritious and intelligent use of what is in the food bag.
- Students need to understand why good nutrition is an important aspect of safe expeditioning.
- They should also know the functions of the basic food groups and where to find them in the ration.

### Nutrients
Nutrients include carbohydrates, proteins, fats, vitamins, and minerals. They are found in a variety of foods and serve different functions in our bodies.

*Carbohydrates* provide the most efficient source of energy to the body. When you are hydrated, they are easy to break down and go to work quickly. Our most common sources of carbohydrates are the sugars and starches found in grains, pastas, drink mixes, cracker mixes, candy, dried potatoes, cereals, and cocoa. Simple carbs (sugars) break down quickly, like kindling in a fire;

complex carbs (starches) break down slowly, like a big log in a fire. Sugars give us quick bursts of energy; starches provide energy for hours.

*Proteins* are used to build muscle tissue, hormones, enzymes, and antibodies. They can serve as an energy source once carbohydrate sources are exhausted. Our protein comes from dairy products, grains, legumes, fish, nuts, and seeds.

*Fats* provide the body with additional calories for energy and gives us the feeling of being full. It is the most calorically dense food type. We get fats from nuts, cheese, oils, peanut butter, fried trail foods, and margarine.

*Vitamins* and *minerals* serve a variety of functions in our bodies. Some help release energy from food while others maintain bodily functions. For example, vitamin A helps with night vision, while sodium provides electrolyte balance. We get vitamins and minerals from foraged salads and by eating a wide range of food types each day. Some instructors use vitamin supplements as well.

Water is an integral part of healthy nutrition. In the mountains, our requirements are greater than in town because of the dry, thin air and the amount of exercise we do each day. Drink enough to remain healthy and energized, usually at least four liters a day, regardless of weather. Drink enough that you urinate clearly and copiously.

### Eating Well at NOLS
Since carbohydrates are easy to break down and provide quick energy, they should be the bulk of your daily diet. It is not necessary to avoid fat at any meal or to eat it only at certain times of the day. It is critical that we eat a variety of foods and adjust our intake according to our changing needs.

### Teaching Considerations
This information should get passed along early in the course. Later in the course, have students describe how diet should be adjusted according to activities or conditions. This may be an easy way to affirm their understanding of nutrition and to help them turn this simple knowledge into habits.

Some courses experience food stress. This can be caused by genuine food shortages, perceived food shortages, poor cooking, or bad expedition behavior in the kitchen. Keep an eye out for students who show chronic low energy or motivation. They may not be getting enough to eat or their kitchen practices may be preventing them from eating well.

Emphasize nutritional awareness and practical applications. Students need to relate how they feel to what they ate during the day. If, however, you do have students who have nutritional concerns beyond the scope of this class, you should be ready to provide them with more information. All instructors should have a more complete understanding of metabolic processes and the nutritional value of the foods provided in NOLS rations.

### Transfer of Learning
One of the greatest leadership habits students can pick up from their NOLS course is to learn to care for themselves. Good nutrition is an important place to start.

## Staying Warm and Dry
Many students come to NOLS thinking that being damp and cold is normal when you are living in the wilderness. Early in the course, show them they can stay comfortable in the most challenging weather conditions simply by dressing and eating properly. A student who is warm and dry is going to be a better expedition member, a more attentive learner, and a more enjoyable companion.

### Learning Objectives
- By the end of a course, students must demonstrate the ability to stay healthy and comfortable while living and traveling in the wilderness.
- Understand how our bodies produce heat and how they lose heat.
- Show a practical understanding of the effects of nutrition, hydration, and physical activity on personal comfort.
- Outdoor leaders must be able to take care of themselves under stressful conditions and still have enough energy left to look after others.

### Heat Production
Under normal conditions, our body produces heat through muscular activity and basic metabolism. A healthy body that is well-nourished, hydrated, and reasonably insulated maintains its temperature at approximately 98.6° F (37° C). When we get chilled, we start shivering. Shivering is an involuntary response intended to generate heat quickly through muscular twitching.

### Heat Loss
Heat flows from warm objects to cold via radiation, convection, conduction, and evaporation. All objects radiate heat. Warmer objects radiate more than cooler ones. Since we are often the warmest object in an area, we have a net heat loss to the environment. The head, hands, and feet have many blood vessels close to the skin, which increases their potential for radiant heat exchange. When our bodies are cooler than surrounding objects, they pick up radiant heat through the same mechanisms.

*Convection* occurs when a moving medium, such as water or wind, sweeps away an object's pocket of radiant heat. This is how you lose heat when you stand in a cold stream or a cool breeze.

*Conduction* is the direct transfer of heat from a warm object to a cool one. A warm butt sitting on a cold rock experiences conduction. Some objects, such as metal, conduct heat better than others, like ensolite.

*Evaporation* is the process of changing a liquid into vapor. It takes heat for this transformation to occur, so evaporating sweat cools your body. This is why a wet bandanna on your head, or dipping your hands or feet into water feels so good on a hot day. Dry climates help evaporation occur quickly; wet climates hinder evaporation.

### Nutrition and Hydration
Nutrition and hydration play essential roles in keeping us warm. The calories our bodies burn come from the food we eat. Carbohydrates burn quickly. Fats, on the other hand, take up to three hours to kick in, but they provide twice as much energy per gram as carbohydrates. When staying warm is a struggle, eating a balance of the two will provide you with the energy you need.

In cold weather, breakfast is critical to maintaining energy and warmth over the course of the day. Eat a power breakfast containing lots of carbohydrates. Eat fats at bedtime to have fuel early in the morning when the carbohydrates have metabolized. When the conditions are harsh, a proven strategy is to snack all day long and throughout the night.

Hydration is integral to heat production. A well-hydrated body utilizes its food more efficiently and has better circulation. Cold temperatures increase urinary output, thus accelerating dehydration. Drink 3-4 liters per day normally, and 5-6 liters in the cold or at altitude.

### Dressing for the Cold
Cotton clothing works well in hot climates because it holds moisture against the skin, promotes evaporation, and accelerates heat loss. For these same reasons, you should not wear cotton on cold or wet days.

Modern fibers and layering systems provide lightweight, functional clothing that can keep you warm and dry if used properly. Layering clothes creates dead air spaces that trap warm air and provide insulation. Clothes made with wool, down, or polarfleece have hollow fibers that create spaces where air is trapped. Breathable wind gear prevents heat loss from convection. Polypropylene underwear wicks moisture away from your skin before any cooling evaporation takes place. Hats and gloves also provide a great deal of warmth by minimizing radiant heat loss.

Rain gear helps keep other layers dry, but since it is not very breathable, you get soaked with sweat if you exercise in it. When temperatures are mild, you will often be more comfortable hiking in polypro and wind gear on rainy days. When it is cold and rainy, hike in rain clothes with a light layer of polypro underneath to minimize sweating. In either case, once you get to camp, change into dry clothes before you cool down. Alternatively, a lightweight umbrella can keep you out of the rain while allowing sweat to evaporate from your clothes.

### Staying Warm
Staying warm takes work, but getting rewarmed takes a lot of work. When the wind is howling through your tent, it is difficult to drag yourself outside to start the stove and cook a meal or melt snow for water, but staying properly hydrated and nourished is critical to staying warm. Staying warm and healthy takes a little bit of knowledge and a lot of self-discipline.

Avoid excess sweating in cold weather. Change your clothes quickly if you get wet. Keep spare clothing dry, particularly spare socks. Watch out for the safety of others in cold, wet, or windy conditions.

Sometimes, due to inclement weather, it can be a struggle to stay warm at night. The resulting loss of sleep from a night spent fighting off the cold can have a compounding effect that reduces a student's ability to stay warm during the day and negatively affects their performance on the course. If you or your students are cold at night, try stuffing dry clothing into your sleeping bag to fill excessive dead air space and to provide more insulation. Sleep in the middle of the shelter between tentmates and put a water bottle filled with warm water in your sleeping bag. Go to bed warm and stay hydrated—if you need to urinate, it is best to get up and go. If these actions don't do the trick, try doing sit-ups inside of your sleeping bag.

### Drying Clothes
If you are warm and healthy, you can use your body as a drier, especially while you are exercising. Your radiant heat will drive moisture out of wet material, but there is a limit to the amount of clothing you should attempt to dry at one time. Two pairs of socks is the maximum for most people. Good drying techniques include wearing damp clothing over a layer of polypro when you go to bed, hanging socks or gloves over your shoulders and under your outer layers while working around camp, and sleeping with damp gear underneath your abdomen. Clothes do not dry out if you stuff them down at the foot of your sleeping bag. In extreme conditions, clothes can be carefully dried near a fire. Remember to be cautious about melting synthetic fabrics, singeing wool, damaging leather, or burning holes with sparks.

### Teaching Considerations
Often conditions dictate that you cover this topic on the first day of the course. Start with simple facts, then expand on them until all expedition members are able to take care of their personal comfort. You can integrate the topic into lessons on cooking, hydration, trail technique, cold injury awareness, and leadership.

Students learn a great deal by watching their instructors manage their own personal climate control. An inappropriately dressed instructor should not be surprised when his students follow his example—model impeccable standards. Put on an extra layer the minute you stop for a break on the trail. Carry a hot drink with you when you make camp visits. Take off your cotton t-shirt when it starts to rain. Your students learn best by mimicking your actions.

### Transfer of Learning
You can use the topic of staying warm and dry to demonstrate a variety of leadership traits, such as role modeling, personal responsibility, and caring for others. Early in the course, it is enough to simply model these traits, but later take time to verbalize what you are doing so your students learn to use similar techniques with their friends back home.

## Staying Found
For some of our students the backcountry is a new and unfamiliar environment. While these students may be confident in their situational awareness at home, they do not have the necessary prior experience, or schema, to apply situational awareness to the backcountry setting. On the first day of a course, give the group expectations for parameters around camp and tools for staying found.

### Learning Objectives
- Early on students should be aware of what is expected of them around camp.
- As the course progresses, students will understand the importance of setting expectations early and then modifying them as the group builds competence.

### Setting Parameters
Early in the course it may be helpful to set up parameters around camp. Establish an area—usually between the kitchen and the shelters—where students are free to roam as they please. Beyond the established parameters ask that students tell someone where they are going and how long they will be away. In bear country, students leaving the established parameters should carry bear spray and consider bringing a buddy.

As students venture past the parameters, give them tools for not getting lost. Remind them to keep their heads up and identify landmarks along their route. Tell them to occasionally look behind them as they leave camp so they will recognize the route back. If they are going out at dusk, ask that they bring a headlamp so they are not caught off guard by nightfall.

### Lost Students
Should a student find himself unable to navigate back to camp, he should know what to do. Coach students to go to a highly visible area nearby and stay put. Teach them to yell loudly or blow a whistle at regular intervals until a search party arrives. The key is to stay put—eventually someone in camp will realize they are missing and a party will be sent to go find them. The further that they venture into the backcountry, the more difficult they will be to locate.

### Leadership Opportunities
Staying found is another area where we encourage students to develop their own judgment. Toward the end of the course, guide students through a reflection of how as novices they were handed strict rules or guidelines, and as they built competence in their backcountry situational awareness they were granted more leeway to practice their own judgment.

## Fire Building
Although on most NOLS courses cooking is done exclusively on stoves and the most common type of fire is a little twiggy fire used for baking, fire building is a fundamental outdoor skill and one our students should leave the course having mastered.

### Learning Objectives
- Students must be able to build and dismantle an environmentally sound fire.
- Recognize when a fire is appropriate or necessary.
- Understand the legal and safety considerations involved in deciding to make a fire.
- Conditions permitting, students can also learn how to cook and bake on a fire.

### Pros and Cons of Campfires
Fires are a good source of heat for cooking food, warming people, and drying clothes. Adeptness at fire building offers students one more survival technique that may bail them out of tough situations. Fires provide a focus for social gatherings. But when used inappropriately, campfires create long-term scarring, nutrient depletion, disruption of local habitats, and soil sterilization. In some areas, regulations prohibit fires. Students should be careful not to burn shoes or clothing by drying them too close to the fire.

### Fire Pans
LNT encourages campers to use fire pans, which most NOLS courses—with the exception of river courses—do not carry. Students should be aware of fire pans, however. You might consider experimenting with one on your course, or at least familiarize your students with their use. Fire pans are metal trays with sides high enough to contain wood and ashes (about three inches). Oil drain pans and backyard barbecue grills make effective and inexpensive fire pans. The pan should be lined with several inches of mineral soil or propped up on small rocks to protect the surface underneath from the heat.

### Selecting a Fire Site
Choose a durable site that is free of flammable material and away from high winds. Avoid low branches, nylon shelters, food bags, dry grass, and duff. The area adjacent to the fire site must be able to endure human traffic. A good location could be a large flat rock or an area of mineral soil free of shrubs and perennial plants.

In heavily-used places, you can usually find an existing fire ring. Choose the largest and most prominent one for your fire, and dismantle any surrounding satellite rings to concentrate use. Where no fire rings exist, find or make a site on bare mineral soil. Mineral soil is sandy and contains no organic material. You can use dry stream beds or sandy beaches, or you can collect mineral soil from under the roots of an overturned tree to build a mound. If you build a mound, make sure the soil pad is at least four inches thick and a foot larger in diameter then the proposed fire. If you have transported soil, consider using a fire blanket under the mound to facilitate cleanup.

### Collecting Wood
Gather wood far away from camp to dilute impact. Select pieces no thicker than the diameter of your wrist. Do not break branches from dead or living trees. Firewood should be dead and down before you pick it up. Walk around when collecting so you don't deplete the wood supply in one area.

### Building a Fire
Start by lighting a small fire with tinder and kindling. Tinder includes dry grass, wood shavings, and thin twigs. This material ignites instantly with a match and will help the kindling—pencil-sized wood—catch. Slowly add to the fire—too much large wood too soon will smother the flame. Avoid break-

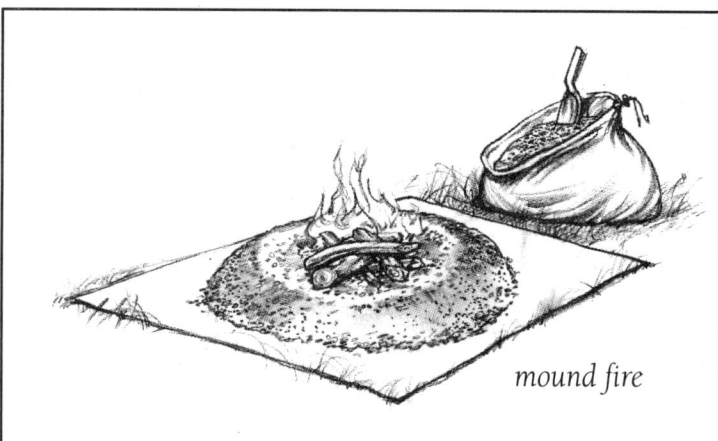

*Use a barrier, like a cloth or fire pan, between the mound fire and the ground. This helps protect the ground below and aides with dispersal of the mineral soil and ashes.*

ing sticks into fire-sized pieces until you are ready to put them in the flames. This retains the natural appearance of the wood and makes scattering leftover pieces easier.

In wet weather, look for dry tinder and kindling under rocks and trees. Whittle dry shavings off larger sticks. In an emergency, use your fuel for ignition, break branches off trees—do what you must—but remember, this is a poor example to show students in any but the most dire circumstances.

Burn all the wood in the fire down to white ash or small pieces of charcoal. Douse the site with water, then place your hand in the slurry of drowned ashes to make sure the fire is extinguished. If it is cool, scatter the ashes over a broad area and return the mineral soil to its original location. Rinse any spilled soil off the rocks and camouflage the site.

### Safety
Be ready with a shovel and water in pots or dromedaries to extinguish the fire if conditions change and it becomes unmanageable. If the day is windy or dry, forgo the fire and use your stove. Never leave a fire unattended.

### Teaching Considerations
Students need to be aware of the local regulations regarding fires in the area where you are camping and of the importance of following fire regulations after their NOLS course. Ask your program supervisor if you are unsure about fire regulations in the areas you are working.

Some students are surprised at the infrequency of fires on NOLS courses. Building, burning, and cleaning up a fire properly is time consuming. Your students must be aware of this commitment before they blithely start in on one. Collect wood as a group and talk about the pieces you select. Have students dismantle the mound and spread the remaining ashes. Getting them actively involved in the entire fire building and dismantling process helps them to absorb the habits and understand the principles of backcountry fires.

### Leadership Opportunities
Fires are a good class to promote judgment rather than rules. At the same time, make it clear that laws and regulations are indeed rules and need to be heeded.

## Fishing
Fishing may be a NOLS student's first exposure to catching, killing, and eating an animal. The experience can be an exciting introduction to a lifelong outdoor sport, and it may stimulate reflections on the implications of being an omnivore. Fishing can provide enjoyment, relaxation, and an opportunity to observe, study, and interpret the aquatic habitat. It also allows for quiet time when students can reflect on their wilderness experience.

### Learning Objectives
- By the end of their NOLS course, students should be able to use and care for fly fishing equipment.
- They should understand basic fish behavior and habitat and have been introduced to the ethical, legal, and culinary aspects of fishing in the wilderness.

### Equipment
A fishing rod acts as an extension of the arm and allows the angler to throw the fly or lure great distances across the water. The reel stores and retrieves line, while metal guides along the rod keep it running straight. Ferrules are the joints where sections of the rod fit together. A leader attaches a fly to the fly line. It tapers down to a thin strand of monofilament that is practically invisible to the fish. Spin reels only contain monofilament line. NOLS fishing kits also include nail clippers, assorted flies or lures, and floatant to keep your fly on top of the water.

Fishing equipment is fragile. As with all camping gear, your options are to carry heavy stuff you can't break or light gear that requires care. Lean the rod against a tree so it does not get stepped on. Assemble and disassemble your rod carefully without twisting or prying the sections. Grease metal ferrules with skin or hair oil. Carry your assembled rod around with the tip pointing behind you and the hook on the hook holder. Inspect your equipment regularly for loose or damaged parts.

### Fly Fishing
Fly rods are assembled and cared for in the same way as spin rods. On combination rods, the fly reel seat is screwed down toward the handle's end. Unlike spin fishing, the fly reel is primarily intended to store line. Rather than reeling fly line in, you pull it in by hand.

Attach a leader to your fly line using a surgeon's knot, and then tie your fly to the leader with an improved clinch knot.

Fly casting is more difficult for novices than spin casting. Practice in an open field first. The weight of the fly line propels the fly out to the fish. Wear glasses and a hat to protect against hooking an eye or an ear. Make sure no one is behind you when casting.

Grip the rod in front of the reel. Keep your thumb on top. Make sure the butt of the reel seat presses against the forearm. Cast with your elbow and shoulder rather than wrist. Find a stable and comfortable stance and use an active upper body to power the cast. The rod moves in a plane 30-45 degrees

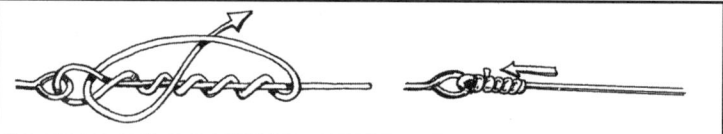

*The improved clinch knot is used to attach the fly to the leader*

laterally off of vertical. Start with 15' of line fed out the tip of the rod.

Now picture a clock face. Your cast should take place between ten o'clock and one o'clock. The rhythm of the cast should be a quick push between the ten and one o'clock position, with a pause at each end of the cast. The pauses are essential to allow the line to roll out completely in both front and back. Watch the line to gauge when to move in the opposite direction. Once a rhythm is established, pull out more line on the back cast and throw it out with the momentum of the forward cast. False casts allow time for more line to be cast and to dry the fly.

Once you have enough line out, let the fly drop softly on the water. Keep the rod tip low and pointing towards the fly while waiting for a strike. Slowly pull the excess slack out of the line between the fly and the rod tip. As with spin fishing, when the fish hits the fly, set the hook by tightening the line. Keep the rod tip up and the line tight while playing and landing the fish. A slack line may allow the fish to wiggle off the hook.

In close quarters where an overhead cast is impractical, try a dabbling technique. This involves flicking line out and letting the stream carry your fly to the fish.

Fly fishing requires stealth to trick the fish into thinking your fly is alive. Sneak up on the stream or lake. Avoid making noises, casting shadows, or creating vibrations which frighten fish into hiding. Stay low near the water.

### Killing and Cleaning a Fish
Once you have the fish near shore, hold the line tight with one hand and reach into the water to grab the fish with the other. Remove the hook and kill the fish as quickly and humanely as possible. One method for doing this is to stick your thumb into the fish's mouth and bend the head back until its neck breaks. Another technique is to hit the fish on a rock, but because of their slippery skin, it can be hard to kill the fish quickly this way. You can also cut off their head with a knife.

To clean the fish, make an incision from the anus to a line just behind the gill junction. Cut the gular membrane under the trout's chin. Grasp the membrane and pull back toward the tail in one motion. The gills, guts and pectoral fins should follow. Clean the kidney tissue along the spine. Rinse the carcass thoroughly before cooking.

In areas, like Wyoming, with Whirling Disease, fish guts should be tossed on shore back in the bushes. This helps prevent diseases from spreading. In some areas, biologists recommend leaving guts in the water. Guts thrown into trees are eaten by birds and pine martens, but if you choose this technique, do it well away from camp to keep animals out of course food. In bear country, fisheries biologists recommend you clean and dispose of fish guts in fast moving water at least several hundred yards downstream of camp. The most fundamental principle in stopping the spread of Whirling Disease is to never move organisms from one drainage to another.

### Principles for Preventing the Spread of Whirling Disease
Whirling Disease and other pathogens are easily transferred from one water system to another. Remember:
- State and local laws prevail.
- In remote bear country, it is okay to recycle fish guts and skeletons in the same fast moving water the fish came out of.
- Avoid discarding anything in the organic sediments found in slowly moving water, because the tubifex worms that help co-host WD live there.
- High-use areas have special needs and can't tolerate fish guts due to concentration problems.

### Fishing Ethics and Laws
Catch only enough fish to feed yourself and your cook group. Kill your fish quickly. Tie knots correctly so that fish won't escape with lures or flies stuck in their mouths.

Fishing licenses are required while fishing or when in possession of rigged fishing gear along bodies of water. Local regulations governing allowable species, size, and quantity of fish taken must be followed strictly. Know and follow the regulations in your course area.

Some students may be repulsed by the thought of killing a fish. It is their decision whether to learn this outdoor skill. This issue can be a catalyst for students to either commit to participating in "the dirty work" of omnivorism or change their lifelong eating habits.

### Catch and Release
If you plan to catch and release, use a barbless hook. Avoid playing the fish to exhaustion. Land the fish quickly and remove the hook with small pliers. Try not to touch the fish, but if handling cannot be avoided, do it gently in the water, trying not to disturb the protective slime on the fish's skin. Monitor the fish after releasing it. See that it swims away; if it doesn't, put it out of its misery and eat it.

### Teaching Considerations
Get your students fishing as quickly as possible. Students have more fun and learn faster when they are motivated by the chance of success. Remind students to have their licenses at all times when fishing. Do not underestimate the difficulty students have killing a fish.

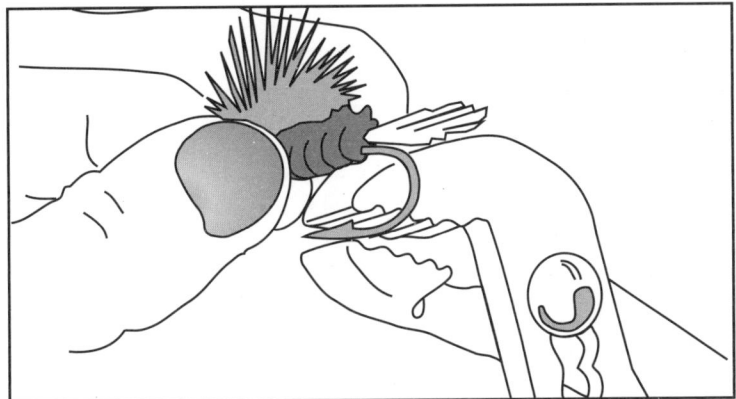

*For catch and release, flatten the barb on your flies with a pair of pliers to avoid injuring the fish.*

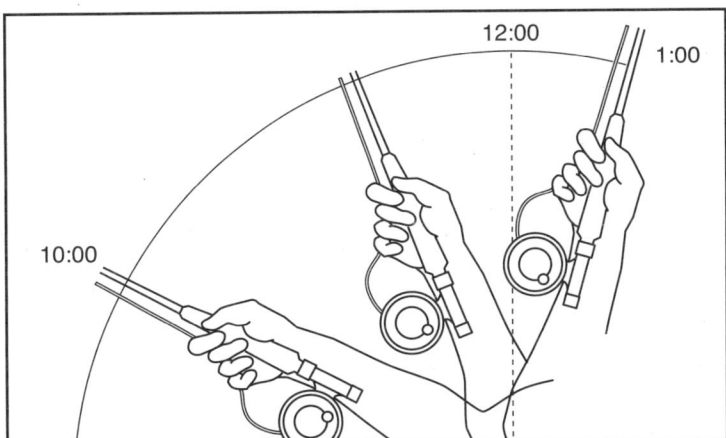

*When fly casting, picture a clock face with your head at twelve o'clock and your feet at six. Try to keep the rod between ten o'clock and one o'clock.*

### Leadership Opportunities
Encourage students who are experienced anglers to coach others. Make sure they are using their expertise to help their peers rather than to increase their power in the group. If you see such a manipulation of power happening, give them feedback accordingly.

### Suggested Reading for Fishing
- Anderson, Sheridan (1986) Curtis Creek Manifesto. Frank Amato Publications.
- Rosenbauer, Tom (2009) The Orvis Guide To Beginning Flyfishing: 101 tips for the absolute beginner. NY: Skyhorse Publishing.

## Trout Habitat and Behavior
A little knowledge about trout feeding habits and lifestyles can aid your students in successful angling. The study of aquatic ecology can be as simple or as involved as the group desires. Keep in mind that the goal is to get them out there catching fish as soon as possible.

### Learning Objectives
- Students should be able to choose a lure or fly that will attract a trout and a fishing spot that is likely to yield a strike.
- Give students an introduction to trout habitat and behavior.
- Show how the science of aquatic ecology directly relates to fishing, a fun and accessible outdoor activity.

### Fish Food
Trout meals include small fish, insects, leeches, and crustaceans. In most cases, anglers use either flies that imitate various stages of an insect's life, or lures that mimic small minnows to catch fish. At NOLS we carry fishing tackle to accommodate fish feeding at the surface, below the surface, and near the bottom of streams and lakes.

### Matching the Hatch
Fly fishing often relies on presenting the trout with some sort of insect imitation. NOLS issues trout flies that imitate terrestrial bugs and aquatic insects in different phases. Terrestrial flies include grasshoppers, ants, inchworms, or crickets that may have fallen or jumped into the water. Aquatic insect flies are more varied. Depending on the genus, aquatic insects go through three to four life phases from egg to adulthood. Mayflies, stone flies, and caddis flies start out as eggs, then crawl or swim along the bottom in a larval stage before floating to the surface and sprouting wings. The mature adults mate, then die. Wet flies include those that approximate the nymph or larval stage. Dry flies resemble emerging or mature adults.

Trout eat insects in all their phases. Try to determine what the trout are feeding on and match this food source with a fly. This is called *matching the hatch*. Look for insects landing on the water and fish rising to eat them. This would be a dry fly situation. The lack of rises may indicate that nymphs, larvae, or baby trout are on the menu. Many aquatic insect species rise to the surface and transform into the adult phase when it is almost dark out. This is called a hatch. Such an event can send the trout into a feeding frenzy.

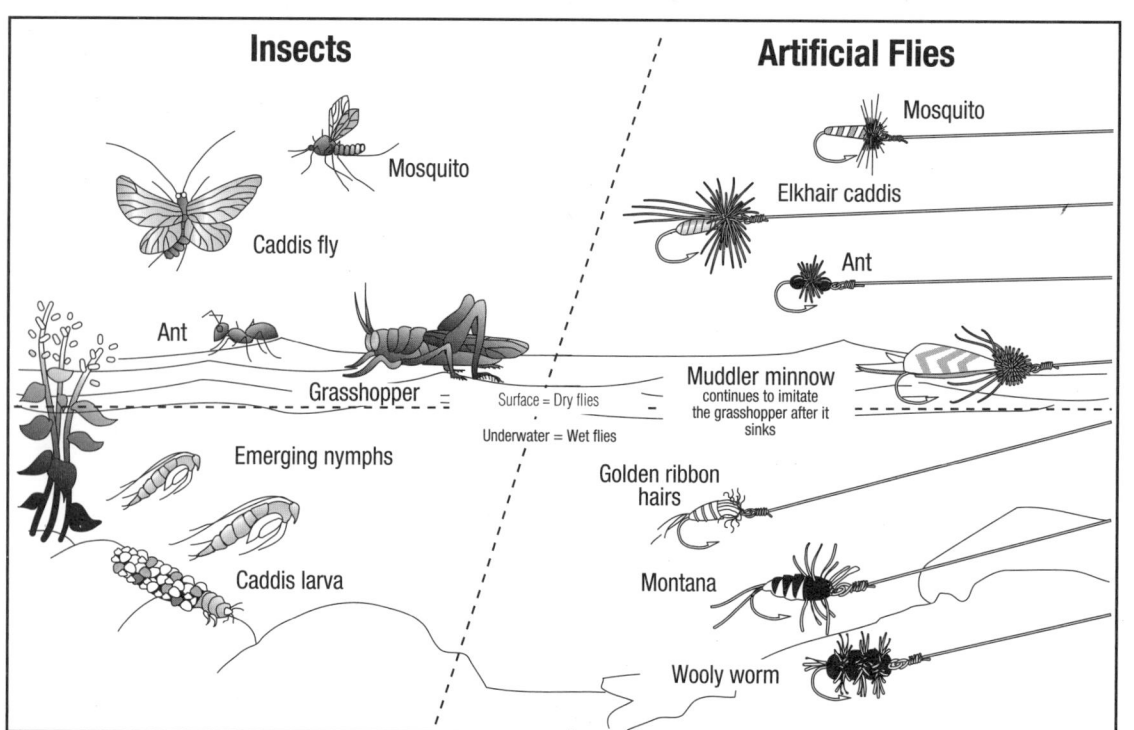

*Matching the hatch is part of the art of fly fishing. Here are some examples of insects and the flies that match them.*

### Fish Sense

Trout have evolved to be good hunters and successful evaders of predation. Their sense organs are especially keen to vibrations, dark silhouettes, and smells. Water transmits sound at a rate of a mile per second, so walking softly on the bank or in the water is essential to avoid alarming the fish. A trout's eyesight is also good. They notice the shape, size, and tonal characteristics of insects. The color of the fly does not need to match the hatch exactly, but if the bugs are light-colored, use a light-colored fly.

Light refracts as it hits the water. This allows trout to detect a predator's approach from 48 degrees or more above the water surface. If you can see the trout, you should approach them in a low, crouched position. The smell of insect repellent, human skin, or petroleum products can also frighten fish. Trout have external taste buds that let them taste their prey just by bumping into it. Tie your flies with clean hands.

### Holding Waters

Read the stream to look for places of shelter and easy feeding. Water velocity is different from place to place throughout the stream. Moving water brings a continuous supply of food, but constant exposure to a strong current tires a trout. Trout pick places that permit them to feed with minimal effort and that conceal them from predators. Undercut banks provide just such a sanctuary, but are difficult to fish. Trout also like to hang out at the bottom of deep runs where the light is diffuse and the water slower. You can often find them in pools just below riffles, usually at the head of the pool where the water is deep and slow.

Eddies behind boulders or submerged logs are also favorite trout hangouts because they tend to harbor delectable insect populations. Watch for trout darting into swifter currents for food and back to slower water to rest. Trout prefer cool water because it is rich in oxygen. If the stream is unusually warm, look for trout in rapid water or where springs feed the stream. Most trout are territorial. This means the biggest, most aggressive fish get the best pools.

The food-producing areas of a lake are limited to the depth that sunlight penetrates. The best combination for trout is a shallow area next to a deep drop-off. This provides good feeding opportunities and a quick escape route. Outlets and inlets create currents that bring food to expectant trout. Lake fish cruise when they feed. Watch for the direction of the rises and cast ahead of them. On windy days, look for current lines holding floating debris. Trout often investigate these lines looking for drowned insects. Peninsulas and land that jut out into lakes are good fishing spots because cruising trout must swim around the obstacles. On these points, try casting parallel to the shore to get your fly or lure into the main traffic pattern.

### Teaching Considerations

As with fishing skills, trout habitat needs to be taught on the water where students can observe and interpret the fish in their habitat. Take your students out and show them rising fish. Explain what the trout might be eating and where the nearest concealment is. Cruise the shorelines and banks while your students are fishing, and quiz them as to where they think the fish are and why.

Don't pass up teachable moments on the trail. If the fish are rising, consider dropping packs and sneaking up on the fish with binoculars to identify them and see what they are eating.

Introduce your students to aquatic insects by wading into the water and capturing live specimens. Examine them under a hand lens. The results are educational and fascinating.

## NOLS Grizzly Bear Practices

Instructors leading courses in grizzly bear habitat need to be competent in following the NOLS Accepted Field Practices (NAFPs) for bears. The following information is derived from those practices, but the NAFP is always the most current source. NOLS' principle goals in bear country are 1) to avoid close encounters with bears and 2) to deter potential attacks. Grizzly bears and black bears cohabitate in many environments; in areas where this is the case, grizzly bear practices take precedent over black bear practices. The practices in this section are tailored to grizzly bear precautions and are appropriate regardless of bear species. Additional information on practices for environments where ONLY black bears live can be found later in this book.

### Learning Objectives
- Understand the purpose and rationale of the NOLS grizzly bear practices.
- Demonstrate the ability and judgment to consistently apply the NOLS grizzly bear practices on a daily basis.

### Principal Goals
The goals of the NOLS grizzly bear practices are to 1) avoid a close encounter and 2) deter an attack if an encounter occurs.

### 1) Avoid a Close Encounter
*Our Practice:*
We strive to avoid close encounters with bears through practices aimed at preventing bears from coming to us and by identifying situations where we are more likely to encounter bears. In particular, courses strive to alert bears to a human presence outside the bear's overt response distance by making loud human sounds—what we refer to as "bear calls."

*Bear Behavior:*
Each bear has a personal space (called an overt response distance) that, when intruded upon, is likely to trigger a defensive response. These personal spaces vary according to the bear's sex, species, and activity. They can range anywhere from less than 20 feet to more than a quarter of a mile. Bears, like all animals, have evolved for survival. If you are far enough away that the bear does not consider you a threat, it may ignore you and continue with its activity. Generally, once a bear gets a whiff of human scent or hears human noises, it will run away unless confronted within its personal space.

## 2) Deter the Attack

*Our Practice:*
Our primary means of deterring an attack are to set and maintain adequate group sizes, stay close to group members, and practice bear encounter drills (including the use of bear spray—see the lesson plan on Bear Spray).

*Bear Behaviors:*
If presented with a threat or some unknown intruder within its critical range, a bear will size up the nature of that threat and act as it sees fit. The threshold at which a bear opts to flee rather than confront appears to relate to the physical size of the threat. Statistics show that most bear attacks are confrontations with solo humans. Bear ecologist Tom Smith cites a large bear-human incident dataset from Alaska and Canada in which he says that two or more people have rarely ever been attacked when calmly making a stand against a defensive bear attack. The same dataset shows that large groups of people that are spread out are more likely to have the solo hiker in front be attacked by a surprised bear. What is key is that a surprised bear sees at least two contiguous people when it makes the snap decision between fight and flight.

Bears may attack humans defensively because we surprise them. More rarely, they may prey on humans. The proper use of bear deterrent spray is highly effective in stopping bears from attacking and greatly reduces the chance of injuries to humans by bears (Smith, 2008). Biologist Stephen Herrero of Canada reports that in every documented case where spray was used, the bear retreated (Smith & Herrero, 2009).

### Bear Awareness Triangle

When in bear country, one is presented with constant decisions about how to implement specific practices. How close do the group members need to stay to each other? How frequently should the group make bear calls? What is an appropriate group size to fetch water or to go defecate? How accessible does the bear spray need to be at any given moment? The ongoing need to make decisions and the number of factors to be considered in each decision can be overwhelming. For this reason, most instructor teams begin courses by simply laying out rules for students. However, as courses progress, instructors may introduce more judgment into this decision making process. This is especially important if student expeditions are a curriculum goal.

The Bear Awareness Triangle (see next page) is a tool to help with this decision making process. The human factor, the bear factor, and the environment are three variables that influence situational awareness and the need to continually reassess changing conditions. Each side of the triangle is accompanied by a few prompting questions.

### Bear Encounter Stoplight

A stoplight metaphor has proven to be a useful risk management assessment and communication tool. The following example is designed to help backcountry travelers assess the likelihood of a bear encounter. The bear stoplight is useful for addressing the degree of risk and how practices may vary for a variety of conditions.

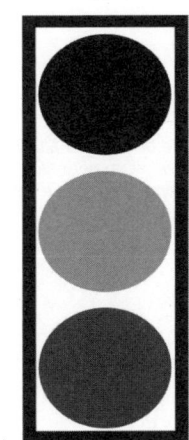

**RED LIGHT** The likelihood of a bear encounter is high or the group's ability to influence the outcome of an encounter is hindered.

**YELLOW LIGHT** Conditions are such that a bear encounter should be anticipated and people should be alert.

**GREEN LIGHT** A close bear encounter is unlikely or can be readily managed.

*Red light: Either the situation should be avoided altogether or a high degree of diligence and preparation is necessary to avoid an encounter or repel an attack.*

specific controlled circumstances (e.g., walking between groups at the tents and the kitchens) group sizes of two or three students may be appropriate. The minimum group size is two.

At any given moment, each individual should be able to identify the group that they are a part of should they need to muster together to face a bear.

### Group Size While Defecating

The expectation to be in a group while defecating consistently pushes the limits of how far group members should be from each other. As a general rule people may spread out 10 or 15 yards in green-light conditions. In red-light conditions however, people shouldn't venture much more than four yards from each other. In a red-light environment, four yards should still offer some small measure of privacy. Instructors need to set these standards consistently from day one.

### Practices While Traveling

Traveling, in contrast to camping, increases the likelihood of coming upon a bear. Even in the best conditions, travel should be considered a yellow-light activity. In general, travel calls for larger groups sizes, closer proximity, and more accessible bear spray than around camp.

### Group Size

Group size is a primary factor in deterring a bear attack. A group only has a deterrent effect if the members are close together at the moment that the bear makes its decision between fight and flight. The default group size is four or more people. This includes time spent defecating. A group of four provides a margin of error for novices and should be the norm in most circumstances.

After careful consideration, demonstrated competence, and in

### Bear Precautions

**1. Avoid A Close Encounter**
- Make frequent and loud bear calls
- Place grey water in a river, a sump, or the ocean
- Avoid camping near human and animal trails

- Students stay promarily in groups of four or more
- Group size rules are in effect at all times
- Prioritize camps with open sightlines
- Separate sleeping and cooking areas
- Choose kitchens near each other
- Pitch tents in close proximity, and arrange so as not to trap a bear
- As appropriate, use bear canisters, electric fences, or bear hangs

**2. Deter an Attack**
- Stay close to other group members
- Keep bear spray at hand in every group
- Practice bear encounter drills
- Have the front traveler carry bear spray
- Sleep in tents or tarps as opposed to in the open

*The principle goals of NOLS grizzly bear practices are to avoid an encounter and to deter an attack. This chart shows some actions that we can take to accomplish the two principle goals.*

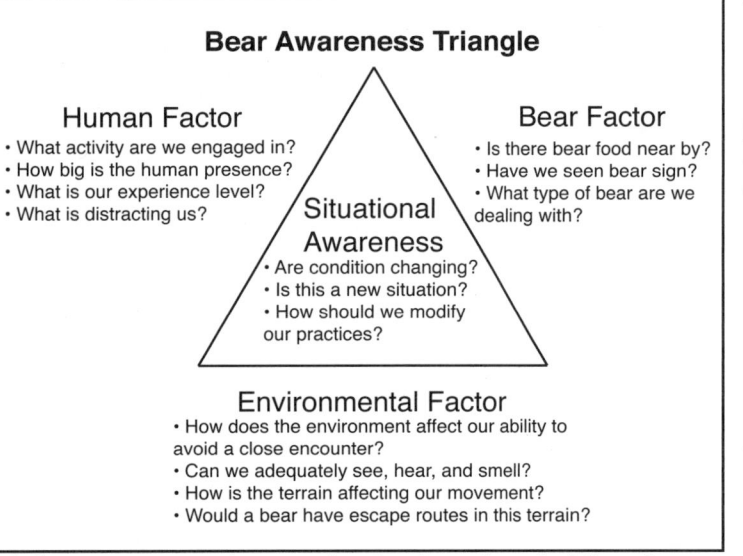

*The bear awareness triangle is a simple tool used to evaluate the different factors at play in bear country.*

### Bear Calls
- Make loud, human noises while hiking to help alert any bears to your presence. In green light conditions this can be done less frequently.
- In red light conditions increase volume and frequency any time a group approaches terrain where visibility is impaired or the wind is in your face. The farther your noise carries, the less likely you are to surprise a bear at close range. Shouting, singing, clapping, and talking loudly are all effective practices.
- Don't make noises like a wounded animal or a bear; these may attract a bear.

### Group Size and Contiguity
- Students should travel in groups of four or more.
- In a red-light environment (e.g., bushwhacking) group members should, ideally, be able to reach out and touch each other. In contrast, in a green light environment, it might be appropriate to be spread out by five or ten yards on the trail.
- Keeping a hiking group together requires communication and discipline. It is a challenge that instructors must address starting on day one. It is paramount that the first hiker has a second person close behind.
- Avoid splitting a hiking group up into smaller satellite groups for scouting. Multiple groups in an area have a higher likelihood of bumping into a bear than one group, and there is the possibility of accidentally surrounding a bear.
- Since instructors often travel as an I-team, it is common for instructors to travel in groups of three and sometimes two. Three and especially two-person groups call for extra caution and increased discipline. Both members of a two-person I-team should have bear spray.

### Bear Spray
Bear spray is a vital tool in deterring an attack and the practices are covered in the next section.

### Practices at Camp
In contrast to traveling, a bear encounter at camp is more likely to take the form of a bear coming upon a group of people. Consequently, practices at camp center around not attracting a bear to camp and being prepared for a bear to wander into camp. Although bears are curious about their surroundings, they are often more afraid of humans than they are attracted to human food sources. However, bears that become conditioned to human food tolerate human scent and may associate it with feeding.

In some locations, camp layout, gray water disposal, and food storage practices will be prescribed by the land management agency. Otherwise, follow NOLS common practices for grizzly bear habitat listed below.

### Separate Tents from the Kitchen Area
- Tents should be located upstream/upwind of the kitchen and, if possible, with visual contact between the two areas. The two areas should be far enough away from each other—100 yards is a good guideline—to provide a comfortable separation if a bear enters the kitchen area while the group is sleeping.
- Keep all cook groups close together so people can gather quickly if a bear is sighted. An ideal kitchen area is in the open and has good visibility in all directions. Good kitchen locations are on gravel bars, along rivers, and in open meadows or clearings.

### Minimize All Odors and Contain Necessary Ones
- Do not eat in or near the tents.
- Where land management agencies require it, or when supervisors and instructors deem it appropriate, we should keep food unavailable from bears using electric fences, bear hangs, or bear canisters. In most of NOLS Alaska's operating areas and in the Yukon we leave food bags unprotected in the kitchen area and have a long record of very low incident rates. This is consistent with recommendations from local wildlife managers. NOLS typically only uses bear canisters where required by land managers because they are extremely inconvenient on an extended expedition. Food-conditioned bears quickly become human safety issues.
- Store all food, garbage, and odorous toiletries such as toothpaste, sunscreen, and mosquito repellent in the kitchen area to minimize the risk of attracting bears to the sleeping area. Remember to transfer trail food from backpacks to kitchen sites. Cook pots, utensils, cups, and bowls should all be stored in the kitchen. Keep food in specified food bags and minimize contact with other equipment and clothes in the pack, boat, and camp. Lining food bags with garbage bags helps to contain odors.
- Avoid spilling food or wiping hands or utensils on clothes.
- Store used feminine products with other attractants in the kitchen. Studies have concluded that menstruation does not attract bears or provoke attacks, but used feminine products may have an odor.
- Used bear spray is considered an attractant and should be stored in the kitchen. Wash off the canister soon after use. Do not stay in an area where the spray has been discharged. If you cannot leave, maintain heightened awareness, and depart the area as soon as practical. If any residue is left on clothes, tents, or equipment, rinse them thoroughly with water.

### Disposal of Gray Water
- Gray water means wastewater other than bodily waste (e.g., dishwater, toothpaste, hand-washing water). To minimize odors, dispose of gray water by either pouring it into a moving body of water or a sump hole. Keep soap out of all bodies of water, since it is harmful to many aquatic organisms.
- Where practical and permitted by regulations, dispose of gray water directly into a creek or a river. Pots can be rinsed directly in bodies of water if all food particles have been removed and bagged. Many rivers and streams can withstand gray water and minor food particles with little ecological impact, especially compared to the impact of food-conditioning a bear. Use of low-volume streams is dependent upon instructor judgment.
- When a stream or river is unavailable or inappropriate, pour gray water directly into a sump hole. Minimize the food particles entering the sump to reduce potential for bears to associate sumps with food. Make sure the hole is large enough to prevent overflow of dirty gray water. The sump should be covered when not in use.
- Groups can disperse their impact by taking soap and water to defecate, and washing hands while away from camp and kitchen.

### Dispose of Fish Carefully
- Fish and other greasy food smells are especially attractive to bears.
- Cook and eat fish right away.
- Any knife used to gut the fish should be kept with kitchen articles.
- Clean fish away from camp and throw the guts in the water to minimize odors. Dispose of bones and other remains in the water also. If this is not possible, deposit them at least one-quarter mile from camp.

### Sleeping Area Layout
- Arrange tents in a line or a semi-circle when possible to prevent trapping a bear inside a cluster of tents where escape routes are not obvious.
- Set up tents where you have clear sight lines in all directions. Avoid being too close to bushes where bears may travel or rest unseen.
- Avoid camping near game and human trails; bears use these trails too. On dark nights, bears rarely leave trails because they can't see where they are going.
- Sleep in a tent. Since it is a larger object than a sleeping person, a bear is less likely to identify it as possible food.

## Bear Camping Distances

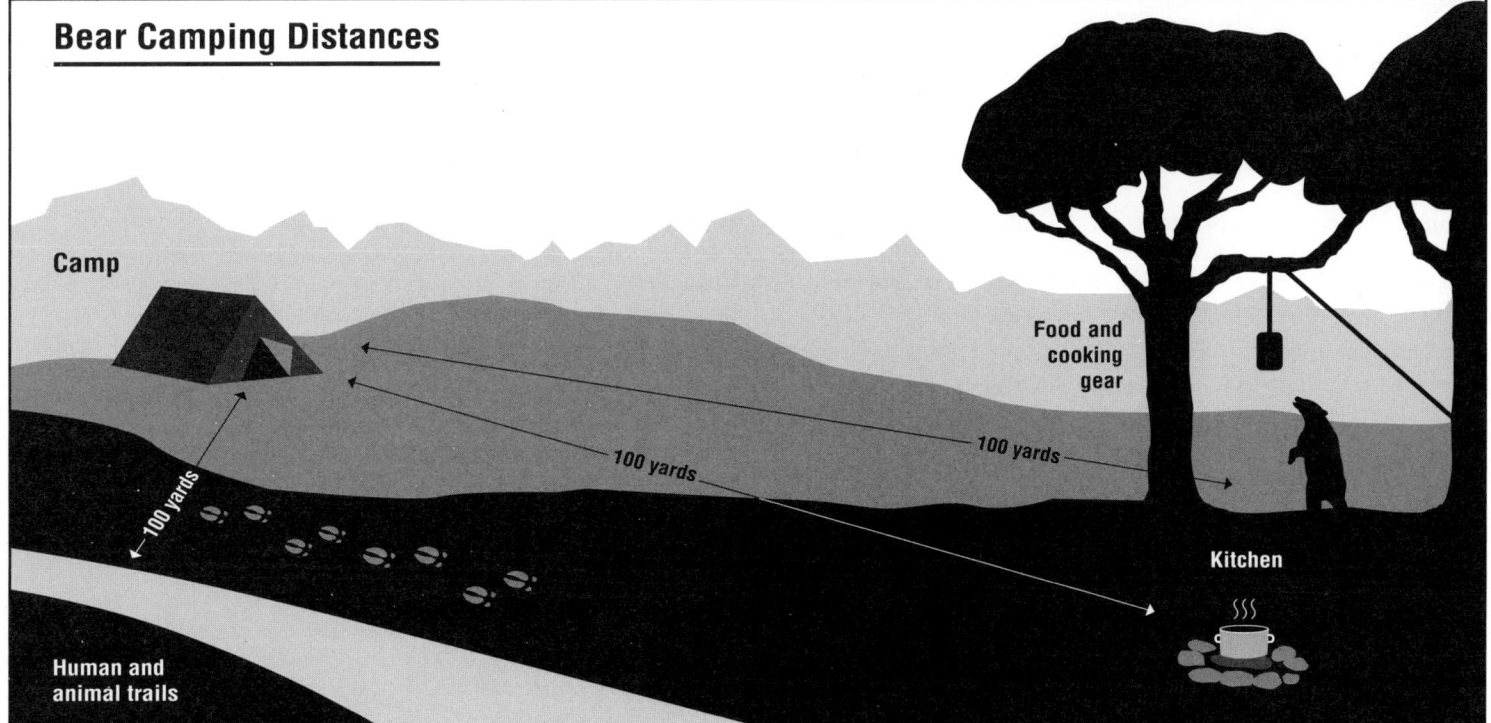

*When camping in bear country it is important to set up camp at least one hundred yards from your kitchen, food storage area, and any trails that may be traveled by bears at night. It is also a good idea to place your sleeping area upwind of your kitchen area.*

### Group Size and Movement Around Camp
- Frequent travel between the sleeping area and the kitchen helps establish a human presence in the area. This presence, if combined with high visibility and strong bear awareness, allows flexibility with group size around camp. Use all of the factors in the Bear Awareness Triangle to assess the likelihood of a bear encounter in camp.
- Bear practices make it challenging to get personal time. In green-light conditions, individuals seeking "solo time" at camp may separate themselves by 10 to 15 yards from supporting group members. These individuals should position themselves to maximize their awareness of the surroundings.
- It is sometimes appropriate to make bear calls around camp. For example, when walking to the kitchens first thing in the morning, or if visibility is restricted.
- Continued alertness is important at camp. Be ready to re-assess your situation if conditions change or as you gather more information.

### Teaching Bear Practices
We cannot completely eliminate the risk of a bear attack, but we can minimize the likelihood and consequences through proper education and practices. It is important that students understand that their best protection against bears is an alert awareness of their surroundings and conscientious practice of the travel and camping techniques we teach.

Start developing a heightened awareness and respect for bears on the first day of the course. Strive to teach appropriate practices and respect for bears without creating fear. Remember that successful practices create invisible results: no bears seen. This can lead to complacency, so camping and travel techniques must be enforced and monitored continuously until they become second nature.

Instructors should continuously verbalize and point out their observations and decisions relating to bear risk. Introduce the sides of the bear awareness triangle in short classes, and then reference them regularly. Gradually delegate decisions about bear practices to student leaders. Coach those leaders on the use of the Bear Awareness Triangle.

### Note on Distances
We use yards as the primary unit of measure this document. In the field, it is often more practical to use paces to measure distances. A pace is about a yard. It is useful to have everyone pace out 100 yards so that they will have a reference for how long their pace is.

## Bear Spray
Bear deterrent pepper spray is specially formulated for use against bears. When used correctly, it has been proven to be effective as a non-lethal means to stop an attack or at worst greatly minimize the consequences of an attack. Keep the bear spray where the people are. It should accompany people on day hikes, to defecate, in kitchens, in camp, during personal time, etc. Bear spray should always be accessible and people should be able to regroup quickly. Keep bear spray in each tent vestibule when sleeping.

### Learning Objectives
- Teach students proper methods for carrying and using bear spray.
- Condition students and instructors to draw and discharge bear spray in the event of an encounter.
- Use bear encounter drills and practice to develop this skill.

### Availability of Bear Spray
- Courses in areas of high likelihood of a bear encounter or long duration exposure such as wilderness courses in Alaska, the Yukon, or the Absarokas are to have one canister of bear spray per person.
- Courses in areas of lower likelihood of a bear encounter or short duration exposure such as courses in the Wind Rivers, the Waddington Range, or Alaska and Yukon mountaineering courses could take one, though preferably two, canisters of bear spray per hiking group/shelter.
- Bear spray needs to be accessible at all times; however, availability may differ whether in camp or while traveling—see below.

### Bear Spray Practices
Bear spray should be carried in such a way to allow for a one-handed draw. It is preferable to carry bear spray on the body so that it is always with the person. A holster will be provided with each bear spray canister.

Bear spray will be worn on the person with a waist belt or chest harness, or attached to the backpack on the hip belt or a shoulder strap (various methods possible). This provides another option if wearing it on the person isn't practical for some reason. Carrying bear spray in wand pockets of backpacks is not acceptable. Carrying bear spray in pockets of clothing is not acceptable except in unusual situations, e.g., a lost holster. Consider carrying bear spray in hand when:
- In areas of high bear density.
- A bear is known to be in the area, but it cannot be seen.
- In areas of low visibility, e.g., dense brush, "tight" terrain, i.e., ravines or gullies.

- During periods of low visibility, e.g., fog.
- Scouting a route ahead.
- Going to defecate.

### Additional Considerations

If not everyone has a bear spray, the front traveler should be sure to carry one. If there are multiple bear sprays in a group, have the first and last person carry a bear spray.

For boating courses, bear spray may be attached to the boat while on the water and should be carried in a holster on the person when on shore.

If canisters of bear spray are lost, the course will adjust the number of hiking groups accordingly and consider options for replacement.

### Bear Encounter Drills

Before leaving for the field it is advised that, when possible, instructors demonstrate how to shoot bear spray and have students practice with an inert or expired canister. If instructors have never shot bear spray, they should practice before going to the field.

Practicing bear encounter drills is intended to help students develop a conditioned response to a potential encounter. Instructors should have students practice what to do in an encounter throughout the course and in a wide variety of situations. Bear encounter drills should be a regular part of the curriculum. They are a chance to reinforce what is taught in the initial bear encounter class and an opportunity to get students thinking about a variety of scenarios and variables. At least occasionally, students should practice all of the actions they are expected to perform, including playing dead and fighting back. When possible, students should practice shooting inert bear sprays before going into the field. Do not fire bear sprays during drills in the field. Also consider the hazard of removing bear spray safeties during every bear drill. It is something every student should practice, but it does not need to be done during every drill.

Drills may take a wide variety of formats. Initially, they will likely be slow walk-throughs of what to do in an encounter. As students gain confidence and experience, drills might start to take on more of a pop quiz format: catch students when their bear practices are compromised and get them to demonstrate how they would respond. For example, how would a group respond if they ran into a bear and had forgotten bear spray?

Drills should emphasize conditioning physical responses to bear encounters, especially the initial response to stand one's ground, draw the bear spray, and group up.

### Teaching Considerations

Be careful to avoid accidental discharge of bear spray. Though NOLS has had more injuries from accidental discharge of bear spray than from bears, this concern should not deter people from having bear spray ready for quick use as necessary.

Students may ask about guns as protection from bears. Scientists who study bear/human interactions have found that bear spray is more effective than firearms at deterring an attack. Furthermore, in instances when an attack did occur, it was shorter in duration and the injuries were less severe when bear spray was used when compared to firearms.

## Bear Encounters

A bear encounter may take many forms. Courses need to be prepared for the worst-case scenario. If a bear is encountered at close range and the bear charges, people will have only seconds to react. It is impossible to predict exactly how a bear will react, but the following standard responses to bear encounters have been shown to avert the situation or minimize injury.

### Learning Objectives
- Students will have a clear understanding of the proper response to a variety of bear encounters

### Responding to an Encounter

Bears can move very quickly. Based on a sprinting speed of 40 miles per hour, a grizzly can cover 100 yards in just over five seconds. It can accelerate from 0 to 40 mph in five jumps. A bear can reach a target from a quarter-mile away in just over 20 seconds.

When a bear is spotted, stop, stand your ground, and draw the bear spray from the holster. Assess the situation: try to identify what species of bear you are facing, and then do the following depending on how the bear acts:

**Unaware Bear—bear does not know you are present**
- Avoid the bear. Quietly leave the area or let the bear move off on its own. If you must move where the bear will see, hear, or smell you, let it know you are coming—talk loudly and calmly, and move your group upwind so it can smell you.
- If you see one bear, be aware of the possibility that there are cubs or sub-adults in the area.

**Aware Bear—bear is aware of your presence**

A bear may stand its ground to display its dominance, inviting you to leave. It may "woof" or pop its teeth together, or both. It may turn sideways to look bigger. Back away slowly, speaking calmly and quietly. If you show no hostility, the bear may leave. A sow with cubs can be more dangerous than a single bear. Her first impulse may be immediate intimidation. Her objective is to stop the disturbance and get you to leave immediately so she can return to her cubs.

- Stand your ground, group together shoulder to shoulder, and face the bear. A bear is less likely to attack two or more people standing next to each other.
  – Do not run.
  – Do not turn your back.
  – Do not back up.
  – Do not kneel down in front of a bear.
- Do not move toward the bear. Watch the bear to see what it does in response to your presence.
- Get the bear spray out of its holster (if it isn't already) and prepare to use it.
- Help the bear identify you as human. Speak to the bear in an assured, audible voice.
- Once the bear establishes your identity, it may move away.
- The following acronym helps students master the fundamentals:

**S**tand your ground

**P**ull the bear spray: draw it from its holster and remove the safety

**R**ound up your group: stand shoulder to shoulder

**A**ct human: talk to the bear

**Y**ield: don't threaten the bear, stand until the bear leaves, or slowly back away.

### Charging Bear

A bear may charge to assert its dominance, but not attack. These false charges or bluffs are designed to intimidate the intruder. It may repeatedly charge a short distance and retreat or charge and pass right by. However, there is no way to know if a charge is a bluff or the bear is going to attack.

Encountering a bear at close range—within 30 yards—means that your immediate response can significantly affect how the bear will respond. Any bear sighting is memorable and any bear encounter can be frightening—more so if that encounter is at close range. Because of the speed at which a bear can move, you may only have one or two seconds to recognize the situation, get the bear spray out, stand your ground, and shoot the bear spray; any other action like yelling, turning away, or trying to run will likely result in an attack.

*If a bear charges:*
- Stand your ground as described above for an aware bear.
- When the bear is just beyond the range of your spray (about 15 yards away) one person shoots a one-second blast of bear spray so that the bear runs into it approximately 10 yards away from you. This should stop the bear from charging. Most bear sprays have a range of 30 feet (9 meters). Check your bear spray for specifics.

*If the bear keeps charging:*
- Shoot the bear spray again continuously. While everyone who has bear spray in the group could shoot it, there is a need to keep some for another possible encounter.
- Aim for the bear's face because eyes, nose and mouth are where the spray is most effective.
- Empty the can if the bear's approach persists.
- Be aware that wind speed and direction will affect your accuracy and that bear spray is likely to affect you too.

### Attacking Bear

If you are actually attacked (being bitten or clawed) by a grizzly:

- Wait to drop and play dead until you have used your bear spray and the bear actually strikes. Dropping sooner may turn a bluff charge into an attack.
- If knocked down, stay down. Get into defensive position. Keep your pack on. Lie face down with your legs apart. This position makes it more difficult for the bear to flip you over and attack your face. Place your hands behind your neck.
- Don't move or resist. The bear generally bites and swats the victim a few times and then runs away. The bear will most likely lose interest once you appear "killed." It may attempt to cover you with dirt or twigs as a cache. Remain still until you are sure it is gone. Getting up too soon could provoke another attack. Most survivors of bear attacks relate that they felt little or no pain at the time of the attack. Victims who play dead are not usually seriously injured or killed.
- If the attack continues despite passivity, then fight back. Use any weapon available. Consider: sticks, rocks, hiking poles, or anything you have access to. Concentrate on the bear's head, eyes, and nostrils.
- If someone is being attacked, someone else should shoot bear spray at both the bear and the person being attacked to drive the bear away. The bear spray will affect the person who was attacked, but these effects are temporary and this action may minimize injuries.

### Teaching Considerations

Grizzly bear encounters on NOLS courses are rare. Through 2013 there have been a small number of grizzly bear encounters—24 in 48 years—and one incident where four students were attacked and injured by a grizzly bear. The attack was very serious and the students recovered from their injuries; however, the incident reinforced the need to diligently follow our grizzly bear practices. An encounter with a grizzly bear can be frightening and the importance of developing a natural response by students and instructors to follow these practices is essential. The proper response to an encounter cannot be taught theoretically or academically, it has to be taught experientially using bear encounter drills and practice.

### Note on Black Bears

If you are being attacked by a black bear, defend yourself aggressively rather than playing dead. Black bears rarely defend their cubs or food from humans, so it is best to assume that a black bear attack is a predatory attack.

## Food Storage in Bear Country

Forest Service regulations in grizzly bear country state that all food, garbage, and other aromatic attractants be stored to minimize the bear's access. Specifically, unattended food and other attractants must be left either in approved bear-resistant canisters or panniers, housed in a bear fence, or suspended from a tree or pole.

Keep all bear attractants, such as food, spices, garbage, used pepper spray (unless thoroughly cleaned with soap and water), and fragrant toiletries stored out of the reach of bears. If bear signs are abundant consider hanging cook gear, cleaning knifes, fishing equipment, and any wind clothes worn cooking.

### Learning Objectives

- Students should know local laws, regulations, and procedures for the area they are visiting.
- Students should know how to set up a bear hang and use a bear fence.

### Bear-resistant Canisters

Although bulky and heavy, these plastic containers are convenient and allow you to store your food securely when there are no trees. They do not hold a 10-day ration, but they do lessen the amount of food you need to hang. The NOLS Rocky Mountain and Alaska branches both have canisters to issue to courses.

### Bear Fence

Bear fences are approved by the Interagency Grizzly Bear Management Committee at the national (US) level, but their local legality still varies. Check local regulations before you choose to use any form of food storage in bear country. Bear fences are extremely convenient above treeline, they weigh much less than food canisters, they avoid the risk of students climbing trees to hang ropes, and they give negative reinforcement to curious bears.

*Hang food from a sturdy branch at least ten feet above the ground, four feet from the trunk, and four feet down from the branch.*

The bear fences used at NOLS are custom made, but anyone can buy similar models from UDAP, the bear spray company. The fences are very effective when used properly, which includes using the marker lights so all animals can see the fence before getting shocked by them, testing the fence every time you install it to make sure the voltage is at 90% or more at the energizer, and generally making sure the fence is used carefully. NOLS has recorded over 50,000 fence nights with no issues except two occasions when people turned the lights off and animals knocked the fences over, highlighting the importance of the marker lights.

Sloppy use of any food storage technique can eventually train bears to defeat the technology and then it will become useless. It is important to practice with the bear fence before leaving for the field so that you know how it functions and to ensure that it is working properly.

### Hanging Food

Federal regulations (where applicable) say food must be hung 10' above the ground and be 4' away from both tree trunks and overhanging limbs or poles. Some grizzlies are known to have a reach greater than 10', so consider hanging the food 15' feet from the ground for maximum protection. The bear hang must be at least 100 yards away from your sleeping area and preferably downwind. There are numerous ways to hang your food. Some require climbing one or more trees; some do not. Basic equipment per cook group:

- One or two 40'-50' 6mm ropes
- One or two carabiners
- Small stuff sack

### Single Rope Hang

A single rope thrown over a stout limb works fine for a lightweight food bag or two. Find a solid, horizontal tree limb 20' feet above the ground with no branches below. Throw the rope over the limb. You can weight the end of the rope with a carabiner or a stuff sack with some small rocks in it to make the toss more effective. Some people throw parachute cord and then haul up the bear rope. Once the rope is over the limb, tie the foodbags on with a bowline, haul them up, and tie off the rope to a nearby tree using friction wraps.

There are some disadvantages to this system. Friction from the rope running over the branch can make it hard to haul up heavy food bags, and both the rope and the tree limb can be damaged. Teach students how to manage the risk of falling limbs by avoiding being underneath them when the rope is being pulled.

### Self-locking Hang
In some areas, there have been incidences of bears clawing or chewing the rope at or near the tie-off to release the food. If you fear food-conditioned bears, you can modify the single-rope technique so that your food will be secure even if the bear chews through the tie-off.

Before you haul up the food, attach a carabiner to the bowline holding the foodbags and clip the haul rope through it. Raise the food as high as you can (well over 10'). Reach up as high as possible on the haul line and attach a stick to the rope with a clove hitch. Release the load slowly. If set correctly, the stick should catch on the carabiner and hold the load. Go ahead and tie off the haul rope for added security, but if this rope is severed, the stick will keep your food off the ground.

To release, raise the load, remove the stick, and lower. The challenge with this technique is getting your food high enough. Also, if the rope is severed, it can be tricky getting your food down.

### Double Rope Hang (reduced friction hang)
Throw one rope over a limb, find an end, tie an overhand or figure-eight on a bight (place a stick in the knot to help loosen it once it has been weighted), and attach a carabiner. Clip the midpoint of your second rope into the carabiner. Haul the rope up until the carabiner is about one foot below the limb and tie it off by wrapping around a nearby tree. Now raise your food on the rope hooked through the carabiner and tie it off.

### Two Tree Hang
If you are unable to find stout horizontal limbs, find two trees near each other that have either solid branches or a crotch in the trunks at about the same height. Using trees at different elevations on a hillside or across a ravine can help. Throw one rope over one tree, and the second over the other. Tie off ropes to food bags. Raise the food by pulling on both ropes.

If you have a big ration, another option is to create a high line with a single rope between two trees. In this situation, tie a couple of butterfly knots in the rope, clip in a carabiner, and attach a haul line to raise your food, then tighten the highline with a 3:1 pulley. You can have a couple of different attachment points along the high line in this type of setup.

### High Line Hang and Tree Climb
Finally, there may be places where you have to climb trees to set your high line. Make sure the branches on the trees are sturdy and have climbers weight them close to the trunk. Use spotters. Attach one end of the rope to one tree by wrapping it around the trunk and clipping the rope back onto itself. On the second tree, place a piece of webbing around the tree trunk and clip the rope through. A 3:1 pulley system can then be built on the ground to tighten the line. The food can be raised as above. Be careful of falls and falling limbs.

### General Tips for Bear Hangs
A small stuff sack can be used to hold your bear hang equipment or to hold rocks for weighting your throw rope. Be careful to make sure that the bag is shut securely; tying a clove hitch around the cinched end works well. This minimizes the risk of the bag coming untied and the stone turning into a projectile. The rope can also be tied directly around the rock with a square knot.

It is best to tie the ropes off away from the actual tree where the food will be hung. This reduces the chance of a bear shredding the rope trying to climb the tree. Plus, hauling away from the load minimizes the likelihood of having people underneath it.

Tying the rope off with several wraps around a tree allows you to use friction to hold the weight and reduces the risk of damage to the tree. Be sure not to tie off one rope over the top of another; tension could weld abrade the ropes.

When lowering the food bags, try using the friction of the tie-off tree to lower the load slowly. You can also use a body belay.

## NOLS Black Bear Practices
This document explains NOLS practices for traveling and camping in black bear only habitat. If traveling or camping in grizzly bear habitat, black bears are likely also to be present, so follow the NOLS Grizzly Bear Practices.

*Local regulations and advice from local wildlife managers supersede, and may differ from, our usual practices*

### Avoid an Encounter
- Be aware of your surroundings.
- Use the Bear Awareness Triangle as a tool to identify the variables that influence situational awareness and the need to continually reassess changing conditions.
- Group size and human presence are deterrents to black bear encounters. However, we do not have set minimum group sizes nor are we as strict about being alone as we are with grizzly bears.
- Bear calls—yelling, "hey bear," etc., are not typically done except if a bear is known to be present or possibly if someone is alone.

### Use an Appropriate Camp Layout
- NOLS does not prohibit sleeping outside in black bear country, but we recommend sleeping in tents/tarps especially if there is recent sign of bear activity. If sleeping out, it is recommended to sleep in pairs. If sleeping solo, make sure others know where you are and stay within shouting distance.

### Respond to an Encounter
A black bear's natural response to confrontation is to flee, so black bear attacks are extremely rare. However a bear's behavior is unpredictable and a bear that is habituated to humans or conditioned to human food can be a danger. Treat all black bear encounters as dangerous situations.

### Follow the SPRAY Acronym
We developed the SPRAY acronym for grizzly bear encounters, but adapted here for black bears.

**S**tand your ground: Don't run away or move toward the bear.

**P**ull the bear spray: If you have bear spray draw it from its holster, remove the safety, and be ready to shoot it.

**R**ound up your group: If others are near you, everyone should group together and stand shoulder to shoulder. If you are alone, wave your arms.

**A**ct human: Make loud noise either by yelling at the bear, banging pots together, blowing a whistle, etc.

**Y**ield: Don't threaten the bear; stand your ground until the bear leaves. If you see a bear from a long distance—100 yards—give it a wide berth or wait until it moves on.

### Predatory Behavior
In rare situations, a black bear may stalk humans and possibly attack. Almost all black bear attacks have been predatory in nature. They may do this during periods of scarce natural food or for other reasons unknown to us. A predatory bear will follow its intended prey for an extended period before attacking.

### Respond to an Attack by a Black Bear
- Defend yourself aggressively, punch, kick, and use sticks or rocks to fight back. Black bears rarely defend their cubs or food from humans, so it is best to assume that a black bear attack is a predatory attack.

## NOLS Backcountry Swimming Practices and Guidelines
We often encourage students to bathe by wading in streams, rivers, and lakes. In some instances, recreational swimming may be appropriate. But swimming in remote water with unknown or unfamiliar obstacles is a challenging risk to manage. Different NOLS branch schools have significantly different hazards and may emphasize or de-emphasize this activity as they deem necessary. In some instances, swimming may simply not be permissible. In a program where student and staff swimming ability is not required or evaluated and where equipment and training for water rescue is not a curriculum priority, recreational swimming and wading should be a carefully supervised activity.

For our purposes, wading involves remaining in water shallow enough to stand up in, and we don't need water deeper than this for simple bathing. Swimming is when your feet no longer touch the bottom and is usually more of a recreational activity rather than just bathing.

## Supervising Swimming and Wading

America averages 10 drownings per day, making it the fifth most common way for people to die from injuries, so water safety habits are important for outdoorspeople to develop. Manage swimming and wading with crisp expectations delivered in a seven-point briefing (below). Then provide a level of supervision appropriate for the maturity of the students. This progression of supervision is similar to the level we provide for hiking groups. We start by maintaining a constant presence, providing adequate coaching to develop good habits. As we learn to trust our students' practices, we begin to provide less direct supervision, while periodically checking that they are staying within our boundaries. On a high mountain course, swimming may be so limited (because of opportunity or environmental factors) that this progression may never leave the beginning stage.

Use conservative judgment when selecting swimming or wading sites and when supervising the activity. Swimming can be a welcome relief from the heat and grime of hiking and it can be fun, but careless or risky stunts have no place in wilderness travel.

All swimmers/waders should wear some type of footwear because a simple foot injury can become problematic.

## Safety Briefing

Students need a good safety briefing before they go swimming or wading the first time. Be sure everyone is there, even if they don't plan to swim that day. All students will need supervision at first. Adult students can be trusted to follow your guiding principles sooner than younger students. It is important that the correct tone be set for this activity.

Instructors will provide appropriate supervision that may include presence at the waterfront, assessment of the site, setting boundaries, and establishing a time frame. Once student ability to manage waterfront risks is adequately assessed, students may use the following steps:

*1) Tell someone where you're going and when you'll be back*
This is a responsible habit students need to develop no matter what the outdoor activity.

*2) Swim with a buddy*
Swimmers need to use the buddy system. In the buddy system, you and your swim-buddy are to watch out for each other. This is a good habit for students to learn and practice, and is applicable in other situations outside of swimming and wading. A trio can work as swim-buddies, but pairs are the accepted norm because there is no question about who is watching whom. The buddy system is not a guarantee of safety and is only as effective as the attentiveness and ability of the buddy to help.

*3) Choose an appropriate site*
Factors include weather, water temperature, depth, current, water visibility, closeness to other people, bottom composition, and hazards. Hazards include lightning, predators, strainers, boats, and pathogens.

*4) Stay in shallow water near shore*
There is no good reason for people to swim far from shore except when swimming is used as a travel technique to get across a river. Wilderness swimmers should stay in water they can stand up in, close to shore. Swimming can occur parallel to shore rather than away from shore. "Close to shore" is defined as close enough for someone on shore to throw them an improvised floating device (not very far). In situations when it is foreseeable that a person could stray into water over their head (e.g., abrupt drop-offs or deep pools), a swimming ability assessment needs to be done. A person needs to be able to easily propel him or her self back to shallow water or shore. Any person who cannot do this needs to remain in water no deeper than waist level to create a conservative buffer between them and fatal traps. This is much more conservative than people are used to at public swimming pools that have clear water and lifeguards.

*5) No diving or jumping*
Diving causes many water-related accidents when people dive into water and hit the bottom. This can be either diving into shallow water head first, or cliff jumping feet first. Backcountry water has less clarity, more hazards, and more irregularity than a swimming pool, making backcountry diving or jumping problematic. Diving and cliff jumping on NOLS courses is inappropriate because of the significant risks and limited benefits.

*6) Watch out for hypothermia*
Sometimes swimmers cool down until they become hypothermic, then start making low quality decisions. Cold muscles result in inefficient swimmers who eventually can't swim (Tipton, 1999). People can survive for extended periods of time in cold water, but swimmers without flotation will drown long before hypothermia becomes fatal. Swimmers should leave the water if their teeth start to chatter or if they feel uncomfortably cold.

Frigid water may be mind numbing when we accidentally enter it. Some people have a panic response where they become paralyzed with fear and discomfort and may not be able to help themselves (Steinman & Giesbrecht, 2001). Others hyperventilate uncontrollably and lose the coordination of swimming strokes and breathing.

*7) Expectations for rescue*
When swimming in the wilderness, far from the nearest lifeguard or ambulance, we have a special responsibility to avoid the need for rescue. NOLS instructors are not trained in lifeguard skills. Instructors are expected to perform within their training and ability. Inform students that expectations for rescue are low.

## Conservative Judgment

While it may squash the spirit of the group if it feels like the staff is holding them back from having fun, a frank discussion of the pros and cons of risk-taking in remote areas may help the course. Use this as a leadership visualization opportunity, asking your students how they would handle the situation if they were camp counselors and had to supervise campers at a backcountry swimming site. Our biggest concerns at NOLS aren't the typical students who show reasonable judgment in the wilderness; our biggest concern is the small percentage of our students who perform risky stunts that have no place in wilderness travel.

## Swimming Rescue

A wilderness program typically does not have lifeguard equipment or the trained personnel needed for lifeguard rescue. It is a problem if your students expect this type of rescue response. It may be your strongest swimmer who defies our instructions and attempts to swim across a cold mountain lake: if your strongest swimmer gets in trouble in deep water, there may be nothing reasonable you can do to help them. The only reasonable option during a wilderness program is to prevent swimming incidents from occurring in the first place. Untrained staff can perform the basic rescue of "throw" and "tow" tasks but should not enter deep water to attempt to save someone.

## Throw, Tow, Go

*Throw*—throw a floating object from shore to provide additional flotation to the drowning person. Of course, this is only an option if you have a floating object handy and if you keep swimmers close enough to shore. Improvised floats may include a bound, rolled up foam pad, an inflatable air matress, a waterproof camera case, a waterproof stuff-sack of clothes, or a log. While these floats aren't optimal, they may provide short-term flotation that helps buy a little time for a better response. Unfortunately, many people who are truly drowning can't see the objects you throw near them.

*Tow*—throw one end of a rope, reach out with a long stick, or use some other extension to pull the person back in. A classic life ring is thrown beyond the person, so you can use the rope to steer the float to the panicked person.

*Go*—only if you are a trained rescuer, you may decide to go help a drowning person. If you haven't been trained in what to do when a desperate drowning person tries to climb on top of you, you have no business going into the water. You can improvise a rescue tube (torpedo-looking float) by rolling up a foam pad, lashing it, and putting a towing leash on it. A 2' loop fits nicely around your shoulder. 2 meters of line between the loop and the tube gives enough room for you to swim while keeping a safe distance from the patient. Practice building and using one of these if you ever plan to use one; you can do it with one foam pad and a few lash straps. The trick in using a rescue tube is to toss it to the person, then tow them in with the leash, so they never even get in contact with your body. There have been numerous incidents of double drownings where untrained people tried to save a drowning person.

# Meteorology

Prior to making an 8000 meter ascent, renowned alpinist Rienhold Messner travels to the mountain and spends weeks observing local weather patterns. We can do the same on a NOLS expedition. Recognizing daily patterns and noting the occasional cold front provide a convenient backdrop for introducing students to some basic meteorological observation and forecasting skills. Understanding these patterns and then using them to plan peak climbs or moving days is a critical skill for mountain travelers. When instructors note weather observations and make forecasts, they manage weather well; when instructors guide students to make weather observations and make forecasts, they teach meteorology well. The information below is broken into small lessons that can be taught as teachable moments as each system approaches.

## Learning Objectives
- Early in the course, students must learn to minimize hazards by being able to anticipate and respond prior to the onset of dangerous meteorological conditions such as lightning, adverse climbing weather, and out-of-season storms.
- Students should understand basic weather observation and interpretation, and be able to differentiate between a local weather phenomenon and a regional weather system.

## Clouds

This can be taught all at once, or as the course experiences each new cloud type. If you teach this one cloud at a time, be sure to have a checklist you use so you make sure you cover them all.

Recognizing cloud types is critical to record the order in which various forms pass overhead. Observing and interpreting this progression helps us calculate how much time is available before bad weather strikes and to predict the weather for the next few days.

Clouds exist in three basic forms: cirrus clouds, cumulus clouds, and stratus clouds. Meteorologists attach prefixes to these cloud forms to describe their height. "Cirro" indicates the highest clouds in our atmosphere. A cirrostratus (stratus is the Greek word for layer) cloud is a high, flat, sheetlike cloud.

*Cirrus clouds* are high wispy clouds sometimes known as mares' tails. They are often the leading cloud form in a warm front.

*Cumulus clouds* are best described as puffy clouds. Cumulus clouds by themselves indicate fair weather. Cumulus clouds occur at all atmospheric altitudes.

*Cumulonimbus clouds,* also known as thunderheads, are a type of cumulus cloud that develops vertically into a towering pile that can reach high into atmosphere. The conditions causing this development—convective currents resulting from temperature differences in the atmosphere—often generate lightning strikes as well. High winds shear off the tops of cumulonimbus clouds, leaving them with an anvil shape.

*Stratus clouds* appear as one or multiple layers and are named for the cloud forms that make up each layer. Recall our cirrostratus example. Other stratus clouds include stratocumulus and nimbostratus (a layer of rain producing clouds).

*Cap clouds* form above peaks when high winds propel moisture-laden air rapidly over a cold summit. These caps are lens-like in shape (lenticular) and appear stationary, though in fact they move rapidly, forming as moist air rises on the windward side and dissipating as it drops on the leeward side. Cap clouds indicate the presence of extremely high winds and freezing temperatures.

Percentage of sky coverage (cloud cover) coincides with common cloud progressions. In this simple observation, note the trends in cloud and sky coverage rather than record a detailed description of cloud progression. For example, "Over the last two days the cloud ceiling has thickened and lowered."

## Local Weather Patterns

Two types of air masses influence all weather: cold-air masses and warm-air masses. To find out the origin of these air masses for your expedition's terrain, look at a large-scale weather map.

If you have a barometer along, explain how to use it to see what type of air mass is moving in. The Brunton Sherpa is especially educational because its bar graph shows trends. Temperature differences affect the barometric pressure associated with each air mass. Since cold air is denser than warm air, these air masses have higher pressure. Warm air masses are low pressure areas. The temperature difference between these different air masses may only be slight to the ground observer.

## Fronts

Fronts occur when warm and cold air masses come in contact with each other. The difference in each air mass' temperature, pressure, wind speed, and direction creates a dynamic that yields predictable meteorological events. Cold fronts occur when a cold air mass bulldozes into a warm air mass. A warm front happens when warm air follows behind cold air and replaces the leading air mass as it advances. In North America, air masses and frontal systems trend west to east, pushed by the prevailing wind.

The size of the air masses, the area where they formed, and the preexisting weather conditions influence the severity and duration of a storm system. Since we cannot see the temperature or barometric pressure of these air masses, we must rely on visual signs to identify the approach and passage of fronts. An observer can often predict how big a "dump" the approaching weather will deliver based on past experience. Such anticipation allows trip leaders to adjust travel plans to avoid exposed travel and unsheltered campsites.

The classic cloud progression for a warm front is: cirrus, cirrostratus, cumulostratus, altocumulus, altostratus, nimbostratus. Basically, the cloud ceiling gets

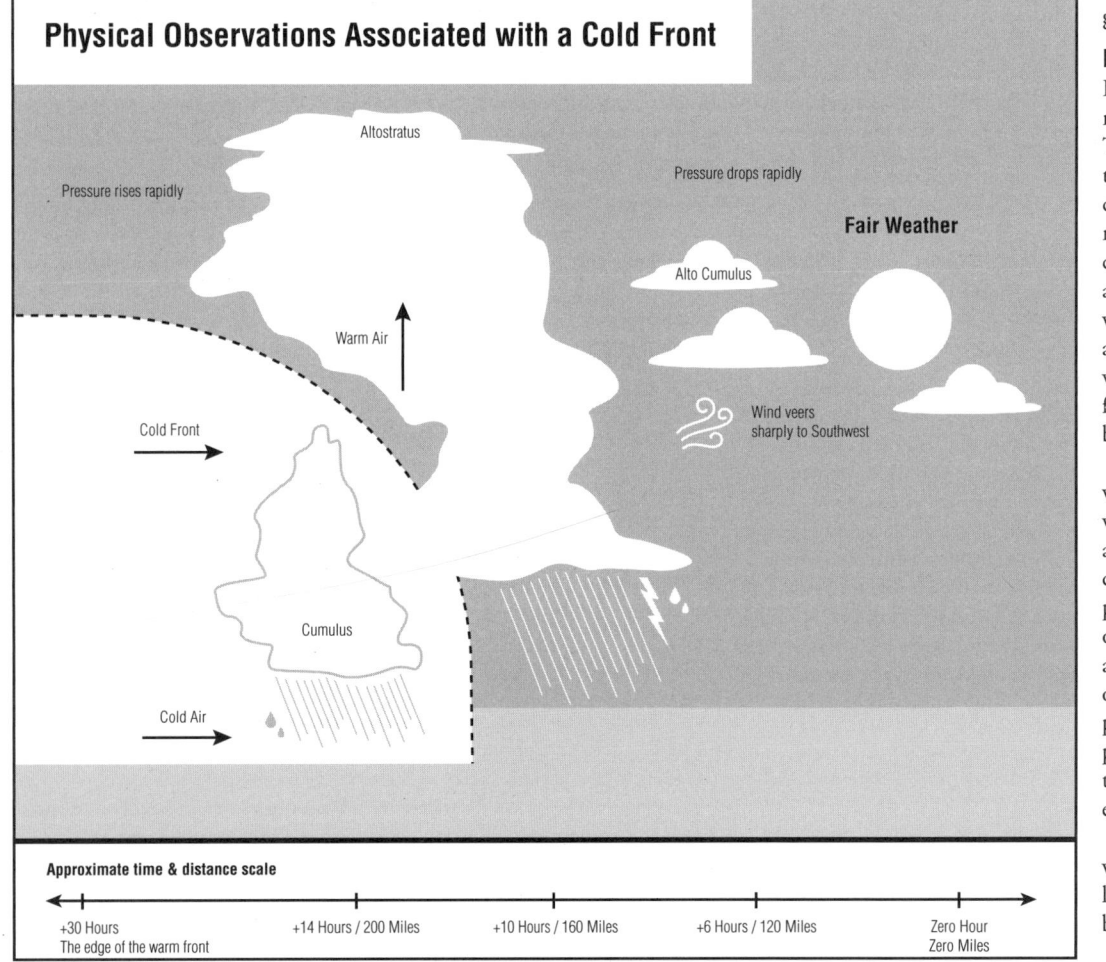

thicker and lower for one to three days before it rains or snows. Cumulonimbus may appear at the end of this sequence and indicate a clearing trend. If you have a barometer, you will see the pressure fall steadily, then plunge rapidly to a low point before it comes back up. Look for the wind to shift counterclockwise and come from the southwest, south, and southeast. The shift should begin with the appearance of cirrostratus. Try to detect a slight rise in temperature and humidity. Warm fronts slide in quietly and build more slowly than rowdier cold fronts.

## Mountain Weather

The dynamics of mountain weather are easy to understand if you know a few simple concepts. Prevailing wind direction is an important tenet, but so is the originating direction of specific storm types. Storm fronts with clockwise or counterclockwise wind shifts interrupt the prevailing pattern: this shift is most observable as a front passes. Air masses from some directions are cooler and drier, while others are warmer and moister. Orographic lifting is important to understand and is explained in any weather book.

## Daily Buildup

As the sun heats the land each day, it cooks moisture out of the ground, developing clouds that heat up and rise. As seasons progress, the timing of this cycle drifts. Help your students observe and predict this cycle. In many areas, daily buildup in summer leads to severe afternoon thunderstorms. If you observe daily buildup in your area, plan to be off mountain peaks and exposed ridges well before the storms arrive.

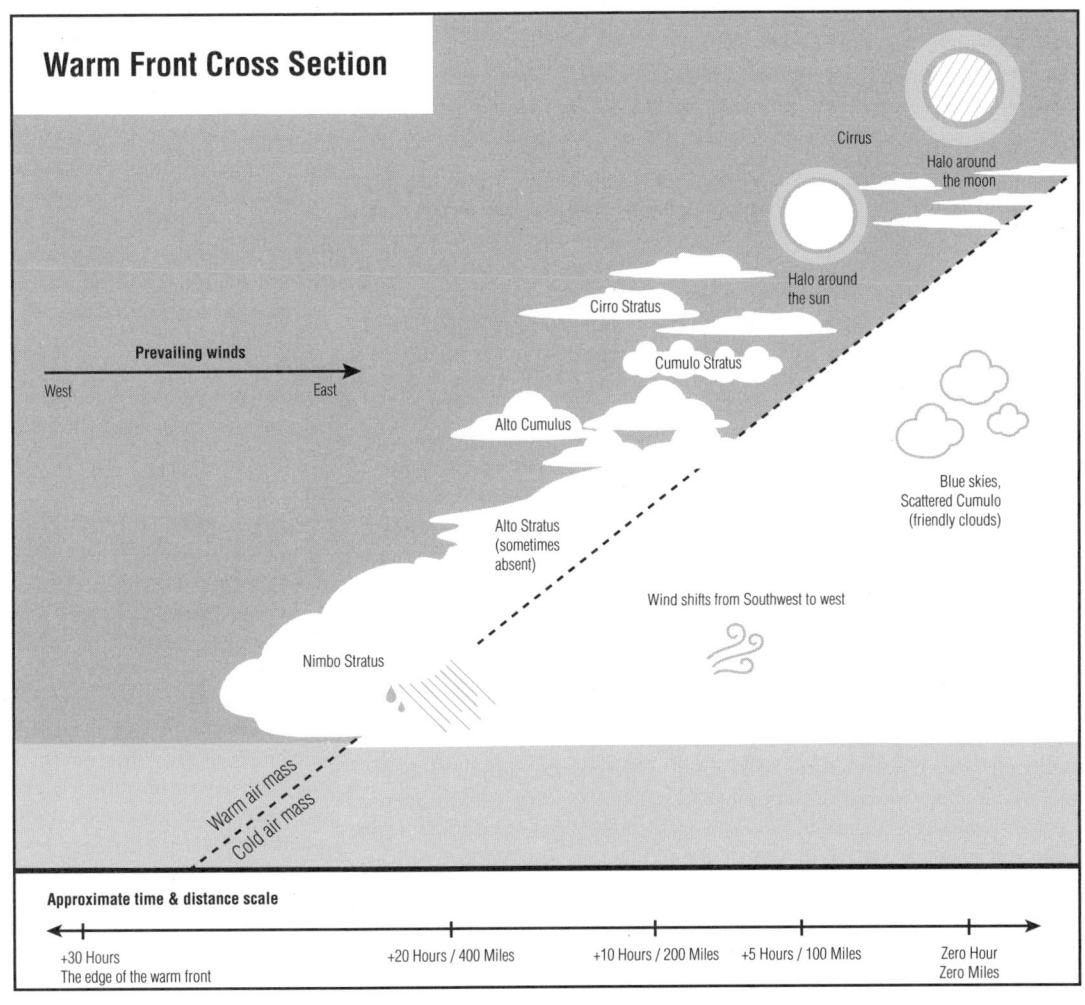

## Teaching Considerations

If a storm hits early in a course, be directive and show your students how a pro guides novices in a risk management situation.

At your first opportunity, point out some cumulonimbus clouds and discuss their potential danger. Students must know how to recognize when lightning is possible and be able to avoid it. Detailed explanations about the causes of lightning can be saved for later.

Include lightning safety in campsite selection practices. Moving camp during a nighttime lightning event is a poor second choice.

Begin basic meteorology instruction by having your students look skyward and describe what they see. Encourage them to document their observations for several days. Show them how to keep a simple weather log. Follow this by teaching basic weather concepts. In the final installment, you can introduce weather patterns, and use their weather journals to interpret the previous days' events.

Remember, no one can see air masses, but cloud progression is visible and, therefore, a helpful observational tool worth stressing. It will help students plan ahead of lightning storms if they can predict how long they take to get to them from the first clues of incoming weather.

## Further Reading for Meteorology

- *NOLS Lightning* (2014) by John Gookin and Scott Morris. Stackpole.
- Gookin, John. (2000) NOLS Backcountry Lightning Safety Guidelines. NOLS.

## Backcountry Lightning Safety

In the past decade, no Americans have died from lightning inside a modern building (solid walls with plumbing and wiring) or in a metal-topped vehicle. When thunder roars, go indoors, until 30 minutes after the lightning stops. Use the Weatherbug app to watch the thunderstorm pass your area in real time. Backcountry lightning education needs to start with these simple frontcountry options and later reinforce them so students don't apply backcountry choices in the frontcountry.

### How Does Lightning Strike?

Lightning strikes fast: the whole process usually takes a few milliseconds. Stepped leaders leave a cumulonimbus cloud and about one in five leaders moves toward the ground. They appear as many branches, but only 1-2 branches will reach the ground. Approximately every 50 meters a new step leaves each leader and heads in a fairly random direction. If a leader gets 100 meters from the ground, positively charged streamers start rising from the closest grounded objects towards the negatively charged downward leader. As soon as the leader is close enough to a streamer, it shoots directly to that streamer and blazes a trail for a significant charge (a return stroke) to shoot from the ground to the cloud. This leader search distance concept is important to understand to reduce injuries.

Lightning tends to hit elevated, sharp terrain features like mountain tops. Lightning tends to hit tall trees in open areas, with objects twice as high receiving roughly four times the strikes. Lightning tends to hit bushes in the desert if the bush is sticking up higher than the flat ground around it. Lightning tends to hit a boat on the water, especially if it has a tall mast. Lightning can still hit flat ground or water, but more randomly than it hits elevated objects.

Lightning tends to hit long electrical conductors. Metal fences, power lines, phone lines, handrails, measuring tapes, bridges, and other long metallic objects can capture and channel currents. Longer objects tend to concentrate more current and reach more strike points.

Most ground strikes occur immediately below a cumulonimbus cloud. Some bolts of lightning can move horizontally and strike out of the blue as far as 10 miles (16 km) away. These horizontal strikes are rare and unpredictable, so they shouldn't affect our decisions, with the exception that we should avoid high exposure areas like summits in these circumstances.

### How Lightning Hurts Us
A lightning strike is hazardous out to roughly 50 feet from the strike point. People are occasionally injured 100 feet away from a strike. The mechanisms that hurt us are the millions of volts of electricity, the heat, and the thunderous blast from the rapidly expanding air.

- *Ground current* occurs with each strike and contributes to half of lightning fatalities. It is the reason we practice the lightning position. You can minimize your exposure to ground current by keeping your feet close together, especially avoiding lying flat on the ground.
- *Side flash* jumps from tall objects like trees when they are struck by lightning, so don't seek shelter near tall trees, other tall objects, or tall vertical surfaces.
- *Contact* is from touching long conductors like railings, cables, and fences.
- *Upward leaders* emanate from high ground and tall objects when downward leaders approach the ground; even if they don't connect with a downward leader, they can be fatal.
- *Direct strikes* cause about 3-5 percent of lightning fatalities. Avoid high places and open ground to decrease risk of a direct strike.
- *Blunt trauma* from the explosive force of lightning can cause fractures or soft tissue injuries.

### Reducing Lightning Risk in the Backcountry
Backcountry settings are at least a 30-minute walk from the nearest vehicles or modern buildings where you can easily find safe shelter. There are four actions that can reduce your lightning risk in the backcountry, but none of them can make you as safe as getting in a modern building or a metal-topped vehicle. These behaviors are listed in order, and each is roughly twice as important as the next.

*1) Time your visits to high-risk areas with local weather patterns.*
Timing activities with safe weather requires knowledge of both typical and recent local weather patterns. There is no such thing as a surprise or freak storm. You must set turnaround times that will get you off of exposed terrain before storms arrive. You need to observe the changing weather and discuss its status with your group. Begin your turnaround if you hear thunder (which means lightning is less than 10 miles away).

*2) Find safe terrain if you thunder*
Safer terrain in the backcountry can decrease your chances of being struck. Lightning tends to hit high points and the surrounding terrain. Avoid peaks, ridges, and significantly higher ground during an electrical storm. If you have a choice, descend a mountain on the side that has no clouds over it, since strikes tend to be less frequent on that side until the clouds move over it. Once you get down to low, rolling terrain, strikes are so random you shouldn't worry about terrain as much. Move to safer terrain as soon as you hear thunder, not when the storm is upon you.

Select tent sites that may reduce your chances of being struck or affected by ground current. If you are in a tent in safer terrain and you hear thunder, you at least need to be in the lightning position. Lying flat increases the risk of injury by ground current. If your tent is in a more dangerous location, such as on a ridge, in a broad open area, or near a tall tree, you must exit the tent and get to safer terrain before the storm arrives and stay there until it has passed.

In gently rolling hills, lower flat areas are not safer than the higher flat areas because none of the gentle terrain attracts leaders. Strikes are random in this terrain. Look for a dry ravine or other significant depression to reduce risk.

The *flash-bang ranging system* measures how far away a thunderstorm is, but sometimes it is impossible to tell which flash is associated with which bang. The flash of light travels fast enough that it is virtually instantaneous. The sound travels a mile every five seconds (1km/3 sec) so ideally you just count the number of seconds between the obvious flash and the obvious bang, and divide by five to determine how many miles away the storm is. Divide the time by three to see how many kilometers distant the storm is. Do not stake your life on the reliability of this ranging system.

*3) Avoid trees and long conductors*
Wide open ground offers high exposure to lightning. Avoid trees and bushes that rise above others, since the highest objects tend to generate upward leaders. Your best bet is to look for an obvious ravine or depression before the storm hits, then spread out your group at 20 foot (7 meters) intervals to reduce the risk of multiple injuries. Assume the lightning position.

Cavers should avoid cave entrances during thunderstorms. Small overhangs can allow arcs to cross the gap. Natural caves that go far into the ground can be struck, either via the entrance or through the ground. People have been shocked standing in water half a mile inside caves. If you are caving near an entrance during electrical activity, don't stand in water, avoid metal conductors like ladders, cables, and railings, and avoid bridging the gap between ceiling and floor.

Boaters need to start getting off the water long before a storm arrives. Avoid tall trees near the edge of the water.

*4) Get in the lightning position*
If lightning is striking nearby and you can't get to safer terrain, get into the lightning position. The lightning position is for waiting out storms in stationary situations when it is impractical to move to a safer location. It is important to reduce your overall footprint on the ground. Reducing your footprint may lessen the likelihood of severe injury due to ground current (the leading cause of lightning injuries). Practice the lightning position ahead of time with your students.

Most people are too careful, getting into awkward positions they could never sustain until a storm passed. The reality is that simply putting your feet together is all that is necessary. Crouching may provide a nominal benefit if you find yourself in extremely exposed terrain, but getting low is not the primary goal of the lightning position, rather it is reducing your surface area in contact with the ground.

### The Effects of Lightning Strikes on Humans
The mechanisms that hurt us are electricity, heat, and the air blast. These cause many different kinds of neurological problems, burns, and trauma.

- *Neuro-electrical damage:* current through the torso or brain can stop the heart or stop breathing. Hearts often restart themselves quickly, but it can take the breathing control center longer to recover. Cardiac or respiratory arrest that isn't restarted quickly will eventually cause anaerobic conditions that make recovery problematic. Current through the tissues can also lead to numbness, paralysis, or other nervous system dysfunction.
- *Burns:* lightning victims can get burned from the high current electricity that turns into heat in conductors that resist its flow. Strike victims can get linear burns from head to feet along the skin, punctate (spotted) burns, or feathering skin marks (not really burns) from the charge flowing over their skin. They can get secondary burns from metallic objects like belt buckles and jewelry that heat up from the current. Burns can also occur from lightning-ignited clothing and the steam generated from sweat on their skin.
- Large entry and exit burn wounds from lightning strikes are rare. Most victims have a flashover effect (current travels over their skin) that saves them from the more severe wounds. But flashover can also travel into orifices, which may explain the many ear and eye problems that result from lightning strikes. Wet people may carry more current over their skin, instead of through their bodies, reducing their injuries. It is not suggested that you intentionally get wet in case you are struck, but it does mean you shouldn't be scared that being wet will increase your risk.
- *Trauma:* the explosive force of lightning can result in direct or indirect trauma resulting in fractures or soft tissue injuries. Watch for explosive injuries at the feet. The high current can also trigger significant muscle spasms that can fracture bones.
- *Psychological effects:* electrical injury can injure the brain. Immediate problems may include altered consciousness, confusion, disorientation, or amnesia. Long term problems may include anything from headaches and distractibility to persistent psychiatric disorders and dementia (Primeau, 1995).

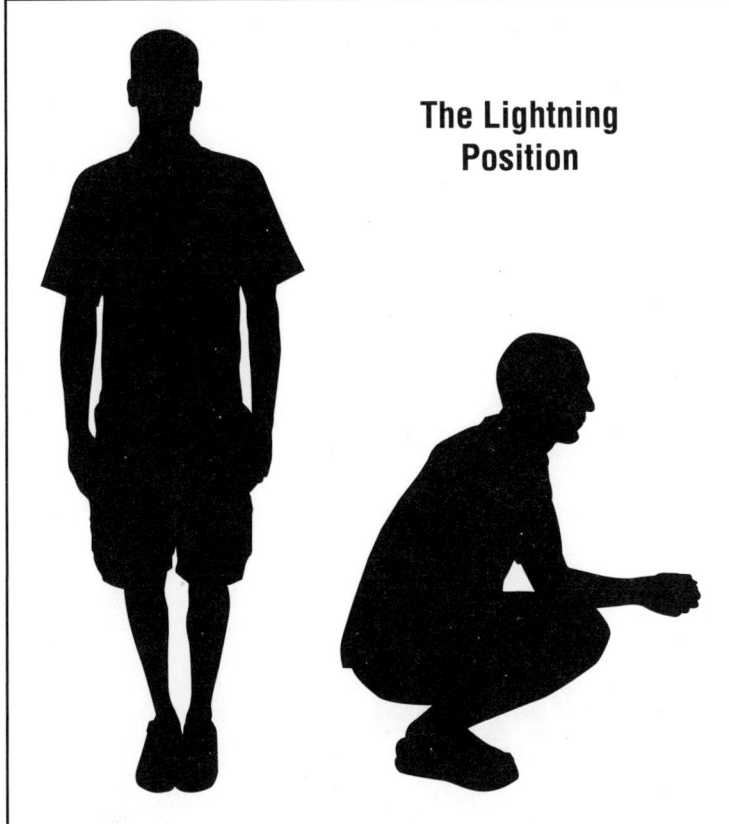

*Two variations on the lightning position emphasize the importance of keeping your feet together and reducing the amount of surface area in contact with the ground. Never lay down during a thunderstorm.*

### First Aid for Lightning Victims

Medical aspects of lightning injury are covered in "NOLS Field Medical And Drug Protocols" and in the book *NOLS Wilderness Medicine*. The following treatment principles do not supersede those documents.

- *Scene Safety:* Avoid further injuries. It may be safer to wait for the storm to pass before treating victims in extremely hazardous locations.
- *Basic Life Support:* Be prepared to provide rescue breathing.
- *Triage:* Unlike normal triage protocols, attend first to those who are in cardiac or respiratory arrest without obvious lethal injury.
- *Assessment:* All patients require a complete body survey and careful evaluation for head, spinal, long bone, or cardiac injuries. Assess peripheral pulses, and sensory and motor status. Check the skin for small hidden burns.
- *Monitor* for cardiovascular, respiratory, and neurological problems.
- *Evacuate* anyone obviously injured by lightning. Be alert for lingering issues that need further evaluation and treatment. Survivors could be disoriented or confused. Their decision-making ability (including judgment, direction finding, and planning) could be dangerously impaired.

### Record Keeping for Lightning Incidents

A precise record of the time and location of a ground strike may help lightning scientists give you some data about that actual strike. Normal near-miss forms need to be completed quickly to accurately document any incident. Near-misses are used to inform others what hazards to be careful of, and to help predict accident types. Any lightning incident also needs a record of actions taken to avoid the hazard before the incident, weather observations, and thunder and lightning observations before the incident. You should sketch and/or photograph who was where relative to surrounding terrain and vegetation, with estimated distances, heights, and elevations, a North arrow, and at least one definitive landmark. If you have time for a detailed sketch, measure using paces that you can convert to meters later. Be sure to record people who were and were not injured by the strike.

### Further Reading for Lightning

- Gookin, J. et al (2013). *Backcountry Lightning Risk Mgmt* (brochure). NOLS/National Weather Service, download at www.nols.edu/research.
- Gookin, J (2014). *NOLS Lightning*. Stackpole.
- Schimelpfenig, T. (2012). *NOLS Wilderness Medicine*, 5th ed. Stackpole.
- The National Lightning Data System records most strikes in the continental US. See a live map and buy data at http://www.lightningstorm.com/explorer.html

### Chapter Six References

- Backer H: Field water disinfection, in Auerbach P. (ed): Wilderness Medicine, Sixth Edition. Philadelphia, Elsevier/Mosby, (2012).
- Boulware DR: Influence of hygiene on gastrointestinal illness among wilderness backpackers. *J Travel Med Jan-Feb.* 11:27 2004
- Derlet, R., Carlson, J., An Analysis of Wilderness Water in Kings Canyon Sequoia, and Yosemite National Parks for Coliform and Pathologic Bacteria. *Wilderness and Environmental Medicine,* 15, 238-244 (2004).
- Girou, E., Loyeau, S., Legrand, P., Oppein, F., Brun-Buisson, C., Efficacy of Handrubbing with Alcohol Based Solution Versus Standard Handwashing With Antiseptic Soap: Randomized Clinical Trial. BMJ, August 17, 2002: 325(7360): 362.
- Giardiasis, The Center for Food Security and Public Health, Iowa State University, (2012) http://www.cfsph.iastate.edu/Factsheets/pdfs/giardiasis.pdf
- Pokorny, T., Leave No Trace Outdoor Skills and Ethics: North American Edition. NOLS.
- Welch, T. Risk of Giardiasis from Consumption of Wilderness Water in North America: A systematic Review of Epidemiologic Data. *International Journal of Infectious Diseases,* Volume 4, Number 2, 100-103 (2000).
- Zell, S. Epidemiology of wilderness acquired diarrhea: Implications for prevention and treatment. *Journal of Wilderness Medicine,* 3. 241-249 (1992).

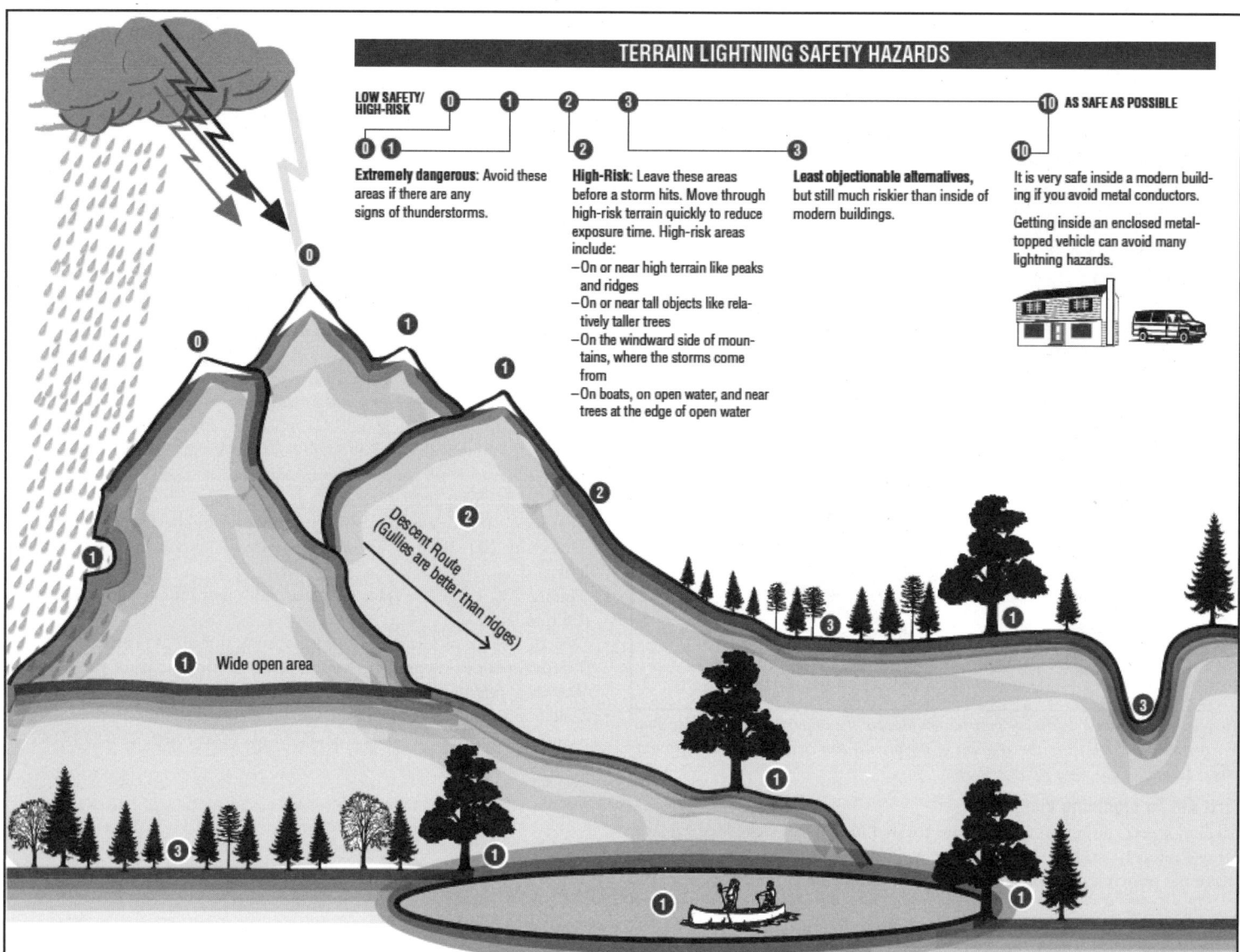

*This terrain diagram highlights the importance of moving to safer terrain during a thunderstorm. The basic principles of locating safer terrain include descending from elevated exposed areas and avoiding tall objects that stick out above their surroundings.*

# Chapter Seven
# Teaching Basic Wilderness Travel and Navigation

*(Climbing related topics are discussed in the NOLS Climbing Instructor Notebook and NOLS Mountaineering Instructor Notebook)*

Basic wilderness travel, including both efficient movement across terrain and accurate navigation, is important to many course types at NOLS, whether it's a 30-day hiking course or a river course with a day-hiking component. NOLS instructors should have a basic understanding of the skills presented in this chapter and how to teach them to students.

## Trail Technique

Efficient hiking techniques are essential for healthy and enjoyable mountain travel. Completing a challenging travel day can enhance a student's self-esteem.

### Learning Objectives
- Students should become careful, cautious, efficient, and environmentally sound hikers.
- They should be familiar with techniques for traveling across boulders, scree, thick bushes, side hills, and even crowded trails.
- A deep understanding of the LNT principles: Camp and Travel on Durable Surfaces and Leave What You Find.

### Risk Management
To reduce the chances for injury, warm up and stretch muscles prior to starting out in the morning or after a long rest break. Pay attention to hot spots and attend to them promptly. Gaiters help keep socks clean, which is important for maintaining healthy feet. Wear boots with heavy packs or on uneven or unstable terrain.

Walk with smooth, deliberate movements to avoid injury. Jumping, running, and twisting with a heavy pack on can cause back and lower leg injuries. On steep downhills, avoid long steps and locked knees to minimize stress on your knees.

Ideally, hike in a party size of four or more. This way, if someone gets hurt, one person can stay with the patient while two go for help. A hiking party should be close enough together to stay within sight of each other.

### Traveling Efficiently
The rest step is a hiking technique designed to conserve energy when moving up steep hills. Take a step. Straighten that leg and lock the knee while stepping with the other leg. Consciously relax the muscles in your straight leg while resting your weight on the bones. It works best with a shorter than normal walking gait. Avoid snapping the knee into the locked position. The goal is to move slowly and efficiently. Now synchronize your stepping with your breathing.

Take rest breaks out of sight of the trail. Rest long enough to give everyone time to eat, drink, and read maps, but not so long that muscles cool and stiffen. Rest breaks should occur often enough to accommodate the needs of the hiking group members, but avoid frequent stops that prohibit developing a regular hiking rhythm. Try resting for five minutes every hour early in a course, then adapt your pattern to terrain, weather, route, and group as experience and fitness change.

A good hiking pace allows efficient movement throughout the day. Ideally, the pace should give you time to observe landmarks and terrain, to maintain an efficient breathing rate, and to arrive in camp with enough energy to choose a good campsite and prepare a hearty meal.

Efficient travel entails redistributing weight when people are having difficulty carrying their load. It requires that hikers are well-hydrated, nourished, comfortably dressed, and carrying packs that are tight and well-balanced. Efficiency also involves making sure nothing is left behind. Check before leaving camp and at rest break sites.

### Mountain Walking Techniques
Hiking in the mountains is different from walking on a sidewalk. Your normal heel-to-toe stride should be replaced by a flatfooted technique, which minimizes foot motion and reduces the chance of blisters. Strides need to be short to walk with flat feet. Lace boots loosely and step around or over objects rather than on and off. Unnecessary up and down steps waste energy.

Allow enough space between hikers to prevent being snapped in the face by branches. Walk with your eyes. Watch the ground ahead, and consciously pick each foot placement. Consider hiking with trekking poles or a stout stick. This will improve your balance and lessen the strain on your knees. Use the rest step or splay your feet when climbing steep slopes in order to shift some of the work from your calves to your thigh muscles. Often sidestepping on steep terrain improves balance and footing.

If you can, find a way around thick brush. If you have no choice, you can try backing through bushes or using a stick to push vegetation out of the way.

### Scree Slopes and Boulder Fields
Walking on boulder fields requires practice and confidence. Step on the uphill side of rocks and boulders so if they roll, you'll be tumbled into the hill and out of the path of the moving rock.

Maintain motion and avoid stopping when unbalanced. Move from rest spot to rest spot. Do not travel over loose terrain with someone directly above or below you. If you have to go through areas that channel rockfall, move one at a time, and wait for an "all clear" signal before heading into this zone. Make sure everyone knows where you are at all times. Another way to travel through dangerous areas is to bunch together, so if a rock gets loose, it won't have time to accelerate between hikers. This technique only works if the group stays in its tight configuration.

If a rock comes loose and someone is below you, warn them by screaming "ROCK!" Use this call for any dangerous projectile.

Handholds can be useful in difficult terrain, but make sure they are secure. Test each hold, be it a tree branch or a rock, before committing your full weight to it. When you are using vegetation, pull on it along the long axis of the branch or vine, and always be suspicious of dead branches.

When descending the fall line, keep your weight over your feet and face downhill. Place your heel first and make sure it has bitten into the surface (scree, loose dirt, or snow) before your weight goes onto it. Bent knees help absorb the shock and place you in an "athletic position" ready to react. Consider helmets, handlines, or belays if the consequences of a fall are serious. Be willing to call halt on an inappropriate descent line.

### Strive to Pass Unnoticed
Use a trail whenever one is available—even if it is muddy. This prevents the creation of the multi-lanes often found in popular areas. Hike single file on the trail to keep from widening its margins. Do not cut switchbacks. Off trail, try to spread out to minimize impact. Walk abreast in meadows.

Take rest breaks well off the trail and out of sight of other hikers. Be quiet and avoid rowdy behavior. Loud noises spook horses and game and can have a negative impact on the wilderness experience of other users.

### Meeting Stock on the Trail
Yield the right of way to horses and pack animals. Move well off the trail and stay still, but in sight. Talk to the riders as they approach so the horses recognize that you are a person and not something to be afraid of. Move to the downhill side of the trail—spooked horses are easier to control if they run uphill.

### Teaching Considerations
Mountain travel habits begin developing on the first hiking day. Correct breathing and hot-spot awareness should be emphasized, modeled, and demonstrated. Blister care can be explained in a teachable moment. Consider having the students examine their feet carefully before they begin hiking. Explain to them what healthy feet look like and how to maintain that status.

Some instructors have their students hike with loose boots on the first few days of hiking. This method forces people to walk slowly, flatfooted, and with their eyes on the ground. Loose boots also cause fewer blisters, because while there is movement inside the boot, there is no pressure to cause friction and rubbing (movement + pressure = friction and blisters).

Students having difficulty walking off trail can learn by following behind instructors and observing their techniques. Before heading into their first boulder field, have students practice boulder walking without their packs. Consider helmets for uncoordinated students. To do this tactfully, be honest with the student. Remind them that their health and well-being comes before fashion or self-esteem.

Hiking with ski poles allows you to transfer some of your weight onto your arms. The poles provide another point of contact when moving over steep or slippery terrain and can make up for the decreased lateral stability found in some students with knee problems.

### Leadership Opportunities
Hiking from camp to camp is the perfect time to practice different leadership styles. Encourage students to experiment when they are leader of the day. To ensure success, have the student leader brief their hiking group and discuss goals in relation to the leadership strategies they hope to employ.

## Hazard Evaluation
To lessen the chances of an accident in the mountains, learn to recognize and manage hazards. Forethought and an understanding of personal and group limitations help to minimize hazard exposure.

Mountain hazards can be categorized in two ways: objective and subjective. Objective hazards are part of a natural process. They include darkness, weather changes, rockfall, and moving water. Subjective hazards are caused by the human attributes of a mountain traveler. These hazards include ignorance, overconfidence, and fatigue.

### Learning Objectives
- Students must be able to identify and mitigate common mountain hazards.
- Students will understand their own technical, physical, and psychological limitations when traveling through hazardous terrain.
- Students should understand how subjective and objective dangers interact to lessen a group's safety margin.

### Objective Hazards
Objective hazards are found in the environment and often involve moving objects or changing conditions. With knowledge and experience, objective hazards can usually be anticipated and managed. The following objective hazards may be encountered on NOLS courses. (See Chapter Ten for more detail on risk management).

### Lightning
For information on how to avoid lightning or minimize your chance of being struck (see the meteorology and lightning sections in Chapter Six of this notebook, and *NOLS Lightning*).

### Rockfall
Learn to recognize signs of rockfall activity. Look at the base of gullies or cliffs for streaked snow, and freshly fractured or lichen-free boulders. Do not travel directly above or below others on loose terrain, and try to limit exposure to rockfall paths by passing through them quickly and one at a time. Helmets may be necessary to minimize danger. Beware passing through active areas mid-morning or late afternoon when natural rockfall is more likely due to freeze-thaw activity.

Choose routes that minimize danger and camps that are well out of the way of rockfall. Look and listen to see what times of day rockfall is most frequent and expect it during rainstorms.

### Snow
Snow can be dangerous without proper gear or experience. To assess the hazard, examine the slope for protruding rocks, check the slope angle, and consider the consequences of a fall.

Soft snow may cause post-holing, and partially melted-out rocks can create elephant traps (that whole people can fall into). Test snow security on steep terrain with a belay, and try to travel at the appropriate time of day to take advantage of harder or softer snow conditions. On steep slopes, look for an adequate run-out, which means checking to see if there is enough low angle snow for a fallen climber to come to a stop naturally without hitting any obstacles.

Probe snow bridges for adequate thickness and make an effort to cross them early in the day while the snow is still frozen and strong. Consider the consequences of falling through the bridge. Will you be in danger of long falls, cold water immersion, or entrapment? Be more suspect as temperature rises, especially mid to late season when overnight freezing stops.

Expect cornices on the lee side of passes and ridges. Stay back from the edge, behind the apex of the ridge, for the safest travel path.

Frozen lakes can make for easy travel when they are solid, but walk around them if the ice is changing colors or showing signs of thinness, such as water around the edges.

### Swift Water
Don't underestimate the power of moving water. River crossings are often the most hazardous obstacle encountered in the mountains. Consider a technical crossing for any moving water deeper than mid-thigh level on the smallest group member and be prepared to alter the route if the river crossing is dangerous. You may find a more suitable crossing if you hike to the divided headwaters of the river or if you cross early in the day. Rivers rise in the late afternoon and evening as snowmelt enters the stream. They subside in the morning after overnight cooling slows melting. (See the river crossing section later in this chapter).

### Wet Surfaces
Be careful of wet slabs, boulders, and scree slopes, and watch out for wet lichen. Steep, wet grass should be viewed as fourth class terrain, especially when exposed or with poor run-outs. When traversing wet, slippery slopes, move slowly, keep your weight low, use solid handholds, and consider the use of handlines or belays in treacherous places. Keep your hands empty.

### Weather
When bad weather rolls in, stop hiking early to avoid getting caught in areas with poor camping. Be aware of rapidly rising water before and after storms, and consider waiting to move until the storm passes. Travel in bad weather only if you are certain you can stay safe and navigate accurately. (See the meteorology section in Chapter Six of this notebook).

### Forest Hazards
Watch for eye level branches when wandering around camp at night. Bring a flashlight, and avoid thick undergrowth in the dark. Walk with your hand in front of your face to protect your eyes.

*Widowmakers* or standing dead trees have fallen on camps during wind storms. When choosing a campsite, check for potential widowmakers and camp out of their range. Test questionable trees.

It is easy to get turned around and lost in a dark forest. It may be embarrassing for you, but to avoid wandering off in the wrong direction and spending a cold night out without your sleeping bag, call out to others if you get disoriented after dark. (See the staying found section in Chapter Six of this notebook).

### Teaching Considerations
Make it an expectation that watching for hazards is everyone's responsibility. An outdoor leader understands that careless, thoughtless, or dangerous behavior affects personal as well as group well-being.

The examples instructors set are critical. Students emulate positive as well as negative role modeling. Often they lack the experience to recognize the latter. Students should observe us staying in control, practicing sound techniques, articulating thought processes, and demonstrating consistent hazard awareness.

Include a hazard update as part of hiking group briefing. Periodic review of hazards keeps students aware of dangers they haven't observed recently.

Start students with one simple way to negotiate a hazard. Then show them new ways as you encounter the hazards again.

### Leadership Opportunities
Social harmony makes for nice feelings, but it doesn't avoid or reduce risk. Speaking up is everyone's responsibility. Complacency invites problems. Look for regular opportunities to reward openness and appropriate confrontation.

### Transfer of Learning
Hazard evaluation is a skill that is easily transferred to life after NOLS. Encourage students to hone this skill in the field, emphasizing that the basics they learn at NOLS will be invaluable later when they are faced with myriad objective and subjective hazards in the frontcountry. A common subjective hazard encountered in the frontcountry is complacency—especially while driving.

# Map Reading

Map reading skills are essential for traveling and leading groups into remote wilderness areas. A topographic map is a two dimensional representation of our three dimensional world. Many of the maps used on NOLS courses are developed from aerial photographs by the United States Geological Survey (USGS). The United States is divided into 7.5, 15, or 30 minute quadrangles for mapping. These sizes refer to how many minutes of latitude and longitude the map covers.

## Learning Objectives
- Students must be able to navigate accurately on- and off-trail using a topographic map.
- Students should be able to interpret basic map symbols (colors, contour lines, scale, grid coordinates, and information found along the margins), and plan a route using this information.

## Information in Map Margins
*Map name:* corresponds to a prominent feature on the quadrangle.
*Date:* indicates when the map was made. Remember, some features on older maps are likely to have changed due to natural and man-made forces (trails are rerouted, forests get burned or clear cut, and ponds dry up). Dates and markings in purple indicate revisions.
*Scale:* measures distance.
*Declination diagram:* indicates the angular difference between MN (Magnetic North) and TN (True North). GN refers to Grid North and tells us the orientation of the Universal Transverse Mercator (UTM) grid system. UTM marks off square kilometers. Most maps have UTM marks on the margins and newer maps actually have the grid squares drawn in.
*Coordinates:* number systems used to locate points on maps. Latitude and Longitude coordinates for the map borders are found at the corners. Lines of latitude (also known as parallels) run east-west but measure degrees north or south from the equator. Lines of longitude (meridians) run north-south but measure degrees east or west of Greenwich, England. UTM coordinates are discussed later in this chapter.
*Contour interval:* tells the vertical distance between contour lines.

## Map Colors
*White* shows non-forested areas.
*Green* indicates a woodland that is dense enough to conceal a platoon—approximately 40 people—in one acre.
*Blue* symbolizes any area covered with water, such as lakes, streams, rivers, ponds. A dashed blue line enclosing a white area indicates a permanent snow field or glacier.
*Red* is used to indicate more prominent man-made landmarks, such as surveys and major roads.
*Purple* shows recent corrections or additions to the map.
*Brown* marks contour lines.
*Black* marks man-made features, such as trails, cabins, bridges, roads, or mines.

## Orienting the Map—Terrain Association
Before you can navigate using a topographic map, you must be able to orient it to the land around you. One way to do this is through *terrain association*. Locate a nearby terrain feature, preferably a linear one (ridge, trail or drainage), then rotate your map until the picture on the paper matches the terrain in view. The better the picture matches the terrain, the more oriented your map is. (Orienting with a compass is covered later in this chapter).

## Measuring Distances on the Map
*Scale:* This is the reduction ratio used when the map was made. A map with a scale of 1:24,000 represents 24,000 inches of the earth's surface for every inch portrayed on the map. The scale will indicate how many miles or kilometers are contained in a given distance on the map.
- On a 15' map (1:62,500 scale), one inch = one mile.
- On a 7.5' map (1:24,000 scale), 2 5/8 inches = one mile.
- 1° of latitude = 69 miles, 1' of latitude = 1.15 miles

## Relief Features on the Map
*Contour lines* connect points of equal elevation. They are used to indicate the elevation and shape of terrain features. They are represented by brown lines. Contour lines are separated by the contour interval, which is the vertical distance between the two lines. Typically this is 40 or 80 feet depending on the scale. The interval is the same between each line, so they are closer together where the land is steep, and farther apart where it is flat.

*Index contours* are the heavier brown lines that include elevation numbers. Every fifth contour line is an index contour. Intermediate contours, found between the index contours and represented by lighter brown lines, do not have their elevation printed on the map. Converging contour lines often appear as one thick brown line. These represent overhanging, vertical, or near vertical relief.

*Supplementary contours* are dotted lines that display half of the interval in relatively flat terrain.

## Recognizing Basic Land Features
Hills and mountains are shown by closed lines that circle back to connect with themselves. Valleys are indicated by V- or U-shaped contours that "point" towards higher elevation. Often you'll find streams running down the apex of the V or U. Ridges are also shown by V- or U-shaped contours, but these "point" towards lower elevations. Remember, creeks never run along ridgetops.

## Steps to Simplify Map Navigation
1) Start with the map oriented.
2) Hike with the map in your hand and stay focused on the passing terrain and landmarks.
3) Know your starting point, look around, and check to see how it is represented on the map. Then, using your map, visualize the terrain ahead.
4) Watch the terrain you pass through. Take mental notes.
5) Fix your position on the map as often as is necessary.
6) Check off features in your mind as you pass them, and remember what time that was.

## Common Map Reading Mistakes
Some of the most common map reading errors occur when you:
- Believe you have traveled farther than you have, especially uphill or off-trail.
- Choose a place on the map where you want to be, and then make it fit your actual location through wishful thinking.
- Confuse a treed open area with a woodland and vice versa.
- Forgot what time you were at a known point.

## Teaching Considerations
This subject is challenging to teach because of differing spatial abilities of our students—three-dimensional visual aids often help.

Teach the "must knows" first and add the less important details later. For example, teach the important map colors—white, green, blue, and black—before you introduce red and purple. Introduce the information in the margins as needed. Avoid any extraneous details that will distract students or will be hard to grasp with limited experience.

Initial instruction should focus on navigation using map colors alone. Orient the map for your students until they become proficient with the greens, whites, and blues. Consider leaving out contour lines until your students need this information. Try to get a map in every student's hands early on in the course.

Introduce contour lines with a three-dimensional model. For example, draw contour lines around your knuckles or knee to make a mountain that can be transformed from three dimensions to two by straightening the limb out. Sand models with parachute cord contour lines also work well.

Travel Plans are a key part of practical map reading. They also provide a way to monitor student progress and help them develop good planning habits. Map quizzes are another effective way to check your students' progress. Having students build terrain models out of snow is a fun way both to practice map reading and to get a good look at your route.

Learning from one's mistakes is an important part of map reading. After initial coaching, constant instructor intervention can create false confidence or dependence in our student map readers. They often learn more after they have walked a couple of unnecessary miles.

## Leadership Opportunities
Teaching map reading is a great time to coach your students rather than simply critiquing their skills. Coaching is a valuable leadership technique that empowers followers by helping them achieve success. Early in the course, you may just want to model this behavior; later talk about what you are doing and help your students develop their own coaching skills.

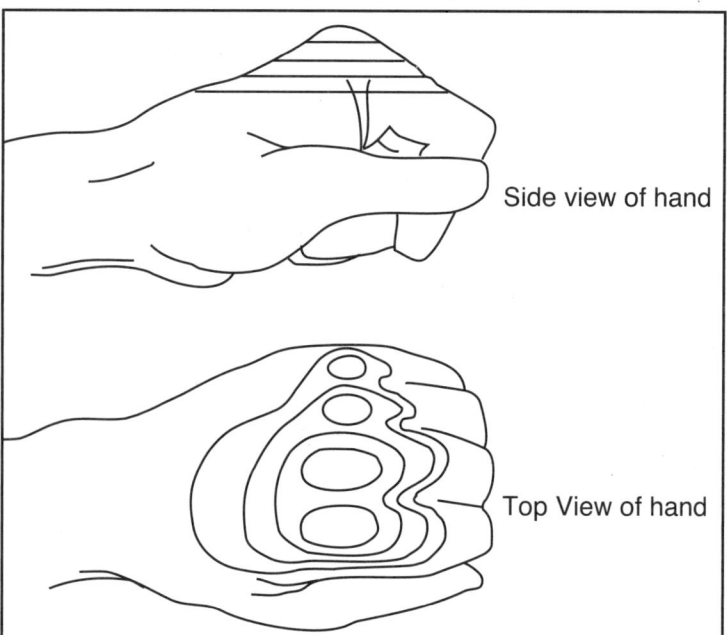

*Drawing contour lines on your knuckles is a good way to introduce the concept of contours.*

## Route Finding

Traveling off the beaten path is part of any NOLS course. Successful cross-country navigation requires sound route-finding skills.

### Learning Objectives
- Students will be able to anticipate hazards and obstacles from their maps and to avoid them as they are encountered during a hike both on and off trail.
- Students will be able to pick energy efficient routes.

### Route Finding
Good route finding conserves energy and minimizes exposure to dangerous terrain. It begins with a study of the terrain features on the map and continues as you find your way across the land in front of you. Good route finding matches the difficulty of the route to the abilities of the party.

### Components of a Well-Planned Hike
A well-planned route is efficient and enjoyable. Avoid unnecessary exposure to lightning, rockfall, steep, loose or wet rock, moving water, technical terrain, steep vegetated slopes, ice fall, and crevasses. Conserve energy by contouring to avoid unnecessary elevation gain or loss. Small elevation changes may help you avoid extensive sidehilling, however. Minimize the time spent on boulder fields and scree slopes, or in deadfall and thick bush. Often the most efficient route sticks to open terrain. To make the route fun, provide opportunities for impromptu teaching and photography, and take time to observe.

### Using the Map
Maps are a good place to start planning your route. Begin by identifying your starting and ending points. The shortest line between two points may not be the safest, fastest, or most enjoyable option, however. Consider all the possible route variations when determining how to get from point A to point B.

Pick out terrain features that will indicate if you are straying off track. For instance, your route may have you keeping a river on your left and a ridge on the right. These *handrail* features serve as boundaries and will channel your route. A *backstop* is a terrain feature that indicates you have passed your destination.

### Using Terrain Features
Field observations, combined with a topographic map, can help you predict the conditions you can expect to encounter during a day's travel. Some things are obvious: steep slopes will be physically demanding and may be slippery, while gradual ascents and descents are less taxing. Subtle factors, such as slope stability, can also be gauged by checking the map for features such as the presence or absence of vegetation. The more trees, the more stable the slope.

Aspect, elevation, and knowledge of ecosystems and habitats provide further clues to travel conditions. In North America, north-facing slopes tend to be more thickly vegetated and to hold snow and cornices longer than south-facing aspects. Boulder fields are common close to the crest of the Wind River Range. Lightning is more frequent at certain elevations and at certain hours of the day. Snow line, tree line, and tundra zones can be expected at roughly the same elevation throughout a given range.

Ridges often have less vegetation and water than valleys. They are also less likely to be choked with deadfall and to have better vantage points. As a result, ridges are often the route of choice in the mountains.

Moving water may be the most dangerous hazard encountered on a route. Weather can also cause unexpected obstacles. Prolonged rains will increase stream levels, promote rockfall, and contribute to flash flooding. Winds are stronger on exposed ridges and passes. But team efficiency is probably one of the greatest factors affecting actual arrival time. Given the unpredictability of many of these factors, alternative sheltered campsites should be planned in the event of impassable conditions.

Maps can clue you in to many of these potential hazards, but remember, they have their shortcomings. For example, a 39-foot cliff might not show up on a map with 40-foot contour intervals. Therefore, expect the unexpected and allow time for contingency plans.

### Finding the Route
Be flexible. The map will only provide the most basic information. Readjust your route or travel plan as more information is gathered. Don't try to determine the entire route at once. Instead, visualize it in stages. One technique you can try in thick vegetation is the "see" method.

A see is the distance you can see from where you are standing. Look ahead and choose the easiest route. If you notice a better see enroute, take it. The second hiker should be looking for a way to improve upon the first person's route. When the end of a see is reached, the process is repeated. The object of this is to keep the group moving as a whole, though individuals may stop briefly. Simply go where it looks easiest, keeping overall travel considerations in mind.

Don't force a route if it becomes dangerous, entails unnecessary impact, or frightens a group member. Be willing to backtrack until a viable alternative can be found.

Ideally, the whole party should know where they are at all times. Pay attention and update the group's position as you pass key landmarks. Look back often in order to make retracing the route easier. If in doubt, stop and scout. If the party suspects they've made a navigational error, stop and figure out where the error occurred. Seek higher ground or a place with a better view, and send members out with maps to gather more information. Regroup and evaluate the scout's findings.

Hiking groups should be self-sufficient so they can relax with the knowledge that if they can't find the way, they can look more the next day.

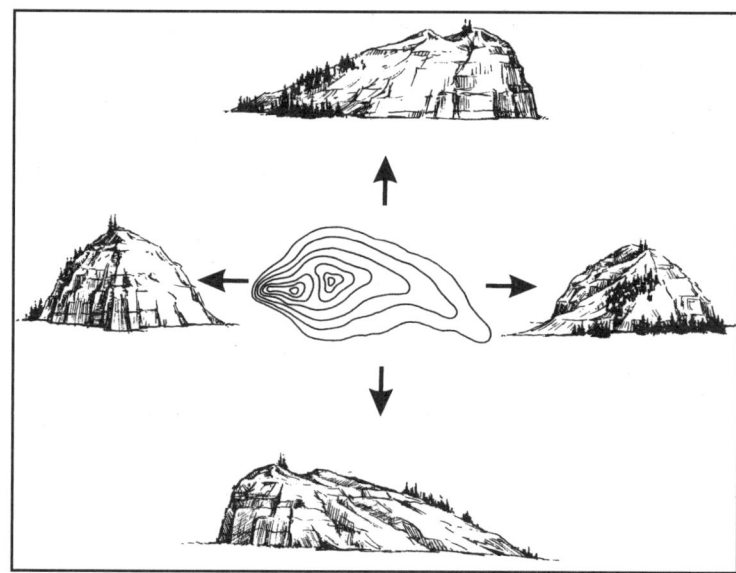

*Try to visualize what a certain terrain feature—such as the hill in this diagram—will look like from different locations. (Diagram courtesy of Brunton.)*

## Teaching Considerations

Route finding instruction begins with sharing your thoughts and navigational decisions with the group. Once students are hiking on their own, route finding should be the subject of hiking debriefings, especially if it did not go smoothly.

Map-reading skills need to be solid before students will succeed at planning a route from the map. Sophisticated route finding incorporates knowledge of local weather, geology, and ecosystems. Have the students extrapolate where moraines and bushwhacks might be by looking at their map. Student route finding can begin before students are honed map readers.

## Leadership Opportunities

Students learn a great deal about making decisions with real consequences when they start route finding. The critical thing for you as the leader is to allow them to make mistakes. If they choose a route that is imperfect but okay, let them use it. If they get lost, get lost with them. If they ask you which route you would choose, don't always tell them. Many students look at these decisions as if there is always a right answer. Help them see that many of the answers to life's questions are trade-offs, not all-or-nothing extremes.

## Compass Navigation

Although most navigation in the mountains can be done with a map only, being able to use a compass is helpful when visibility is limited or terrain features are subtle. Compass navigation skills should be seen as a complement to sound map-reading skills.

### Learning Objectives
- Students should know how to orient their map using a compass.
- Students will be able to take and follow a compass bearing.
- Students will understand how to triangulate their position.

### General Concepts

A compass provides us with a consistent reference point and allows us to navigate without landmarks. The compass points to the earth's magnetic force which emanates from the magnetic north pole around Hudson Bay. These lines of force are caused by the flow of the earth's molten metal core. True north is the top of the planet towards the center of spin. Declination is the angular difference between true north and magnetic north at your location.

### Basic Compass Parts

*Base Plate*: This contains the direction-of-travel arrow.
*Bezel or Housing*: The movable plastic circle with the degree readings and an orienting arrow printed on it.
*Needle*: This floats on a pivot inside the housing. The red end of this needle points to magnetic north ("Santa is red and lives up North").

### Boxing the Needle

Boxing the needle is the first step in compass navigation. To do this, hold the compass flat in your hand at mid-chest level. Rotate the housing until the direction of travel arrow lines up with north on the bezel. Now rotate the entire compass by moving your whole body until the north-seeking arrow lines up with—or is "boxed in"—the north-indicating arrow printed on the housing. The needle is now boxed and pointing toward magnetic north ("Red Fred is in the shed").

### Orienting the Map

A compass can be helpful in orienting a map when visibility is low because of clouds, thick vegetation, darkness, or featureless terrain. The technique for orienting your map using a compass follows these steps:

1) Set the declination by dialing the bezel to the left or right according to the declination diagrams in the bottom left of your map.
2) Lay your map on a flat surface or hold it level.
3) Place the compass on the map so that the base plate is aligned with the left or right margin and the direction of travel arrow points to the top of the map.
4) Without disturbing the compass, rotate the map underneath it until "red Fred is in the shed." Your map is oriented to true north.

### Taking and Following a Bearing

To take a bearing, orient your map and then draw a straight line from your present location to your destination. Without disturbing the map, lay the compass edge along the intended line of travel. Rotate the housing or bezel to box the needle. The direction-of-travel arrow should be pointing in the direction you want to travel. The number on the housing dial is your bearing.

*Following a bearing (Diagram courtesy of Brunton)*

Now, keeping the needle boxed, lift the compass up to eye level. Sight along the direction of travel arrow and pick out a landmark which lines up with it. To follow the bearing, walk to your landmark and repeat the process of sighting along the direction of travel arrow with needle boxed. Keep doing this until you reach your destination. Fewer sightings result in fewer errors, so it helps to choose distant landmarks.

To take a field bearing without the map, choose a landmark and point the direction of travel arrow at it. Rotate the bezel to box the needle. Follow the bearing as described above.

### Triangulation

*Triangulation* is used to determine one's position using two or more known points. Start by orienting your map and placing it on a flat surface. Choose two landmarks that you can see on land and locate on the map.

Take a bearing on one of the landmarks. Place the edge of the compass (keep the needle boxed) on the map, so that it runs through the center of the landmark you just sighted. Double check to see that the needle remains boxed and that the map's orientation has not changed.

Draw a line along the edge of the compass through the landmark. Extend the line in each direction. You are on that line somewhere. Now repeat this procedure on a second and (for more precision,) a third landmark. It is helpful to pick landmarks that are at least 60° apart in order to improve the accuracy of the triangulation.

The intersection of all three lines is your position. Given human error, however, all three lines rarely intersect. Often they form a triangle. Your location should be somewhere in that triangle. Notice that triangulation with a compass is just a more refined way of orienting yourself using terrain association.

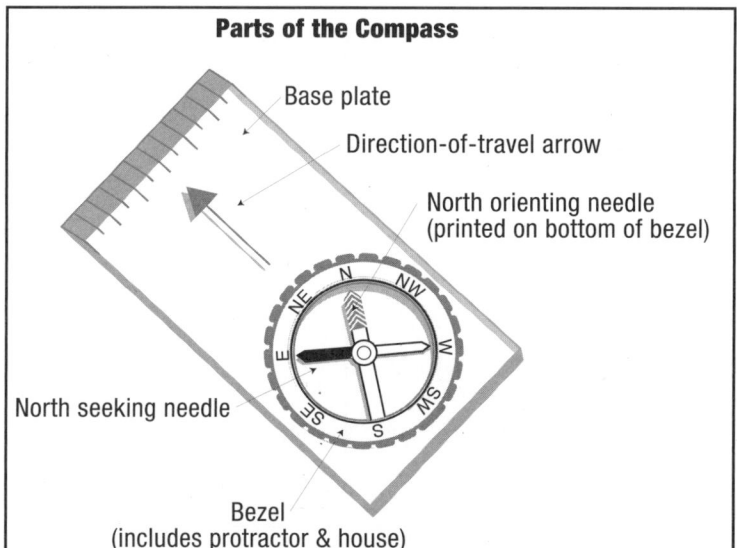

Triangulation is easier when you are traveling along a defined linear feature (ridge, trail, drainage, or river). Once again, start by orienting your map. Then trace a line along the linear feature you are following. Take a bearing on a landmark and transfer the line to the map. The intersection of the bearing line and your travel feature is your position.

### Teaching Considerations

Introduce compasses once the students are comfortable with basic map reading and terrain association skills. Compass use can be a distraction that impedes students' map-reading development, and the topic can be confusing if the instructor is unable to teach compass use in a simple manner.

Compass use should be taught in a step-by-step progression that builds upon previous skills. For ease of understanding, consider teaching it in three installments. A sample progression could look like: general concepts (boxing the needle, orienting the map), measuring a bearing off the map and following it, and then triangulating a position.

Compass instruction is most effective in a setting that has clear, easy to identify landmarks. A simple orienteering exercise can be a fun way for students to practice their skills. Make sure the distance to each waypoint is long enough to require accurate techniques. Accuracy in setting the points is critical to successful orienteering exercises.

### Leadership Opportunities

Some students come with a background in compass navigation and are comfortable with their use. Let these students help their less-experienced colleagues learn the skill. The trick is to get them practicing appropriate leadership. They should understand that their goal is to help the others, not to tell people everything they know about compasses.

## Using UTM Coordinates

USGS topographic maps (quads) are marked with both latitude/longitude and Universal Transverse Mercator (UTM) coordinates. Because the UTM system is based on uniform 1000-meter grids, and uses base-10 math, it is simpler and easier to use. Students who want to use a GPS, or who might work in land management, should learn to read and plot UTM coordinates.

### Learning Objectives
- Have a basic understanding of the UTM grid system.
- Be able to read coordinates from a known point on a map.
- Be able to plot points on a map from coordinates given.
- Understand where to locate datum on maps and why datum need to correlate with coordinates.

### General Concepts

The UTM grid system divides maps into numbered grids, each representing a square kilometer. By carefully measuring the location of a point within a UTM grid on a map, navigators can reference a precise location on land or sea without relying on landmarks. The UTM system divides the world into several hundred zones. Each UTM coordinate is expressed in units of meters east and north from the left corner of the "zone."

Coordinates are expressed by two values, an *Easting* value and a *Northing* value. The long version of these values is located on the top left and bottom right borders of each USGS quad. They look like this: 442000m.E, 3665000.m.N. The digits that represent thousands of meters and tens of thousands of meters are enlarged to help you quickly locate which kilometer reference lines to use.

Although some newer USGS quads come with printed UTM grid lines, most do not. In order to more accurately plot coordinates, these lines can be drawn on each map. UTM ticks are printed in blue along the border and usually have a corresponding number in black next to each tick. A 24" straight edge can be used to draw grid lines in connecting these ticks. To draw lines in the field, fold the edge of the map over to use as an impromptu straight edge. If you are carrying some maps that do not have grid lines, have students draw them in before continuing.

In order to read and plot UTM coordinates, it helps to have a UTM grid reader which should match the scale of the map (1:24,000 for USGS quads). Some Brunton compasses have these grid finders on their baseplate. Grid readers can be made in the field by transferring the 100 meter marks from the map's metric distance scale to the upper right corner of a straight edged piece of paper.

### Reading Coordinates

To read the coordinates for a known point "X" on the map, place the grid reader directly over the grid where the X is located. Read the Easting value first. Start from the closest vertical gridline to the left (West) of the X. In the diagram below, the Easting gridline is 442000. To get the Easting coordinate for the X, simply add the number of 100m squares you count to the X from the 442000 line. In this case, the number of 100m squares is 3. The easting value should be 442300m.E. Read the northing value by counting up from the lower (South) horizontal gridline. The Northing value for this X should be 3664700m.N. This is your location to the nearest 100m, plus or minus 1/2 a soccer field.

To be more precise, we can read to tens of meters. Imagine ten tick marks along the bottom of the small 100m square (on the map) surrounding the X. The X is .2 to the right of the edge of the # 3 line. The Easting value should be 442320m.E. Because the X is exactly on the #7 Northing line, the 10m reading for the Northing value is 3664700. The value stays the same. Have students determine the coordinates of some map locations.

### Plotting Coordinates

To plot a point on the map from given coordinates, simply reverse the process for reading. Carefully place the grid reader over the kilometer-sized grid square in which the coordinates fall. Count 100 meter squares and visualize the point you wish to mark on the map by looking through the grid reader. Move the grid reader and mark the X. Lastly, reposition the grid reader and double-check your mark. Have students plot coordinates you give them.

### Datum

The datum (dated map data set) is an important informational piece that must be included with UTM coordinates. The datum is printed in the margin on the bottom left corner of USGS quads. USGS maps will be in either North American Datum 1927 (NAD 27) or North American Datum 1983 (NAD 83). The most common GPS operator errors relate to mis-entering waypoint coordinates by entering the wrong datum for the map you are using. Also, if a party needed to call or radio for a helicopter evacuation, the correct datum should accompany any coordinates given. Have students locate the datum on their maps.

### Teaching Considerations

This class should be taught after students have had a chance to practice basic map and compass skills but before introducing GPS.

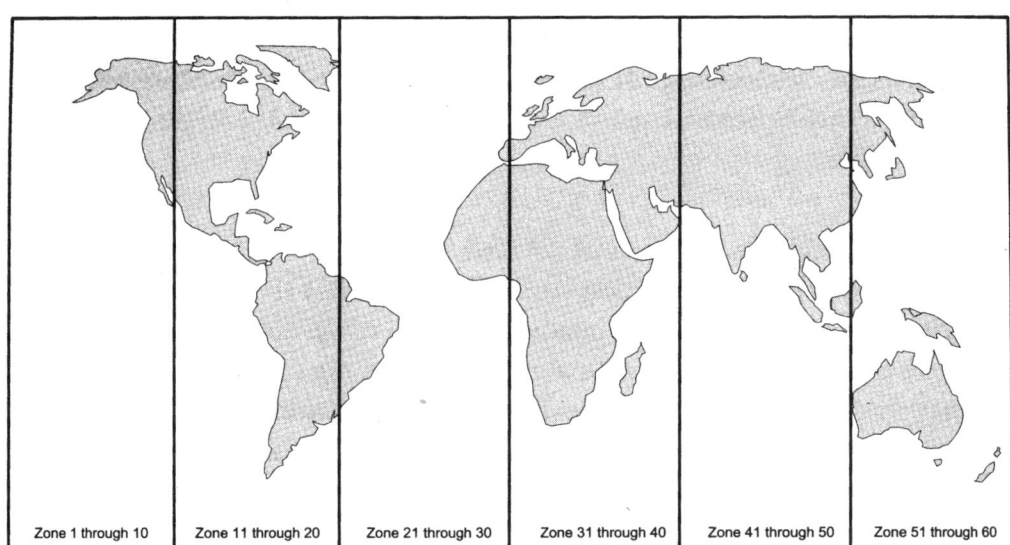

*UTM Zones (diagram courtesy of Brunton)*

Consider having students draw in gridlines while folding maps prior to heading in to the field. Remind everyone to bring a pencil with a good eraser.

In non-emergency situations where time is more a factor than accuracy, you may choose to eyeball coordinates and work without a grid reader.

If you are artistically inclined, draw the map diagram on mylar so everyone can follow along as you teach. Using different colored markers for grid lines, contours, etc. can greatly simplify things.

After introducing how to read coordinates, have students read several coordinates from points you have chosen on the map.

Experienced UTM users might also consider making UTM part of an orienteering course or giving students the "X" for their next hiking day in UTM coordinates and letting them mark their own maps.

## Using Latitude/Longitude Coordinates

The latitude/longitude system was the first coordinate system and is still used by pilots, sailors, some land management agencies, and many GPS users. While it is slightly more cumbersome to use than UTM, instructors should understand lat/long coordinates, and be able to teach and plot using this system.

### Learning Objectives
- Have a basic understanding of latitude and longitude.
- Be able to read coordinates from a known point on a map.
- Be able to plot a point on the map from given coordinates.

### General Concepts

As with the UTM system, the latitude/longitude coordinate system is used to indicate an exact physical location on Earth using numbers. Latitude and longitude are measured in degrees, minutes, and seconds. One degree = 60 minutes. One minute = 60 seconds. Rather than dividing minutes into 60th's to get seconds, it is often simpler to measure in 10th's of minutes. Forty-two minutes, thirty seconds (42'30") equals forty-two point five minutes (42.5'). The 1:24,000 scale maps are maps of 7.5 minutes of latitude and 7.5 minutes of longitude, hence the "7.5 minute series." On 7.5 minute USGS maps, measurements of latitude and longitude appear in the margins at 2.5 minute intervals. Measurements of latitude appear in the left and right margins, and measurements of longitude appear on the top and bottom. Black tics indicate the lat or long on the margins and four small black cross-marks appear within the map where the lines of latitude and longitude intersect. This makes drawing these lines (by folding a map edge over to use as a straight-edge) very easy.

### Reading Latitude

Latitude represents North-South position on Earth. Because lines of latitude are parallel and evenly spaced, a degree of latitude represents a constant distance on the ground.

Place the ruler so that it spans the lines of latitude that the point to be measured or plotted falls between. Orient the ruler vertically (North to South.) The zero minute end of the ruler should be on the southern line of latitude, when you're in the northern hemisphere. To measure the latitude of a point on the map, read the value from the ruler at the point, and add it to the latitude of the line at the zero end of the ruler.

### Reading Longitude

Longitude represents East/West direction on Earth. Longitude increases as you move away from the Prime Meridian, or 0 degrees, in Greenwich, England. Because the lines of longitude converge at the poles, a degree of longitude represents a varying distance on the ground, depending on latitude. Globes illustrate this point very nicely.

Place the ruler so that it spans the lines of longitude with the point to be measured or plotted between. The ruler must be diagonal to fit! To measure the longitude of a point on the map, slide the ruler vertically, keeping the ends on the lines of longitude marked on the map, until the edge of the ruler touches the point to be measured. You may need to extend the longitude lines above or below the map to properly position the ruler. If you can't get the ruler in the right position, try the "other diagonal." In Diagram B, X is at the 1.62' mark, for a resulting longitude of 109 degrees 39.12 minutes W.

### Plotting Lat and Long

To plot the location of given coordinates, measure the latitude and make a small tic on the map to indicate the line of latitude the coordinates fall on. To plot a longitude coordinate, make a small tic on the map to indicate the line of longitude. Double check your marks, then extend those lines using a straight edge and a light pencil. The X should be marked where the plotted lines of latitude and longitude intersect.

### Teaching Considerations

An inflatable globe can really help students understand why longitude needs to be measured diagonally.

## Travel Plans

Besides their planning and communication function, Travel Plans are valuable for enhancing your students' map reading and navigation skills. A well-developed travel plan not only gets the students to camp on time but also provides them with a useful tool for executing their own post-course adventures responsibly.

### Learning Objectives
- Promote student planning and navigation skills.
- Students should leave their course understanding the importance of making accurate time/distance calculations and recognizing how this practice relates to efficient wilderness travel.

### Uses for Travel Plans
- As a planning tool that allows you to calculate the energy and time required to travel and surmount obstacles along a chosen route.
- As a navigational learning tool. This is particularly effective because it forces students to convert spatial relationships into language that can be decoded by others.
- As a means to track overdue parties.

### Travel Plan Format

A written travel plan should include:
1) The names of the participants (duties and equipment)
2) Travel plans
   - Origin, destination, date
   - Route description (using named map features and cardinal directions)
3) Time-distance calculations
4) Contingency plans (as needed)
   - Alternate campsites/rendezvous points
   - Anticipated obstacles/hazards
   - Potential causes for delay
   - Phase lines (e.g., won't turn back once we cross the pass)

### Estimating Travel Time

One part of the travel plan is a multi-step calculation to determine the total time required to travel a given route.
1) Start by measuring the mileage on the map from point A to point B. Measure the crooked line that predicts your route.
2) Next determine the adjusted distance. This equals the linear distance + elevation gain adjustment.
3) Travel time (hours) equals the adjusted mileage (miles) divided by the rate of travel, measured in miles per hour.
4) Total time of travel equals travel time + delays.
5) Estimated time of arrival = estimated time of departure + total time of travel.

> **Time/Effort Conversion Table**
> - Traveling two miles (3.2km) on a flat trail with a heavy pack takes roughly one hour.
> - Traveling one mile (1.6km) off trail with a heavy pack takes roughly one hour.
> - Any uphill travel slows pace. 1,000 feet (305 meters) of elevation gain equals roughly the effort needed to walk one mile on a flat trail (i.e., 1/2hr).

### Teaching Considerations

Students do not need to be expert map readers prior to this class, but they should be able to recognize obvious map symbols, count contour lines, and make distance calculations using the map's scale. Having a long travel day under their belts can help them realize the importance of having a travel plan.

Travel plan instruction should be geared towards successful navigation, rudimentary time/energy management, and the development of an anticipatory mindset towards route-finding hazards and obstacles.

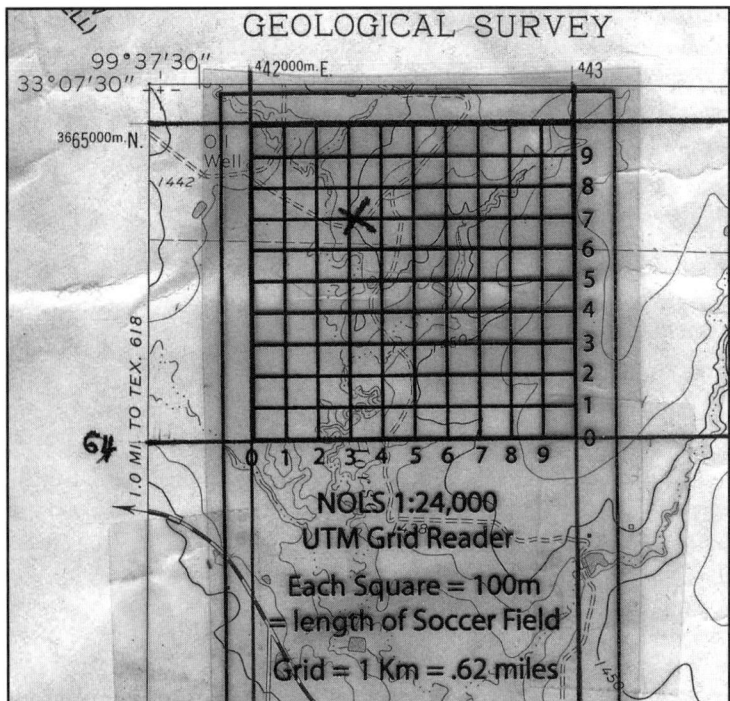

*A grid reader used with a map with UTM lines make the coordinate system easy to use.*

Subsequent travel plan assignments must be followed up and critiqued. Students tend to devalue the utility of these plans if they do not receive timely feedback, and may come to see them as a burden if they are not framed properly. Plan enough time so all the students can do one on their own.

Consider having students navigate solely by a well-written travel plan. This exercise helps them focus on navigating within the big picture and sharpens their ability to judge distances and elevation changes more accurately. The exercise works best when terrain features are easy to see. It also needs to happen later in the course when students have the skills to succeed at this challenging task.

### Leadership Opportunities
Travel plans are about planning, self-discipline, communication, and preparation. These habits are much more important than any specific format. Early in the course, have your students follow your format; later ask them to add anything they would include if they were leaving the itinerary with friends.

## Using The Global Positioning System (GPS)

Just as good compass skills are a complement to map-reading skills, being able to use a GPS receiver is a valuable skill, particularly in emergency situations and featureless terrain. GPS can serve as the perfect double check for anyone learning to use map and compass. It also encourages students to learn coordinate systems. Additionally, GPS receivers make gathering route and camping data for land managers much faster and simpler.

### Learning Objectives
- Students should understand basic GPS theory and recognize the limitations of GPS.
- Students should be able to locate their position using GPS.
- Additional goals include: entering waypoints into a receiver by UTM coordinates or by physical location and routefinding with GPS.

### A Brief History
The US Department of Defense launched the first GPS satellites in 1978. Today, GPS technology is not just for the military. It is used to navigate urban buses, new passenger cars, ships, airplanes, and sailboats as well as in mining, forestry, surveying, agriculture, and many other fields. Many cellphones made after 2002 transmit GPS coordinates to a 911 dispatch center. Some give precise locations, while others just give the location of the local cell tower.

### How GPS Works
The "NAVSTAR" satellite system is made up of 24 satellites whose orbits follow one of six different paths about 1200 miles above the earth. These satellites interact with a network of government-monitored ground stations which track the satellites and keep them in the proper orbit. GPS receivers determine their position by measuring the time it takes radio signals to travel from each of four satellites to the receiver. In 1998, handheld receivers were accurate within 100 feet 95% of the time. Today, they are often accurate to within 10 feet. The next generation will drop this resolution to a single foot.

New GPS receivers have a number of integrated features such as altimeters, digital compasses, and built in topo map software. This class, however, will focus on the primary skills of:
1) Locating your position on a map with GPS.
2) Entering waypoints by physical position (when at that location) and by UTM coordinates taken from a map.
3) Basic routefinding.

### Locating Your Position on a Map Using GPS
The most basic function of any GPS receiver is to determine your current position. In order to make use of position information, users must be able to accurately plot coordinates on their map.

Most units will acquire signals from at least three satellites within three minutes of being turned on or less if they have been used recently in the same area. This is called getting a position fix. For the receiver to work well (3D mode), it needs to have a lock on (line of site) at least four satellites. While receivers will read data when in range of only three satellites (2D mode), the inaccuracy of this mode (often more than a mile) makes the data unreliable. In the same way that triangulating from more known points spread out over a greater distance with a compass means more precision, more satellites in range and in proper geometry means faster and more accurate data. While signals can travel well through tents, you may not get enough signals in a tight canyon or under dense forest canopy.

WAAS means wide area augmentation system. It uses ground stations to add correction factors to satellites. This technology is steadily advancing and may help your EPE (estimated positional error) get smaller on some GPS units in some situations.

Each position fix is displayed in UTM coordinates or latitude/longitude. A secondary function of the receiver is that it can translate UTM coordinates to lat/long or vice versa.

### Entering Waypoints
Waypoints (also called landmarks) are representations of points on earth that are stored in your GPS receiver's memory. By guiding you from waypoint to waypoint, your receiver can aid in routefinding. Entering waypoints creates a route description or record of the places you've visited. Waypoints can be stored in two ways: by entering coordinates or by pushing a sequence of buttons to record a "snapshot" of your physical location into the receiver's memory. While your position fix changes as you move, stored waypoint coordinates do not change unless you edit them.

You may want to enter UTM coordinates in your GPS to use the GPS to find a physical location on land. The coordinates may have been given to you by a third party to find a difficult to reach spot—a new climbing area or good fishing spot, for example. You might also wish to enter coordinates you have determined from your map using a UTM grid reader. In either case, your receiver will have an "enter waypoint" or "edit location" function that allows you to manually enter the numerical coordinates. There are four bits of information you should have for each coordinate. For example, the position of Ice Lake is:

| | |
|---|---|
| Zone — | N11 |
| Easting — | E599600 |
| Northing— | N4790750 |
| Map datum— | NAD-27 (US) |

The most common operator errors relate to mis-entering waypoint coordinates: entering the wrong datum for the map you are using, or entering the wrong zone in the UTM coordinate system. The wrong datum can be up to ~200' off, but the wrong zone will put you in the wrong state. The datum and zone are printed in the margin on the bottom left corner of USGS quads. USGS maps will be in either North American Datum 1927 (NAD 27) or North American Datum 1983 (NAD 83). While some receivers today feature an "autozone" function, others do not. The UTM system divides the Earth into 6-degree zones numbering 1 to 60. That means there are 60 places on Earth with the same UTM coordinates. The continental US consists of zones 10-19, with zone 10 covering Washington and zone 19 covering Maine. Make sure you have correctly entered the right zone and datum.

You should be able to enter a waypoint into your receiver in the field, recording a snapshot of your physical location. By recording waypoints at crucial route junctures, you could (for example) return to camp following your GPS waypoint to waypoint even in whiteout conditions or complete darkness. This means that, properly using GPS, you should always be able to retrace your steps. Entering your position as a waypoint does not require plotting or entering numbers but merely pressing a sequence of buttons under the waypoint menu in your receiver. The receiver will also ask for a name for each waypoint. You can name waypoints by date, time, a nearby recognizable land feature, etc. The name should prompt your memory of that place and why it is significant.

### Routefinding with GPS

When entering waypoints for routefinding, consider critical trail junctions or large land features that force you to change directions as places to enter a waypoint. For example, if you need to cross through a steep canyon, you might enter a waypoint at the place where you begin descending into the canyon and again at the place where you exit the canyon on the other side. Without these waypoints, the receiver might lead you right up to a cliff edge, which happens to be directly in line with your next waypoint. Remember, the receiver does not recognize potentially hazardous terrain, only waypoints.

Once you have entered waypoints in your GPS receiver, you can use the receiver to navigate between these points with the "Go To" function. All receivers have some sort of arrow diagram that will literally point you in the direction of your next waypoint and give you magnetic directions. With GPS, however, you must be moving in order for the GPS to have directionality.

An easy way to use your compass to follow a GPS-given bearing is to align the compass and GPS receiver when the receiver is pointing towards your destination. Then, without moving the compass, rotate the bezel and box the needle. Now you can put the receiver away and follow your compass bearing to the next waypoint. Again, GPS is not a compass (although some units now include imprecise digital compasses). It cannot tell you your heading unless you are moving.

The receiver will also tell you your distance to the next waypoint. Keep that distance and your pace in mind as you travel toward the waypoint. You should be able to estimate your time of arrival (ETA). If the receiver is left on while you are travelling, it can estimate your ETA at your current pace, but this is an unnecessary strain on the batteries.

Following a compass bearing around large obstructions is often problematic and involves some guesswork to get back on your bearing after circumnavigating the obstruction. GPS receivers can give you your new bearing as you go around the obstruction without the chance of compounding errors. Get the new bearing from the receiver, reset your compass to the new bearing and continue on your way. Because saving battery power is critical on long expeditions, always travel using your map and analog compass (more accurate than current digital compasses).

### Additional Limitations and Common Mistakes

Multipath Interference (MI) can negatively affect receiver accuracy. MI happens when a signal bounces off an object (a cliff or building) on its way to your receiver. This creates multiple paths for the same radio signal. It is hard to know if your position fix is inaccurate, so avoid cliffs if possible when taking a position fix.

As with all electronics, GPS receivers and batteries are best kept warm in winter conditions. Try to keep them insulated or in a jacket pocket. Many receivers will not operate below −10°C. Most receivers are waterproof, though a few are not.

Always be on the lookout for operator error—entering the wrong coordinates, wrong datum, or wrong zone for a waypoint.

### Teaching Considerations

GPS should be taught only after students have been introduced to and gained some experience with map and compass skills, including triangulation and UTM coordinates. Students should have some confidence in their basic navigation skills before learning GPS so that GPS is seen as an additional educational tool.

While teaching "How GPS Works," a diagram of satellites in varied locations helps students visualize how receivers triangulate.

Before teaching this class, instructors should have gained some experience using GPS. Instructors new to GPS should spend some travel days early in the course familiarizing themselves with the receivers they have been issued.

If your group has enough receivers and time, you may consider doing an exercise where small groups of students have to find points using coordinates you give them or routefind to waypoints you have entered before class.

## River Crossings

*This document is an abridged version of NOLS River Crossing Practices. NOLS instructors should refer to the full text in the NOLS Accepted Field Practices.*

Mountain travel requires the skills and abilities to assess moving water hazards, judge and decide if and where to cross a river, and execute appropriate river crossings. Rivers can present a major hazard on mountain courses, and crossing them presents significant risk. Decisions to cross rivers, creeks, or streams need to be made carefully.

The methodology for river crossings is complex and is influenced by environmental conditions and subjective human factors. This document cannot address every possible situation. The methodology and techniques described are based on NOLS' collective experience teaching this skill, executing successful river crossings, and from review and investigation of river crossing incidents.

### Learning Objectives

- Recognize river hazards and assess risks to hikers.
- Know and have practiced dry and wet crossing methods.
- Be able and willing to decide not to cross a river if conditions are judged to be too difficult.
- Be able to organize and properly execute river crossings.
- On courses with independent student group travel (ISGT), students may need to cross moving water without supervision.

### Teaching Considerations

Anticipate where rivers and creeks will be encountered and plan the instruction progression accordingly. Teaching and practicing this skill takes time, and that needs to be factored into travel plans. This material is best taught in a series of classes as river hazards are encountered. In some cases, small creeks are encountered first and can be crossed using dry techniques or shallow wades; however it may be necessary to perform a deep wade early in the course.

This is a complex and nuanced subject with many personal preferences and environmental variables. Instructors need to discuss personal biases and preferences in advance and resolve conflicting opinions. The goal is consistency in curriculum to avoid confusing the students. Be careful not to overwhelm students with too many techniques. Teach site assessment (scouting), decision-making, and crossing execution at the same time. Teach the roles, responsibilities, and limitations of spotters. **Always teach students that they never have to cross a river if a crossing site that matches their ability cannot be found.** Teach students to be aware of perceived external pressures, such as: camp is on the other side, the other group crossed here earlier, instructors are expecting us, etc. These are factors that are secondary to making decisions about suitability of a crossing site.

River crossing is an experiential activity best taught under the "describe, demonstrate, do, and reflect" maxim. Significant practice is necessary to develop competency, but practice time is often limited due to cold water temperatures. Instructors are the best role models. Choose good crossing sites, demonstrate techniques clearly, use spotters, and model effective execution of the crossing to address pace, communication, and maintaining the formation. Remember, what may be easy for an instructor is often difficult for novices. Ask yourself what you would want students to do if you are not there.

Specific dry crossing techniques taught will depend on the creeks/rivers encountered. Dry crossing techniques are commonly taught when hiking in small groups with an instructor as creeks are encountered.

For wet techniques, start with one (possibly two) techniques, and practice until a situation arises where an additional technique can be taught. Clearly state the pros and cons of each technique. Wet crossing techniques require a detailed teaching approach. It is best taught as one large group at an appropriate river. Consider doing the first wading class while camped near a river so it will be easier to warm up and dry out. Introduce wading techniques on land so students can better focus on how to work as a team. Have students practice in the river both with and without backpacks. The more time students can practice, the better. As they gain confidence, challenge them with harder water to improve their confidence. Get them to feel the force of moving water so they respect its power, understand what method of support (stick, hand holding, grasping packs, etc.) is most comfortable, and get a feel for their personal limitations. In a low water year or late in the season, courses may not get a chance to practice or need to use wading techniques. It is possible to teach wading techniques at the outlets and inlets of lakes.

## River Features

Understanding river features is critical to making appropriate assessments and decisions about river crossings.

*Current* is the flow of water in a river. The flow is the volume of water measured at a specific spot in units per time, such as cubic feet per second (CFS) or cubic meters per second (cumec). Velocity is the speed of the current measured in distance per time such as miles per hour (mph) or kilometers per hour (kph).

- The terrain influences velocity. Steeper gradient equals faster current. Use maps to anticipate areas of steeper gradient. Wide sections of rivers can decrease the current, whereas narrow sections may increase the current. Current tends to slow in deeper areas of a river. When speed is doubled, force is quadrupled.
- One assessment tool for estimating current speed is to throw a stick into the main current and walk next to it on the bank. If the stick goes faster than walking pace, the current is likely too strong to wade. If the stick matches walking pace, the current might be slow enough to wade.

*Volume* is determined by the size of the watershed and seasonal factors like spring melt or periods of heavy rain. A high volume of water has much greater force than a low volume of water in the same river.

*Depth* is determined by gradient, riverbed configuration, and volume. Steeper gradients typically mean shallower depth, but faster current. Flatter gradients typically mean greater depth and slower current. Unstable riverbeds may have deeper channels scoured out by the current. Deeper channels may not be obvious from shore and may not be identifiable while crossing until you step into them. A narrow river channel can constrict the volume of water to create greater depth. A wide river channel can allow the volume of the river to spread out and create shallower depth.

*Water clarity* influences the ability to see the riverbed through the water when assessing the depth and is affected by turbidity (suspended solids such as those found in muddy or glacier fed rivers), depth, waves, rapids, and vegetative tannins. A river can be opaque and shallow or opaque and deep.

The only effective way to determine depth is to probe with a long stick or attempt a trial crossing. Some instructors advocate throwing rocks into a river to get clues as to the depth of the river by listening to the sound. If you can hear the rock hit bottom it can provide a clue that the river may be shallow enough to wade. If you can't hear it hit bottom it indicates the water is likely too deep. Some instructors think this is an important assessment tool while others do not. It takes a practiced ear to distinguish the sounds; the technique can provide false positive results and alone doesn't provide a complete understanding of the depth of the entire crossing.

*Riverbed composition* determines the type of footing one can expect when wading a river. Sand, silt, or gravel riverbeds can offer good footing. Large river cobbles (e.g., softball to basketball-sized) can create unstable footing. Submerged boulders can present a foot entrapment hazard. Submerged boulders that you can hear moving downriver indicate an unstable riverbed (and likely a strong current). Boulders partially exposed above the river surface can create eddies. Muddy riverbeds (commonly seen in the canyons) can cause people to become trapped in quicksand (quick mud).

*Eddies* form when the current slows (or may actually move upstream) behind the downstream side of an obstacle such as a large rock. An eddy can also form along the shore where the water is slowed due to friction from the riverbank and riverbed.

*Bends* in the river can create areas of deep and shallow water—an inside bend is shallower while an outside bend is deeper.

*Braided rivers* have a wide graveled riverbed that is dissected by numerous channels of water and interspersed with dry gravel bars or islands. Rivers may be braided all the time or just during periods of low flow.

*Full flowing rivers* have distinct banks and water is present from bank to bank (no gravel bars). Rivers may be full flowing all the time or just during periods of high water.

*Riverbanks* that are steep or tall may indicate a deeper channel while riverbanks that are undercut may indicate strong current. The riverbank can present significant obstacles for people entering or exiting a river during a crossing or during a mishap.

*Seasonal fluctuations* can change the volume of a river. Spring and early summer in the mountains are generally when the water can be at its highest and fastest. During late summer and fall seasons, after most of the winter snow has melted, river levels are usually lower and the current is slower.

*Diurnal fluctuations* in river flow can occur due to changes in temperature between day and night. They are most pronounced during spring and early summer in locations with broad daily temperature fluctuations such as mountain streams at high altitude and mid-latitude. In a diurnal pattern, the river rises as the heat of the day melts snow, which increases runoff. In the morning hours following cooler nighttime temperatures, the river level is lower. Diurnal flow patterns are not universal and can be affected by many variables such as the distance between the crossing site and the melting snow. Rivers at high latitude generally have smaller diurnal fluctuations, due to the long summer days creating much smaller daily temperature fluctuations. Diurnal flow patterns can be gauged by placing a marker such as a stick or rock cairn at the water level and checking it periodically over a 12–48 hour period to see if and when the water level rises or falls.

*Debris* in the river such as strainers (trees that have fallen and are partly in the river and partly on land), logjams (logs piled up across the river channel by floods), and other debris floating downstream can present hazards. A person who gets caught in a strainer or logjam can become trapped, possibly underwater.

*Rapids or waterfalls* indicate an area of a river with steeper gradient. Some mountain rivers may have rapids for long stretches. Rapids and waterfalls have strong current, unstable riverbeds, and entrapment hazards.

*Glacial rivers* are characteristically silty and opaque—you cannot see through the river to the riverbed. Glacial rivers are not as subject to seasonal or diurnal flow fluctuations because melting forces within the glacier can keep the flow more constant. Glacial rivers often have unstable riverbeds, particularly near the glacier. The depth and shape of the riverbed is subject to change from the force of the water on the unstable material. This can result in deeper channels being formed without any visible change at the shoreline. In other words, the water level may not appear to rise or fall at the shore, but a deeper channel may have been formed further out in the river. When assessing rivers with unstable riverbeds, be wary of hidden changes in the riverbed profile.

*Tributaries* flow together to form a larger river. Crossing individual tributaries may be a better way to get to the other side of a larger river that may otherwise be too large to cross.

*Water temperature:* Cold temperatures can impede one's ability to wade due to numbing and weakening of the body and must be considered in the event that someone falls in.

## River Crossing Methodology

River crossings are divided into two types—dry and wet. *Dry Crossings* can range in difficulty from a few easy steps on the tops of exposed boulders to difficult balancing acts on logs or wet rocks.

The risks from dry crossings include injuries from slips and falls due to slippery surfaces on rocks and logs, falls due to logs or rocks rolling or shifting when weighted, or losing one's balance. Injuries include athletic injuries from performing awkward steps and jumps while wearing a backpack, fractures or head injuries from falls onto rocks above or below the water surface, and hypothermia or drowning from immersion in cold moving water. Consider the consequences of a fall when anticipating, assessing, deciding on, and executing a dry crossing.

*Wet crossings* may be the most hazardous type of river crossing we do, however, they are frequently performed successfully. Wet crossings need to be done in a mindful way with astute situational awareness of the variables that may lead to or inhibit success and an understanding of the consequences of failure.

The keys to successful wet river crossings are planning, assessment, decision-making, and skill in executing the chosen technique.

## Dry Crossing Techniques

*Rock stepping*, means stepping on the tops of exposed rocks. Rocks need to be closely spaced so that steps are short. The sequence of steps needs to be planned. Flat-topped rocks are best for obvious reasons. Rocks can be slippery due to wet lichen, moss, algae, or thin layers of ice, all of which may be difficult to see. Throwing sand onto the tops of the rocks may improve traction. Testing the sequence of steps first without a pack is recommended. Consider using a trekking pole or stick to aid balance. Jumping from rock to rock is unwise. A spotter may need to be stationed in the creek at a particularly difficult step to lend a hand or help protect someone from injury if they fall.

*Log crossings* are done by walking along trees that have fallen across the creek or on logs placed across to form a bridge. The trees need to be well anchored so that they don't roll or lift when stepped on. Assess the risk of a fall off the upstream side of the log, which may make the log a strainer. Logs that are high above the river increase the severity of a fall.

*Logjams* are substantial piles of logs pushed together from floods and can provide effective bridges. Individual logs in a logjam may be unstable and difficult to detect until stepped on. Use caution.

*Tyrolean Traverse* uses a rope system to suspend people above the river as they pull themselves across. See separate information for practices for constructing a Tyrolean Traverse in the next section.

## Dry Crossing Considerations

The following are considerations for preparing and executing a dry crossing. Balance and pack stability are integral to success—you should redistribute loads, if necessary, to avoid having top-heavy packs. Consider having stronger students take more weight, shuttle packs, or pass packs across. Make sure all loose items are secured inside the pack. Keep hands free and avoid dangling things off the pack or around the neck that can alter balance or block visibility. Use or offer assistance with trekking poles, long, stout sticks, or a helping hand from a group member. Hand lines may be a useful aid to balance. To be effective, they need to be strong and secure, such as a rope stretched tight with a pulley system. Do not tie into a hand line—it's not a belay, just a balance aid.

## Wet Crossing Techniques

The WADE principle provides a way to focus attention on the important elements of judging wet crossings. WADE stands for:

**W**atch: Planning, before the course or during daily route planning, and awareness of environmental conditions that may affect river crossings. Begin to consider alternatives in case a planned river crossing cannot be done.

**A**ssess: Evaluate a specific crossing site based on the river features and the ability and skill of the group.

**D**ecide: Can the river be crossed by the group? Does the assessment match the group's abilities and physical and emotional state? If yes, what crossing technique will be used? If no, make alternative plans.

**E**xecute: Devise a crossing plan, communicate how the plan will be executed, and perform the crossing.

Wet Crossing Techniques may be as simple as walking through a slow moving, shallow (boot-top) river or as complex as executing a wading technique in deeper faster moving rivers. The following wading techniques are accepted practices at NOLS. They are not listed in order of priority.

## The Tripod

The *tripod* is a solo technique that uses a stout pole for balance. The pole needs to be long enough to allow its use for probing the riverbed while allowing for proper body position. It needs sufficient strength to support a person leaning on it. Trekking poles may be adequate in some cases, but may lack strength in more difficult situations.

## The Group Pole

The *group pole technique* incorporates a long stout pole held by all group members to provide a way for the team to stay in formation and provide team members support. The pole can be a 2–3 inch diameter log, a pair of trekking poles, and even a mega mid tent pole. The team can either face upstream or across the river. This is technique provides excellent support for all team members. If one member loses his or her footing, the pole, held by all members, provides a secure handrail. This method also does not rely on people holding onto each other or their packs, is comfortable while wearing a pack, enhances the team's ability to negotiate obstacles, and allows for effective oral communication among team members during the crossing. This can be done effectively with 2 – 6 people.

*The Group Pole Technique*

## The Eddy Technique

The *eddy or eddy line technique* is a common technique at NOLS. The first person in a line uses the individual tripod technique and group members line up one behind the other in the eddy formed by the leader. Team members grasp the pack of the person in front of them near their center of gravity (at hips or hip belt) because grabbing the back of the pack in front of you can pull the person off balance. The group sidesteps across while facing upstream. It works best in groups of three to five; larger groups are difficult to coordinate. The front person should be a strong group member. It is an effective method, but has some shortcomings: oral communication within the team can be difficult because people are basically shouting into the pack of the person in front of them, the ability of people to see is hindered from being so close to the pack in front, it requires careful attention to coordinate foot movement, experience has shown that if the water gets above the waist people can loose their footing and the whole team washes out, and it is not as good for crossings that require negotiating obstacles such as boulders.

## The Mutual Support Technique

The *mutual support technique* has been advocated by the New Zealand Mountain Safety Council and is the preferred technique used by NOLS New Zealand. Line up people shoulder-to-shoulder with stronger people on each end.

*The Eddy technique*

The ideal group size is three to five people. Undo chest straps and loosen shoulder straps. Waist belts are fastened because in New Zealand self-rescue uses the pack for flotation. Insert arms between each neighbor's pack and their back, and grasp either their waist belt or their pack shoulder strap (down low) on the opposite side. Move into the river as a single unit facing the opposite bank. If the group needs to retreat, they should back up slowly while shuffling feet.

### The Chain

The *chain technique* is done in a team holding hands and/or linking arms. Variations include facing upstream and sidestepping across perpendicular to the current or facing the opposite bank and crossing parallel to the current. This technique is good for water below knee deep and allows the team to flex to move around obstacles. It can provide less confident students with support for crossings where others may use the solo tripod.

### The Pyramid

The *pyramid technique* is a variation on the eddy technique where the second and third persons stand shoulder to shoulder behind the lead person. The fourth, fifth and sixth persons stand shoulder-to-shoulder behind the second and third. This technique provides lateral and longitudinal support for each group member.

### The Pack Float

The *pack float* technique may be useful in rare situations when faced with a wide, slow moving river that is too deep to wade. Using the buoyancy provided by a backpack, lay on it facing upstream and ferry across the river. This can be done individually or in a group of about three people with the packs forming a raft. This technique requires a long runout with no downstream hazards, and people's torsos will likely get wet.

### Prepare for the Crossing

The following are considerations for preparing and executing a wet crossing. As with dry crossings, balance and pack stability are integral to success. Wade in boots or camp shoes to provide protection from rocks on the riverbed. Decide whether to wear socks or not. With plastic boots, decide whether to just use the shells or use the liners too. Decide whether to use gaiters or not. The disadvantages of gaiters are that they can add drag and Velcro closures can fail, while the advantages are that they can keep sand and gravel out of boots and help keep plastic boot shells in place. Clothing can balloon up with water and create drag, which may make it difficult to move. For deep crossings (≥ knee deep), remove wind or rain pants. Snug-fitting long underwear provides some warmth with minimal drag. Wearing extra upper body layers helps people stay warm, but can make it difficult to jettison a backpack or swim in the event of a fall. Secure the pack flaps and zippers and strive to keep as much clothing as dry as possible.

### Anticipate the Need to Remove the Backpack in the Event of a Fall

Sternum straps should be unfastened and shoulder straps loosened. The big question is should hip belts be fastened or unfastened? There are two schools of thought on this topic: 1) unfasten belts to ease getting the pack off if a fall occurs; or 2) keep belts fastened to aid in balance and prevent falling and to use the floatation of the pack while wearing it to aid in rescue. The latter is advocated in New Zealand (see below in the section Rescue of a Fallen Team or Team Member for a description of how this works). The following applies to NOLS courses:

   a) Hip belts can be left fastened during crossings in water above the knee IF self-rescue with a pack on has been practiced in the water and students show competency (see below).
   b) Hip belts will be unfastened in water above the knee if self-rescue with a pack cannot be practiced.
   c) Hip belts can be fastened or unfastened in water that is below the knee pending instructor's prerogative.
   d) For students who may encounter wet river crossings while on ISGT instructors need to set rules for when hip belts can be unfastened or fastened. These rules should be consistent with any instruction and practice the students have received.

### Establish Spotters

During wet crossings, spotters are people without backpacks positioned downstream of the crossing site on shore, in shallow water, or in eddies where they

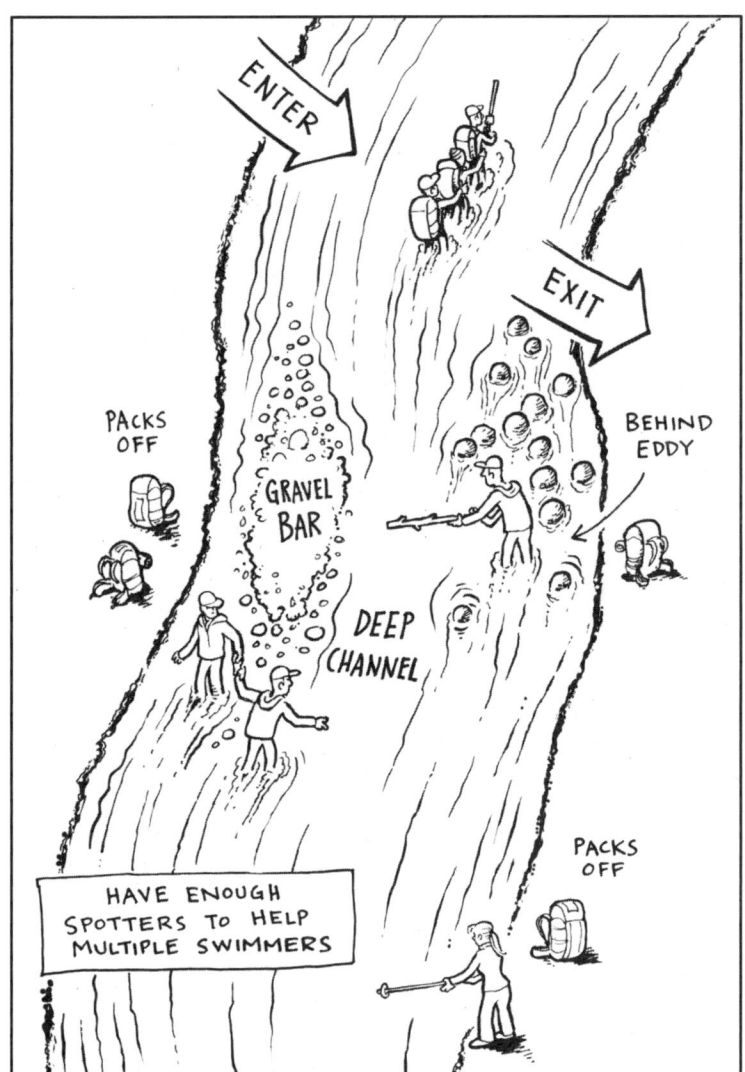

*Spotter Locations*

may be able to provide assistance to a person who falls in and is being swept downstream. During dry crossings, spotters might be used to help protect someone's head if they slip and fall or offer a helping hand.

### Spotters are not Lifeguards

Spotters are not likely to be able to pluck someone from a fast moving current, but they may be able to provide assistance to someone who is either able to get themselves to shore or has been carried to shallow water by the current. As a spotter, be prepared to safely reach as far out as possible to grab the swimmer and guide them towards shallow water/slow current. A chain of people linking arms may extend the reach. Long sticks may be used as aids to reach people, but it may be difficult for a struggling swimmer to grab and hold onto a stick. Study the flow of the current to determine where someone may be carried. It may be useful to throw a log into the main current to see where it goes. Positioning spotters depends on terrain variables, such as whether a river is braided or full flowing, riverbank topography and vegetation, and the flow of the river. For example, on a full flowing river with heavily vegetated banks it may not be possible to place spotters in effective locations.

Positioning of spotters is a decision-making factor in determining the suitability of the site—if they can't be placed adequately, find another site. Spotters need to be used during any scouting attempts to cross the river and be in place before the first team crosses. Once a team is across, position them as spotters for the remaining teams. Keep spotters in position until everyone is across and on the shore. DO NOT create more swimmers. Prioritize helping the swimmer and less on gear recovery.

### Executing a Wet Crossing

In general, techniques where people face across the river (versus upstream) are easier and faster to execute, but are more difficult to reverse if the conditions are found to be to challenging. Facing downstream may cause the current to buckle knees, causing a loss of balance. Choose a diagonal line that angles downriver. This avoids having to fight the current every step across. Look for eddies near shore and midstream, as they can be good places to enter and exit the river or rest. Be sure everyone understands the crossing route. Everyone should take small steps, move one foot at a time, move slowly, and weight the foot carefully in case the footing gives way. If using a pole, move it first to feel for any obstacles or deeper channels. Avoid staring at the river; moving water can be mesmerizing and interfere with balance. Keep moving, but don't rush. Concentrate on keeping the team formation intact. Have pre-planned communication signals such as "zero" for stop – keep communication simple. Have a communication/signal plan for once the first group reaches the other side. The first group should signal when they are ready to have the second group cross.

### Rescue for a Fallen Team or Team Member

The first response is for the team to attempt to keep a fallen member from being carried downstream by holding onto him or her. The strength of the team may be able to assist the person to remain upright, get back on their feet, or keep them from being swept downstream. If that fails and the person or persons are swept downstream, they become "swimmers." A swimmer's best chance of rescue is self-rescue. Swimmers need to be able to quickly and effectively respond to the situation and contend with being immersed in cold and swift moving water while being carried downstream, likely without much control and possibly having a large and unwieldy backpack on. There are three options:

1) The conventional wisdom is to get the backpack off, roll into a seated position with feet up and pointed downstream, deflect rocks with feet, do not try to stand, and use hands to skull or steer towards shore.
2) A different school of thought, but one that requires extensive practice in the water and is advocated by the New Zealand Mountain Safety Council, is to use the backpack for floatation. A backpack will float and can be used to the swimmer's advantage. Options include:
   – With hip belt and shoulder straps secured the swimmer can lean back onto the backpack and use their arms outstretched to either side to skull across the river.
   – If the hip belt is unfastened, the swimmer can hook their thumbs through the shoulder straps where they join the pack near the waist, lean back and use their feet to help guide themselves to shore.
3) A third option is to remove the backpack while in the water, roll or hold onto it, and float or kick to shore.

*Swimmers should only attempt to stand when in shallow water and no longer being carried downstream by the current.*

### The WADE checklist

A checklist is not instructional. The instruction and practice occur separately. A checklist is a way to confirm that important steps have been done and establish a mechanism for each group member to express their opinion about the crossing. The checklist does not lead to a go/no go decision; at each step a decision not to cross can be made.

**W**ATCH (plan in advance before the course and for a particular day's route)
- ❏ Have environmental conditions that affect the river features been identified and assessed?
- ❏ Have possible river crossings on the route and likely crossing sites been identified?
- ❏ Have alternatives to river crossings been identified in the event that conditions prohibit crossing?

**A**SSESS (once a river is encountered)
- ❏ Have all applicable river features (depth, current, exit/entry points, bottom, run out, etc.) been assessed?
- ❏ Have spotter locations been identified?
- ❏ Has the group's physical and emotional state been assessed at the specific crossing site?

**D**ECIDE (once the site has been assessed)
- ❏ Can the river be crossed?
- ❏ Have all group members voiced their opinions about the assessment of the crossing site?
- ❏ Is the condition of the river (current, depth, width, etc.) reasonable for each group member?
- ❏ Is the technique chosen to cross within each group member's ability?
- ❏ Are there any secondary factors that might influence a decision to cross (time schedules, sticking to a plan, time of day, time invested on the crossing assessment, etc.)? Have these been reconciled?
- ❏ The group has decided that river can or cannot be crossed.
- ❏ What are the alternatives to the crossing?

**E**XECUTE
- ❏ The crossing plan, including rescue response, has been discussed among the group.
- ❏ Everyone understands the rescue plan and what to do if they fall in.
- ❏ Spotters are established at strategic locations.
- ❏ Crossing teams are organized to distribute strong group members within each team.
- ❏ Expectations are established for communication among the group during the crossing.

### Teaching Considerations

River crossings demand good teamwork and organization. Find a practice site that is appropriate for solo crossings, as well as one that will challenge people and force them to work together.

### Conclusion

The ability to cross rivers is an important skill for wilderness travelers. Knowledge of the environment, familiarity with the power of moving water, an understanding of the WADE principle, and experience with specific crossing techniques all come to bear when making a decision to cross a river. Respect this hazard, and if in doubt make the conservative decision not to cross and look elsewhere for a more suitable crossing location.

## The Tyrolean Traverse

A Tyrolean traverse can be a thrilling event on a NOLS course. Some course routes routinely use the technique to cross rivers, especially during the spring-thaw. The skills learned building a Tyrolean traverse can be applied to boating, mountaineering, rescue, caving, river crossings, and many other situations. The Tyrolean is also an excellent leadership exercise for a small team.

A classic Tyrolean traverse is a double taut line across a river that allows you to cross the obstacle on ropes rather than in the water. The lines are tightened using a 3:1 pulley system. Rarely are any two Tyroleans the same. Success with the system comes from being able to adapt the basic concepts to any appropriate site.

*Spotter Technique*

### Learning Objectives
- Instructors must determine whether the students need to master the skills required to erect a Tyrolean traverse or just experience the thrill of crossing a river on a rope.
- If you want your students to able to build Tyrolean traverses on their own, they should understand basic rope handling, pulley systems, tensionless anchors, and force vectors before you begin instruction on a traverse system.

### Equipment Needs
1) Four ropes
   - two long ropes - anchor to anchor taut lines: preferably static lines
   - two short ropes - bank to bank
2) Two cordelettes
3) Ten locking carabiners
4) 20 non-locking carabiners
5) 15 double slings
6) Ten single slings

### Site Selection
Selecting a safe site often involves extensive scouting. The ideal spot is a narrow portion of the river where a single rope can easily reach from shore to shore. You will need two large, healthy anchor trees at least ten feet back from the river's edge, and high banks so the ropes are well above the water to prevent the people crossing from dragging through the river. The site should also have safe spots for easy loading and unloading.

### Getting the Ropes to the Other Side
One of the main reasons for making a Tyrolean traverse is that only one person has to swim the river. Ensure the swimmer's safety by choosing a short crossing site with minimal objective hazards. Station spotters downstream. Have dry clothes and a hot drink ready to send with the first person across the ropes when the Tyrolean is complete.

Throw the ropes across the river. Make sure a poor toss will not get the rope caught in the river. For long tosses, you may want to tie a rock to a section of parachute cord. You can then use the p-cord to pull the rope across. Once over, keep the rope out of the water to prevent snags. Use prearranged hand signals to communicate above the roar of the river.

### Basic Construction
Use two wraps of rope around a large tree trunk to create a tensionless anchor strong enough to hold the force exerted by people crossing the traverse. The end of the rope is tied in a figure-eight on a bight and clipped to itself. Two ropes should be attached in this manner to a single tree on one side of the river. On the opposite shore, the ropes pass through a pair of guide biners clipped into a sling attached to the guide tree. The ropes then go to independent anchor trees where they are pulled tight with a 3:1 pulley system. Two additional ropes, attached by carabiners to the taut line, are used to make a hauling system.

### System Safety
The weak links in a Tyrolean system are the anchors, which carry much larger loads than in anything else we do, and the tightened ropes, which are very prone to abrasion when under load. Be especially sure your tight ropes are not being abraded by rocks between the anchor and the river—pad these spots.

Tyroleans put a tremendous amount of stress on ropes. Don't use a lead rope for a Tyrolean because the stress will take some of the spring out of the lead rope. Static lines are preferable because they carry loads better, they don't sag as much, and they are more abrasion-resistant under a load.

Tighten the system enough to keep people dry, secure, and able to move without undue effort, but do not remove all the slack from the ropes. According to vector physics, the force on the anchors increases as the angle of sag in the system decreases. In other words, the tighter the system, the greater the force on the anchors when the system is loaded in the middle. Sag equals strength. Bouncing puts unnecessary stress on the anchors. Consider using a haul line to help people across.

Use two supporting ropes in two independent systems so everything is backed-up. Use two carabiners for pulleys. This creates a redundant system and results in less friction by providing a better bending angle than one or three carabiners. You can use the improved prusik hitch to create your 3:1, but tie the system off so the prusik is no longer in the system. Have no more than four large people tighten the pulley system to avoid rope damage. If your rope still needs to be higher off the water, build an X out of strong logs to prop it up it more. This X needs to go as close to the river as possible. Avoid breaking branches and friction burns on the trees used.

### Crossing Tips
Clip into both support ropes with two non-locking carabiners. The gates should be reversed but not opposed in order to make unloading easier. If an individual's harness does not hold the carabiners so the supporting rope goes through without twisting, add two biners more to twist the orientation 90 degrees.

Haul your gear across when you have roughly half your people on either side: this is a great opportunity for practicing all four leadership roles.

### Retrieving the System
When half of your group has crossed the river, reverse the entire system to make it retrievable. The old guide tree now becomes the new anchor tree and vice versa. New pulley systems are set on the far bank. Keep the rope out of the current during this transition.

When there is only one person remaining, release the system, undo your tensionless anchor, and join the ends of the support ropes with a Flemish bend. The Tyrolean is now one system without a backup. Make sure the knot is clear of the trunk on the upstream side, then retighten and have your last person cross. Pull the rope from the upstream side to keep the tail from being washed around the front of the tree and creating excessive friction. Pull the rope as quickly as possible to limit its time in the current and reduce the chance of it getting snagged in the river.

### Teaching Considerations
If you want your students to know how to do a Tyrolean on their own, start by teaching them the preparatory skills. Once they understand the basics of knot tying, anchoring, and 3:1 pulleys, demonstrate a simple dry land Tyrolean and have them practice. Avoid trying to jam all the preparatory instruction into the morning before your Tyrolean demonstration. Build these skills through a series of experiences that reinforce the techniques.

Discuss how judgment must accompany safe use of this skill. Students need to know that other methods for crossing a river have been considered before putting in the time to build a Tyrolean. Equally important is their ability to choose a safe site. If students have the opportunity to practice the system before an actual crossing, instructors can then focus their riverside instruction on site selection, site safety, retrieval, and adapting the theoretical system to the actual location.

Self-sufficiency with this skill requires practice in different settings. Besides learning the construction skills, students must know how to adapt the system to less than ideal locations. Once again, this technical skill is a fantastic medium for nurturing judgment, decision-making, and leadership.

### Leadership Opportunities
Building a Tyrolean traverse is a great exercise for developing leadership and teamwork. Your debrief of the activity should not only be linked to the technical skills learned but should also address what behaviors and actions helped or detracted from their success. Questions to ask include: Who is uneasy without structure? Who organizes and how is he or she reacted to? Who teaches others? Who doesn't do much? How were differing opinions resolved? Was there one leader or was it more of a collective leadership experience?

*Brunton diagrams are from Michael Hodgson's book "Compass and Map Navigator" (copyrights are retained by Brunton Inc.).*

# Chapter Eight
# Teaching Environmental Studies and Biology

Teaching materials for the environmental studies thread of our core curriculum can be found in the *NOLS Environmental Educator Notebook*. Most students come to NOLS with a strong environmental ethic (Lindsey, 2006). What they are looking for is not confirmation of that ethic, but rather tools to broaden it in their own future expeditions and for applying that ethic in their home communities. They generally arrive at NOLS with lots of knowledge about nature and ecology that they got from school and the media, but they lack the hands-on experience you can only get from immersion in nature (Louv, 2005). The NOLS expedition offers an immersion in nature that complements our students' strong knowledge and ethics in this area.

### Learning Objectives
The goal of the environmental studies curriculum is to teach our students observation skills that aid in the interpretation and enjoyment of the mountains, an understanding of how they interact with the natural world, and, most importantly, to develop personal feelings for the natural world they are a part of. The information that connects natural history to stewardship is ecological principles. The curriculum provides tools they can use to examine the ecosystems they travel through and to explore the changes these places undergo as a result of both time and human interaction. Ultimately, we hope our students feel they are part of the global ecosystem, explore it with a sense of wonder, and return home better citizens and stewards. Students will be able to:
- Consistently perform Leave No Trace living and traveling skills.
- Display natural history observation and interpretation skills.
- Apply ecological concepts as they relate to wilderness living and traveling.
- Discuss the history and potential solutions to pertinent environmental issues.
- Name the land management agencies for this course area and understand their mandates.
- Understand the transference of wilderness ethics to daily life.

## Teaching Ecological Principles
The *NOLS Environmental Educator Notebook* contains in depth information on teaching ecological principles and should be included in every course library. For many areas in which NOLS operates we have developed regionally specific Safari Guides, which are ecological handbooks for hikers. An important outcome for a NOLS wilderness course student is that they return home feeling they are actually part of an ecosystem, both locally and globally.

> *"The science of relationships is ecology, but what we call it matters nothing. The question is, does the citizen know that he is a cog in an ecological mechanism? That if he will work with that mechanism, his mental wealth and physical wealth can expand indefinitely? But that if he refuses to work with it, it will ultimately grind him to dust? If education does not teach us these things, then what is education for?"*
> -Aldo Leopold

Students need to know enough names of species to be able to recognize and discuss the life zone they are in during the course. These life zones are usually described as specific ecosystems. They are detailed for many NOLS expedition areas in the NOLS Safari Guide series.

Staff should use the ecosystem concept to discuss why we alter LNT camping practices. For instance, the higher ecological productivity of a grassy meadow makes it more resilient to impact than the forb understory in a dark forest. Ecological concepts are universal and transfer to life at home. An understanding of the habitats we are living in while immersed in these ecosystems provides tangible examples and the direct wisdom that only comes from personal experience.

### Teaching Considerations
When teaching ecology, avoid the abstract and limit your discussions to what can be seen in the immediate surroundings. Use teachable moments to teach about habitats. Use habitat information and awareness to emphasize the importance of sound minimum-impact skills.

## Teaching Biology on Semester Courses
Many NOLS semesters earn biology credit in ecological concepts. Instructors on these semesters need to use the expected student outcomes on the University of Utah course description. In general, the outcomes include learning about ecological concepts, applying them to the course, and envisioning how students can apply these concepts to their lives beyond NOLS. Some students use biology credit as the one required science course in their liberal arts education, so it is critical they develop the thinking habits described in the Inquiry section of the *NOLS Environmental Educator Notebook*. These concepts are easily applied to LNT practices and can help students develop judgment about things like where and when to use catholes. Inquiry can be used to judge whether off-trail groups should walk spread out or single file in a certain type of vegetation. As with most general areas of our curriculum, it helps to teach across the curriculum, mixing biology with LNT and risk management.

### Biovocabulary
One area where we often fall short is in development of academic vocabulary: when our students return to their home school and are explaining to the biology department chair why the University of Utah/NOLS biology credit should transfer, their use of vocabulary is one way the professors can assess the effectiveness of our program. Our students generally ace the mastery of concepts with broad application to the real world, but don't necessarily develop the academic vocabulary that is a somewhat superficial but a typical measure of whether a student understands a field of discipline like Ecology. If they have taken a college level course in Ecological Concepts, they need to be comfortable using terms like *primary succession*, *island biogeography*, and *cascading trophic levels*.

### Grading Biology
An easy way to give grades in Biology is to teach ecological concepts and have students keep journals of how they saw those concepts on each section. In the final semester section they can be asked to envision how to apply these concepts to their lives beyond NOLS. Some students will need coaching early in the semester so their field journal meets your expectations. A grading rubric is the ideal way to manage this so the standards are consistent among different instructor teams on the semester.

## Environmental Studies Field Guides
*NOLS Environmental Studies Field Guides* (formerly *Safari Guides*) are available for many of the school's operating areas. Look for the field guides at NOLS locations or as PDFs on the curriculum page of rendezvous (http://rendezvous.nols.edu).

# ENVIRONMENTAL STUDIES AT NOLS

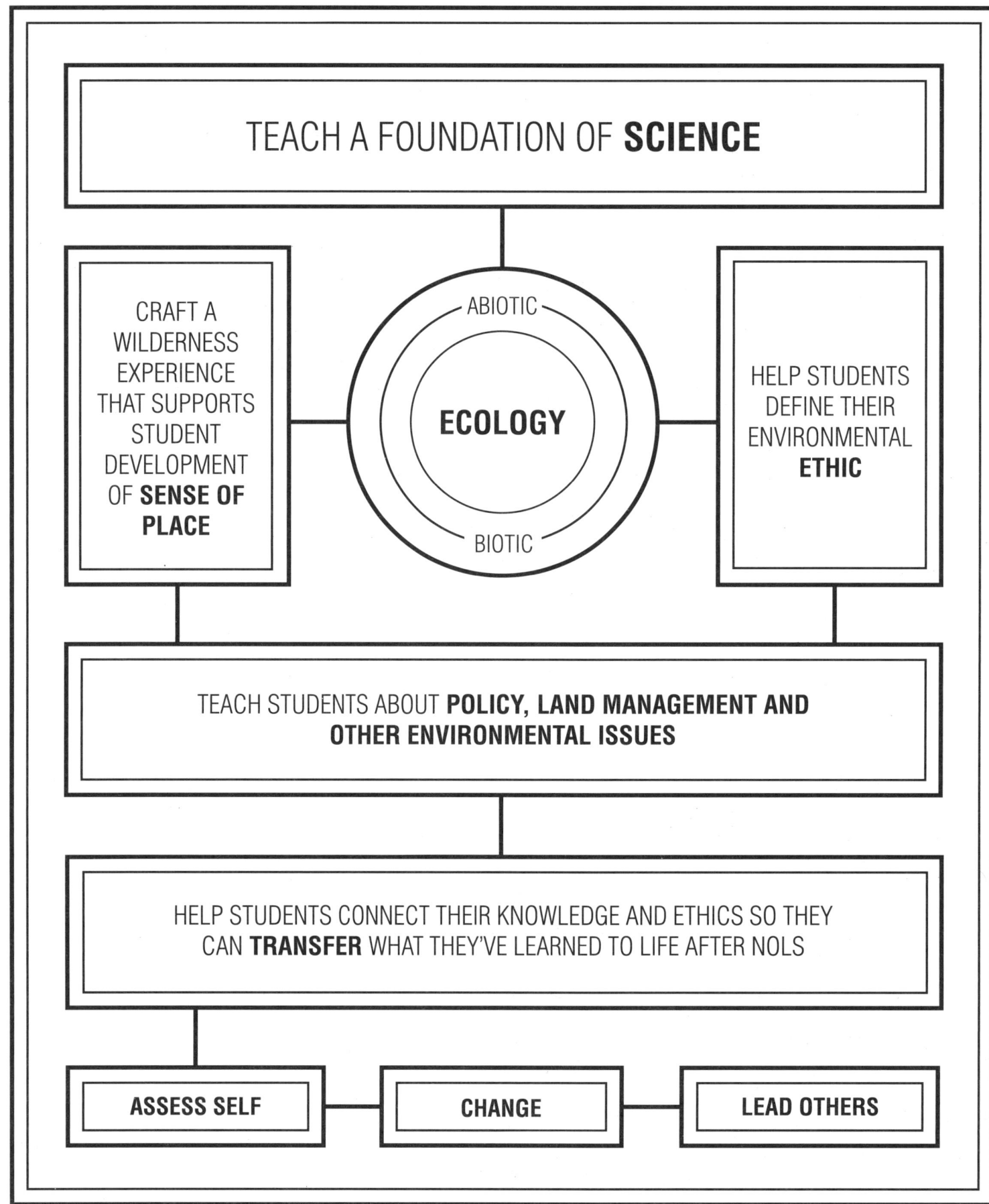

# Chapter Nine
# Teaching Leadership

## Using The NOLS Leadership Model

The *NOLS Leadership Educator Notebook* has specific lesson plans for teaching leadership at NOLS. Every chapter of the LEN has tips on leadership opportunities, since leadership is a thread that connects everything we do at NOLS. The NOLS student guide to leadership is the pamphlet called "Leadership At NOLS." Leadership outcomes are based on the four leadership roles and the seven leadership skills that are described in the pamphlet "Leadership At NOLS."

### Learning Objectives
At the end of a course we expect successful NOLS students to:
- Work effectively as a member of a team.
- Communicate ideas and concerns on an individual and group level appropriately.
- Accurately identify personal strengths, skills, and areas for growth in developing outdoor leadership styles.
- Take responsibility for learning by setting and attaining personal goals.
- Plan and carry out their own expeditions.
- Use abilities and initiative in a leadership role with peers.
- Respond to problems using decision-making and planning skills.
- Display an awareness of group strengths and limitations.
- Use experience and judgment to implement sound decisions and follow them through to completion.

### The Four Leadership Roles
Designated Leadership
Active Followership
Peer Leadership
Self-Leadership

### The Seven Leadership Skills
*Expedition Behavior*: Demonstrate teamwork, respect for others, a positive attitude, and commitment to group decisions.
*Communication:* Effectively communicate on interpersonal and group levels.
*Judgment and Decision-Making*: Demonstrate good judgment and decision-making skills.
*Self-Awareness:* Understand personal tendencies, strengths, and weakness as a leader.
*Tolerance for Adversity and Uncertainty:* Maintain a positive attitude and tolerance for adverse and uncertain conditions.
*Competence:* Master the wilderness living and travel skills of this course.
*Vision and Action:* Demonstrate the ability to plan and implement course activities.

Besides the four roles and seven skills, we expect staff to help students identify the signature style, or styles, that seems most effective for them.

An overarching goal of NOLS is to develop "competent, responsible wilderness travelers and leaders." While a background in theory is helpful in leadership development, at NOLS we pride ourselves on practical leadership education. Outdoor leadership is the ability to make decisions. Leadership is well-timed, appropriate action, not a theoretical attitude or behavior. NOLS believes that outdoor leaders exercising good judgment based on common sense, knowledge, and experience provide the best service to people and the environment. Everything we do at NOLS can be taught within a leadership context, hence the routine tips on leadership opportunities throughout this book.

## Student Teaching

Successful teachers and effective leaders share many of the same traits: clear communication skills, organizational abilities, enthusiasm, and a sincere desire to share information. Student teaching can be, therefore, a way to help further a student's leadership skills. To enhance the effectiveness of the experience for your students, help them prepare their material, offer them hints for effective presentation, and provide prompt feedback after the class has taken place.

The primary goal of student teaching is the successful presentation of information to a group of peers. The material presented should be relevant and appreciated by the audience. The activity should be voluntary.

### Topics
Help your students choose a topic that interests them and fits into the group's goals. Once a subject is decided upon, encourage them to focus on the aspect that intrigues them most. Ask them what the group would want to know about their topic. Defining the subject and narrowing the focus helps new teachers avoid getting lost in a maze of material.

### Preparation
With the student teacher, determine whether additional research is necessary prior to presentation. Discuss the resources available to supplement your student's knowledge; these can include everything from the course library to instructor notes and other expedition members' personal experience.

Have student teachers clarify their goals. Ask them what they want their audience to know. Are they teaching a skill? Or, is their objective to have the audience develop a basic understanding of an issue or object? Encourage your students to focus on fostering curiosity rather than creating experts. Too much information can be overwhelming or boring.

Figure out what teaching format will be most effective. A class on junipers works best as a teachable moment. Predator-prey relationships can be taught effectively with a game. Knot tying lends itself to the basic demonstrate-and-do formula. If the student decides to do a lecture, help develop some visual aids to illustrate the topic and enhance the presentation.

### Presentation
Have students come up with an outline for their class. Make sure their progression is logical, easy to follow, and covers the major points. Have them include a review or wrap-up at the end. One of the most common pitfalls for new teachers is the failure to include any kind of closure in their class. Such an oversight leaves the audience hanging and can be avoided by simply reviewing the material covered and inviting questions.

Most students benefit from rehearsing their presentation. Have them make a practice run through the class with you. Ask them questions. Give them feedback on everything from their posture and tone to the specific information conveyed. Remember, even a well-researched class can be painfully boring if presented in a droning, monotone voice.

Timing can be critical to the success of a class. Student classes, like instructor classes, need to be integrated into the overall course progression. Choosing appropriate locations and making sure that conditions are optimal will increase the likelihood that your student will have a successful experience. Student teachers should not be expected to motivate and inspire the unmotivated or the uncomfortable. Make sure the group is in a frame of mind to be courteous to, and supportive of, their peer.

### Feedback
After a student class, take time to evaluate the content, delivery, and effectiveness. You may choose to debrief the student privately, or to have the entire course offer constructive feedback after the presentation. Make sure you point out the positive aspects of the class, as well as the things that could be improved upon. Consider everything from the visual aids to organization and the group's reaction. Commend the student for their effort and encourage them to build upon the experience. Some good ground rules for feedback are:
- Let the speaker self-critique first.
- Speak for yourself.
- Don't repeat what's already been said.
- Avoid suggesting alternative approaches unless they ask for that specific advice.
- During later activities, apply the new information, then let the student teacher know how much it helped.

### Teaching Considerations
A student teacher's experience should be positive. If the material needs to be taught again, then the instructors have failed in their coaching role. A successful presentation results from close work between a motivated student and an instructor familiar with the material. The instructor must be involved with

everything from choosing the subject, to coaching the student, timing the presentation, and providing feedback afterwards.

Such close involvement requires a significant investment of time. This investment must be weighed against the potential benefits of the student-taught class. Would the student's leadership development be better served by an instructor-student feedback session or another chance to lead a hiking group? Poorly done student classes can erode self-confidence, waste time, and scare off other would-be teachers in the group. But good student classes are invaluable steps for both the student teacher and the peers who are encouraged by the success.

For the first-time teacher, consider limiting the length, scope, audience size, and exactness required by the subject matter. A simple formula might be to have a student prepare a mini-class about something commonly found along the trail. Let the student choose the appropriate moment during a moving day to present the information. This small, informal group setting is often less intimidating than teaching to the whole group. An instructor should be present in order to critique the student. That evening the information can be shared at a group meeting by one of the hiking group members.

### Leadership Opportunities
The reality of standing up in front of a group and presenting a topic is a great leadership opportunity for students. They can work on their organization and public speaking skills. Student teaching should be a successful learning experience. To ensure this, coach your student before and after their class.

## Expedition Planning
In most cases, students already have a sense of an expedition by the time you present a class on expedition planning. They understand the skills and relationships necessary to live in the mountains for extended periods of time. Your presentation, therefore, should be aimed at inspiring them to use this knowledge to plan personal trips in the backcountry after they finish their NOLS course.

### Learning Objectives
- Provide your students with guidelines that enable them to plan, organize, and carry out an extended trip in the wilderness.
- Understand the logistical requirements, personnel and fiscal considerations, and equipment needs of an expedition

### Choosing an Expedition Goal
It is important to select an objective for your expedition. The goal you come up with may be as simple as catching fish or identifying birds, or as complex as summiting K2 or kayaking the Colorado River. The critical thing is that all team members have the same basic mission in mind. Consider having a backup objective in case certain factors, such as weather or group motivation, force a change.

### Choosing Your Team
Select a team of people who work well together and enjoy each other's company. Make sure that you have people with the skills and experience necessary to attain your objective. All team members should be aware of the expedition goals and willing to share in the trip's expenses.

### Coordinating Your Logistics
Do your homework before you get to the trailhead to avoid logistical nightmares in the field. Your research should include looking into routes, knowing regulations, and planning for emergencies. Logistics also include planning for food, finances, transportation, and fuel.

### Planning Your Route
A) Information Sources:
- Guide books, trail guides, outdoor magazines, mountaineering journals
- Outdoor retailers
- Park rangers and public land managers at regional and local offices
- Locals who have been to the place before at the same time of year
- International trips should consult "Lonely Planet" guides or State Department "Background Notes"

B) Map Sources:
- U.S. Geologic Survey, Denver, CO
- Retail map dealers, outdoor stores
- Local, public, and university libraries

C) Permits and Backcountry Regulations:
- Check with local land agencies for specific regulations

D) Emergency Resources:
- Plan how to handle any emergency encountered during your expedition
- Know the nearest hospital to your roadhead
- Find out who handles rescues and helicopters in your trip area. Check to see if there are any specific requirements or limitations for this kind of assistance

### Travel Plans
Figure out exactly where you are going and how you will get there. Take care of any airline tickets, bus transportation, or car expenses required. Find out if there are luggage requirements or restrictions. Make sure you have all the necessary visas, shots, and papers.

### Money
Finances are more easily dealt with before the excursion begins. Consider requiring a deposit to cement members' commitment during the planning stages.

Depending on the nature of your expedition, you may want to approach equipment manufacturers and food producers for donations. Offer to do product testing or provide testimonials and photographs in return for their support. However, sponsorship is difficult to get. If it is your first big expedition, don't count on getting many freebies.

### Equipment
Choose clothing, equipment, and shelters that are able to accommodate the weather found in the region you will be traveling.

Leave with gear in good order. Pick items that do not require special equipment to fix. Bring a basic repair kit that includes: stove parts, duct tape, wire, needles, thread, and ripstop nylon.

Prior to leaving, discuss who will pay for any personal gear used by the group that is either damaged or lost.

Pack a first aid kit. Stock it with supplies that have multiple uses, such as tape, 4X4 gauze pads, and disinfectant. Keep this kit small and practical.

### Food and Fuel
Keep in mind personal tastes, caloric requirements, weight, cost, packaging, and ease of preparation when creating the menu. Cheap bulk food can be obtained in the bulk food sections in some supermarket chains, at food co-ops, ethnic grocers, and from restaurant supply distributors.

### After the Expedition
Make sure you put the gear away clean, dry, and repaired. Make notes on what worked well and what you would do differently next time. Share photos and notes.

### Teaching Considerations
This class works well towards the latter part of the course when the students have experienced expedition life and have started thinking about where they are going to use their NOLS skills next. Often instructors preface the class by reading a story or telling humorous anecdotes from a personal experience that demonstrates the pitfalls of poor expedition planning. Remind your students that they have the skills to do their own trips and that all they need is some organization, a group of friends, full food bags, and rides to and from the roadhead.

Provide students with guidelines for making their own first-aid and repair kits. Show them the ration planning sections of the *NOLS Cookery*, and encourage them to go for it.

### Leadership Opportunities
Expedition planning is about leading or participating in a personal expedition—it is a summary of what a NOLS course is all about and should be part of your instruction. At the end of your course, start a discussion by asking your students how they would organize their own trip. Ask them whether they would take their inexperienced friends into the terrain they just traveled through. Most NOLS grads will know the perfect answer: "It depends."

# Chapter Ten
# Teaching Risk Management

Risk is a vital component of a NOLS education. Our philosophy of risk is expressed in the NOLS Core Values: "We accept risk as an integral part of the learning process and of the environments through which we travel. The recognition and management of risk is critical to both the development of leadership and to the safety and health of our students and staff." The risks that NOLS students and field instructors face are varied and include:

1) Risk from learning new skills and pushing their personal limits through experiential learning
2) Emotional risks from living and working closely with others in challenging environments
3) Physical risks associated with the hazards of traveling through remote and rugged terrain and environments.

Modern society generally views risk as a negative. However, educators understand the need to challenge students in order to motivate them to learn. In adventure education these challenges include exposure to natural hazards and subsequent risks. Some in the adventure education field have chosen to expand the current definition of risk to include the potential to gain. The gains in this case may be new skills, increased confidence, or improved health (Williamson, 1997).

While NOLS is not risk averse, we are not cavalier about risk. In the outdoor-adventure education pedagogy, risk is often managed to the point where it becomes a perceived threat rather than a real risk. At NOLS we seek to manage risk in such a way as to mitigate potential for harm, but in many situations the risks remain quite real. The inherent risks and hazards of the NOLS "classroom" are necessary to achieve our educational goals. Finding the right balance between educational goals, exposure to risk, and student well-being is the core attribute of effective NOLS instructors. Too little risk and the education suffers and the goals are not met. Too much risk and students get scared and people might get hurt; the education suffers and the goals are not met.

Risk management at NOLS reflects our organizational culture with two core elements:
1) Risk management at NOLS supports educational experiences by integrating all aspects of the organization to promote the health and well-being of students and staff.
2) NOLS expedition risk management is the process of understanding and anticipating the risks of leading groups in remote wilderness environments and applying appropriate responses to reduce the likelihood of having an injury, illness, fatality, or close call.

We develop and apply risk management systems that include and rely on following accepted field practices in concert with appropriate instructor judgment to minimize the harm to students and staff. We put special emphasis on injury and illness prevention strategies, hazard assessment, instructor training and performance, and continual examination and refinement of our field practices.

## Risk Management—a Three-Part Framework

Risk management at NOLS is a strategy that includes all aspects of the organization. Attention to the health and well-being of students and staff is an integral part of the NOLS culture and permeates all levels and departments.

The overarching framework within which the NOLS risk management strategy has been designed is comprised of three essential elements: *alignment, management,* and *information*. This framework, which was developed by Charles (Reb) Gregg, attorney and former NOLS trustee and legal counsel, is adaptable to any adventure education program (Gregg, 2005). Our approach to risk management and legal liability is to conduct quality, well-run programs. If we do our jobs well, legal problems should be infrequent or relatively easy to resolve.

The risk management elements of alignment, management, and information are not static and need to be frequently evaluated. For example, if staff competency becomes inadequate to reasonably lead and teach a specific activity, then either the staff need to be better trained or the activity needs to be scaled back to be in alignment with the staff's abilities.

### Alignment

Alignment means that NOLS activities align with our mission and purpose, and with our students. In other words, we do not do things that do not help us achieve our mission, nor do we teach people who our staff are not trained to lead or teach. It also means that our instructors' competencies and abilities are aligned with our educational goals and curriculum. Alignment involves answering the questions: why, what, where, and who.

NOLS courses are open to the general public; however, there are some populations not suited for NOLS. NOLS is not a therapeutic program. Our instructors are not specifically trained in therapy or counseling. The minimum age is 14 years. It is our view that physical and cognitive development by this age is adequate to meet the demands and expectations of a NOLS course. In some cases certain courses are for specifically defined age groups, i.e., adventure courses for 14 and 15 year olds. For all courses, students need to be physically and mentally fit.

NOLS activities have certain risks associated with them. These risks are called inherent risks and are those risks that, if removed from the activity, would fundamentally change the nature of the activity. For example, if whitewater rafting helps achieve the mission and goals, then the risks, such as being thrown from a raft, hitting rocks, or drowning are understood to be inherent with the activity. Inherent risks cannot be completely eliminated from the activity but can be managed to minimize the likelihood of causing injury.

### Management

Management refers to having appropriate practices and procedures and adequately trained staff to manage and lead the activities and provide support services. Risk management means anticipating what can go wrong and having methods to avoid or mitigate the risk of harm. NOLS addresses management in a variety of ways including careful course planning, comprehensive pre-course briefings, instructor training and evaluation, established field practices, emergency response and management systems, and extensive curriculum resources and materials.

### Information

Information refers to our students knowing what they are getting into when they enroll. Prior to being enrolled on a course, prospective students are provided detailed information describing the course. Students must be informed of the objectives, challenges, curriculum, hazards, and other aspects of the course they are enrolling on. One important element in the inherency of risk is that the participants understand the risks. Student information needs to depict the reality of the experience. Participants need to understand the extremes of weather, the physical challenges they may encounter or need to endure, and the living situation they will be in.

## NOLS Risk Management Goals

Risk management is imbedded in the culture and community of NOLS. The health and well-being of NOLS students and staff is one of our highest priorities. Our risk management program is an organizational strategy designed to achieve specific goals to provide clarity and focus, and to set metrics for gauging performance. Our performance in achieving these goals is monitored regularly.

- Prevent fatalities, disabling or disfiguring injuries, and serious illness.
- Reduce all injuries and illnesses.
- Anticipate emergency response and crisis management needs and design suitable protocols and plans.
- Identify the accepted field practices for managing life threatening risks and hazards and the expectations for their consistent use.
- Be a leader and resource of wilderness risk management practices and outdoor education curricula.

## Organizational Structure

The NOLS risk management program involves everyone at the school. It is a robust system that allows for appropriate proactive and reactive measures given the variability of the situations that arise. Within the NOLS organization there are five main components of the NOLS Risk Management Program.

*1) Oversight*

Risk management oversight is provided by management and implemented by students and field instructors. The elements of successful oversight include the formation of a risk management committee and regular meetings held by the executive director team to assess the state of risk management at the school. Direct oversight by the risk management director, the human resources department, branch directors, field instructors, and students is also key to sound risk management.

*2) Curriculum & Practices*

NOLS curriculum and our practices provide direction for essential skills taught and each curriculum topic is integral to risk management. The NOLS core curriculum of risk management, leadership, outdoor skills, and environmental studies helps maintain consistency throughout all NOLS courses.

The curriculum is supported by NOLS text books, NOLS instructor/educator notebooks, the NOLS Accepted Field Practices (NAFPs), libraries at each location, and use of the internet to provide access to curriculum materials.

*3) Instructor Training*

Instructor training is essential to the manner in which we conduct courses and requires a substantial commitment of resources. Training starts with instructor courses—intensive backcountry expeditions that prepare instructors to lead NOLS courses. Initial training is supplemented by continuing education in the form of instructor seminars, the Instructor Development Fund (IDF), and extensive performance review and evaluation.

*4) Administrative Processes*

Administrative processes provide infrastructure for informing students about NOLS and evaluating program performance. The admissions department manages pre-course information, reviews applicants, answers applicants' questions, and conducts applicant medical review and screening.

NOLS performs periodic risk management audits (both field and administrative). A well-structured incident review process, regular program evaluations, and an extensive risk management incident database all contribute to an infrastructure that supports progressive risk management.

*5) Field Support Services*

Field Support Services provide core infrastructure for conducting courses. NOLS uses equipment that is durable, reliable, and well maintained. We provide nutritious food to sustain active wilderness living for extended periods. Our transportation systems include operator training, licensing, and vehicle maintenance. Field instructors are supported by a physician advisor and medical protocols to aid in making medical decisions. An extensive emergency response system, including field emergency procedures, administrative emergency response systems, and crisis management protocols, gives field instructors clear guidelines for managing emergencies.

## Incident Reporting

For decades NOLS has embraced the importance of reporting field incidents. We have consistent records since 1984 recorded in a single database. A core element of the NOLS organizational culture is based on the trust that incidents (injuries, illnesses, and near misses) can be reported and discussed among instructors and managers to gain knowledge from our experiences and better manage risk. Dr. Scott Sagan, in his book *The Limits of Safety* (Sagan, 1995), describes how safety can be achieved through the implementation of appropriate organizational design and management techniques. Sagan identified four components that can be found in effective and reliable organizations that are involved in high risk operations:

1) Stated leadership safety objectives
2) The need for redundancy
3) Decentralization, culture, and continuity
4) Organizational learning

All four of these elements are present at NOLS, with an emphasis on *organizational learning*, which simply means that the organization learns from

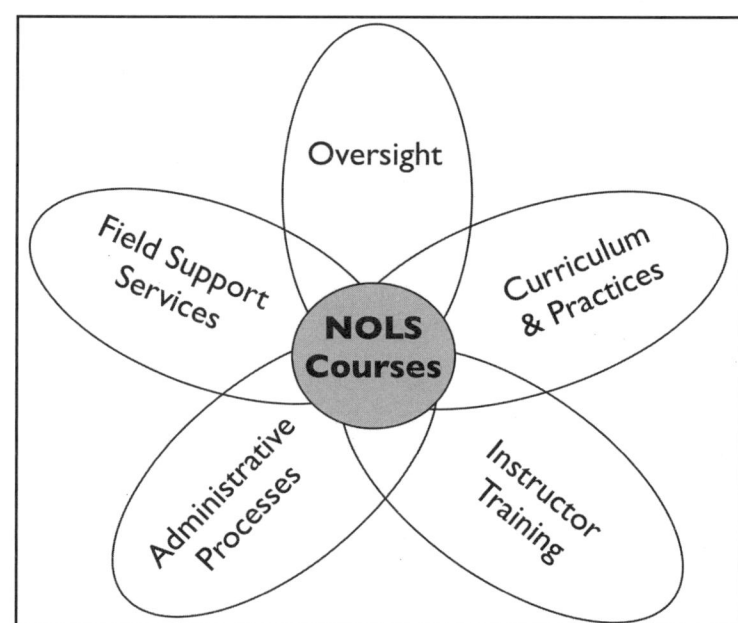

*The different organizational components at NOLS interact to effectively manage risk.*

its experiences and mistakes. This suggests that the analysis of incidents is significant for effective risk management. NOLS has, for decades, embraced the concept of organizational learning as a pillar of our risk management strategy.

James Reason (1990), a professor of psychology and the author of the book *Human Error,* states, "effective risk management depends on establishing a reporting culture. Without a detailed analysis of mishaps, incidents, near misses, and these 'free lessons,' we have no way of uncovering recurrent error traps, or of knowing where the 'edge' is." When we collect this type of information we no longer need to rely on anecdotal accounts and myths and instead can focus on known and documented problem areas. As a result we can develop a better understanding of which types of incidents and injuries are most common and/or important and, in turn, can modify training, education, or policies accordingly.

An undeniable aspect of human nature seems to be the desire (or fear, depending on the circumstances) to identify responsible parties whenever a serious incident occurs and place blame on their failures. But, incidents are rarely the result of a single event or cause, such as instructor incompetence or disregard for another's welfare. Instead, the people involved in the incidents—generally good people who truly care for their students—simply do not see the entire picture as it unfolds. Their decisions are based on the continually changing and often subjective information they have at the time. It is only in hindsight that their decisions might be seen as flawed.

Incident analysis can be counterproductive if the goal is merely to find someone to blame. According to Reason, the ultimate outcome following any investigation should not be to assign blame, but to reduce the potential for future incidents. We need to be less concerned with who made a mistake and more concerned with how the controls—which are intended to prevent an incident—failed.

What is unarguable is that, given the subjective and ever-changing nature of our work, achieving perfection is impossible. Risks from hazards can be moderated or hazards can be avoided altogether, but at what cost? Eliminating the risk completely means eliminating the gain from participating in adventure education.

While our learning might indeed be limited, we can consciously choose not to get caught in a situation of needing to blame someone. Instead, we can acknowledge that incidents will always exist, and do our best to reduce their numbers and severity. The lessons we can garner from the study of incident data and investigations, while not a substitute for actual experience, are very useful in our ability to manage risk.

# Teaching Risk Management

Teaching risk management is one of the four core elements of the NOLS curriculum. This section is intended to provide key concepts for instructors to use to guide the development of students' ability to manage risk and develop their judgment and decision-making. When teaching risk management to students, they should be provided some theoretical information, but more importantly they need to have opportunities to gain practical experience. The theoretical information provides context, but a well-designed progression of experience leads to the development of strong risk management skills.

This section provides theoretical and practical concepts, but does not address specific hazard identification or risk mitigation practices.

## Learning Objectives
- Understand how incidents happen.
- Use risk management terminology to communicate about risk management decisions and actions.
- Be able to assess risks using these concepts commensurate with their experience and judgment.
- Understand and apply the concepts of situational awareness and mindfulness.
- Be able to identify and assess hazards present in the environment in which they are traveling.
- Use technical skills as appropriate to manage risks.

## Vocabulary
- *Hazard*: a source of danger.
- *Risk*: the possibility of loss or injury; peril.
- *Peril*: exposure to the risk of being injured, destroyed, or lost; danger.
- *Danger*: exposure or liability to injury, pain, harm, or loss.
- *Management*: the process of dealing with or controlling things or people.

## Risk Management at NOLS—a Two Part Definition
1) Risk management at NOLS supports educational experiences by integrating all aspects of the organization to promote the health and well-being of students and staff.
2) Expedition risk management is the process of understanding and anticipating the risks of leading groups in remote wilderness environments and applying appropriate responses to reduce the likelihood of having an injury, illness, fatality, or close call.

## The NOLS Risk Management Mission Statement
"To promote the health and well-being of students and staff as one of our highest priorities." We are mission-driven and student-oriented.

## Hazards
There are three categories of hazards that govern our risk management decisions. They are also often referred to as factors.

*Objective hazards* are environmental hazards, and are those aspects of the natural world and its forces that present risks. These include such things as weather, darkness, falling objects (i.e., rocks or tree limbs), and moving water.

*Subjective hazards,* also called human factors, are the characteristics, personalities, and behaviors of people. These include such things as fatigue, physical strength, complacency, overconfidence, and differing perceptions.

*Program hazards* are aspects of the program that may influence decisions in the field and define an organizational risk tolerance or profile. Examples include independent student group travel, students leading rock climbs, and other objectives such as summiting a specific mountain peak or sticking to a schedule.

## Standard Risk Management Strategies
In the world of risk management (not just wilderness risk management) it is understood that there are four primary responses to risk.
1) *Avoid* or isolate the hazard/risk because it is too frequent and/or severe, e.g., class IV whitewater (NOLS courses paddle up to class III).
2) *Mitigate* the risks to an appropriate level through the use of controls, e.g., the use of common or accepted field practices.
3) *Retain* the risk because the consequence is unlikely and/or not severe. It is already at acceptable levels, e.g., weather. We don't cancel courses because of weather, but decisions about day-to-day activities are guided by weather patterns. In this way we also retain the risk because we can mitigate it.
4) *Transfer* the risk to someone else. In a field setting this is done through organizational policies and procedures (e.g., our helmet policy: helmets will be worn when...). Organizationally, this is done with the Student Agreement and Acknowledgement and Assumption of Risk form—students assume the risks.

## How Incidents Happen
At NOLS we refer to injuries, illnesses, and near misses (close calls) as *incidents*; however, in the literature these events are often still referred to as accidents. Understanding how incidents happen provides context for preventing them from happening at all.

*Dynamics of Accidents Theory* (Hale, 1984) stated that objective hazards + subjective hazards = accident potential. A modification of Hale's diagram to include program factors and referring to it as the Dynamics of Risk Potential allows for it to be more applicable to adventure programs. For example, the combination of wet, uneven terrain and a person acting in haste because they are in a hurry to get to the trailhead to be picked up increases the overlap of the three factors and increases the risk potential for a fall. If the person travels through the terrain carefully, slows down, and realizes it is OK to be late to the trailhead, the overlap of the hazards lessens and the potential for a fall is reduced.

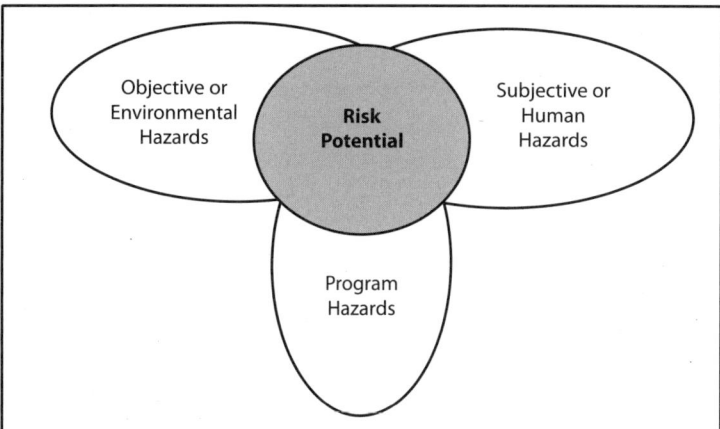

*Risk potential occurs when objective hazards, subjective hazards, and program hazards all align to create risk.*

The matrix *principle causes of accidents in outdoor pursuits (see next page)* developed by Dan Meyer and Jed Williamson lists the objective factors and further divides the subjective factors into two subcategories—potential errors in judgment and potentially unsafe acts. The addition of potentially unsafe acts considers the mechanism. Building on our example above, the person hiking on wet, uneven terrain in haste most likely is hiking too fast. The potentially unsafe act in this case is unsafe speed (fast/slow).

*Domino effect, cascade of events*, and *ripple effect* are all ways to represent the idea that incidents are generally not isolated events, but rather are often the result of the culmination of smaller preceding events and/or decisions. The full impact of each of these preceding events or decisions may not be fully recognized or understood in the moment, but in retrospect, become contributing factors to the incident itself and a causal chain of events can be identified.

## Risk Assessment and Communication Tools
With an understanding of subjective, objective, and program hazards NOLS students will have a basis for understanding the many variables in assessing and managing the possible negative outcomes of risk.

### Likelihood and Consequence
A common formulaic concept for assessing risks is: risk = the likelihood of an event X the consequence of that event. Likelihood is the probability something will happen and is somewhat like calculating the odds, except that not all possible negative outcomes can be known, the numerical values simply don't exist or are too subjective to be useful, and people have the ability to influence the outcome—it's not just up to chance. So likelihood is a subjective assessment, and a more appropriate way to frame this concept is: **Risk is an assessment of likelihood and consequence.**

## Principle Causes of Accidents in Outdoor Pursuits
*A matrix devised by Dan Meyer & Jed Williamson 1979-1998*

| Potentially Unsafe Conditions Due to: | Potentially Unsafe Unsafe Acts Due to: | Potential Errors in Judgement Due to: |
|---|---|---|
| Falling objects: rocks, trees, etc. | Inadequate protection | Desire to please others |
| Inadequate area security | Inadequate instruction | Trying to adhere to a schedule |
| Weather | Inadequate supervision | Misperception |
| Swift or cold water | unauthorized or improper procedure | Disregarding instincts |
| Equipment/clothing | Unsafe speed (speed or slow) | Fatigue |
| Animals/Plants | Inadequate food, drink or medication | Distraction |
| Physical or psychological profile | Poor position | Miscommunication by staff or participants |
|  |  | New or unexpected situation |

Our success in determining likelihood depends on a few personal attributes:
- Our ability to understand the environmental conditions.
- Our ability to be alert to and able to perceive and identify the hazard(s), and understand the risks and possible consequences.
- Our prior experience on the type of terrain or with the particular hazard and risk.
- Our ability to take appropriate action in response to the hazard/risk, such as our skill in negotiating the terrain (i.e., boulder field) or responding to the risk (i.e., lightning).
- Our ability to assess the subjective abilities and behaviors of ourselves and the group.

When we consider that risk is an assessment of likelihood and consequence, we get a simple set of questions to ask when we assess a situation.

How likely is it that someone will fall while hiking down a steep slope? Your assessment will be based on your understanding of the terrain on which you are hiking (geology, slope angle, and surface), your ability to choose a route everyone can follow, and if group members can or will actually follow it. The consequence is the severity of the outcome to you or your group if something does happen. If a participant falls, will she slide or tumble a long or short distance, crash into a rock, or go off a cliff? Based on your determination of consequence you may deploy risk mitigation measures (controls), e.g., a fixed rope, belay, or handline to minimize the consequence of a slip or fall or avoid the slope altogether.

We won't (and usually can't) have all the information to make a risk-free decision (if such a decision actually exists), so there is a level of uncertainty in our ability to perceive, understand, and identify hazards and risks. To manage risk and make good decisions we need to strive to gain information and stay alert to changing situations and new or different information that arises—attempt to make uncertainty more certain—and that may warrant changing or making different decisions as we proceed.

Judgment, then, is necessary in assessing risk. Outdoor leaders need to judge what the hazards are, whether the group is or needs to be exposed to the hazard, what the likelihood is of the hazard presenting a risk, and what the severity is of the consequence of that exposure.

A graphic way to consider risk assessment is with the *Likelihood and Consequence Chart* below. Using this chart a group can categorize the risks they expect to encounter on a given travel day, a specific activity, or perhaps an entire trip into one or more of the four quadrants. This can provide clarity as to where or when they need to focus their risk management efforts, since travel on any given day could expose people to all four quadrants.

### The Risk Continuum
The Risk Continuum is a way to understand how different people may per-

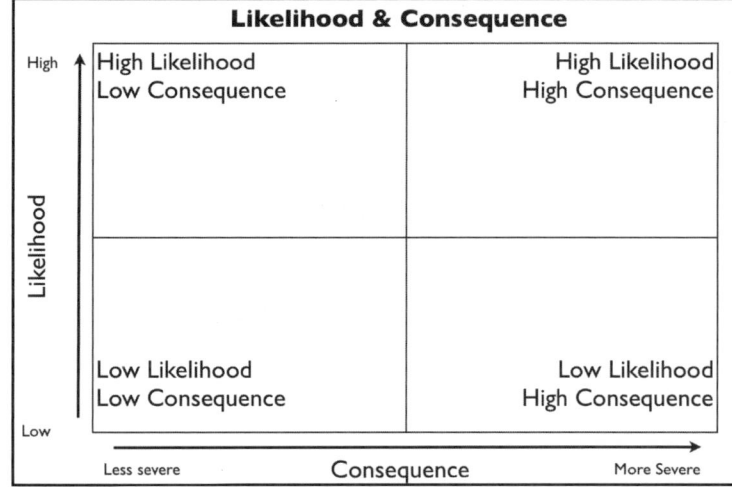

ceive and tolerate risk and how it might affect teaching and learning. Risk perception is an individual's awareness of the likelihood of loss or injury. Risk tolerance is the amount of risk an individual is willing to accept in pursuit of a desired goal. Some goals may be judged as worthy of higher levels of risk than other goals.

If we view risk on a continuum, we would put *absolute risk* (the worst case scenario) at one end and zero risk at the other end. Depending on the situation, we can mitigate the risk to an acceptable level as deemed appropriate by the leaders and/or participants by using controls.

The *residual risk* is the risk that remains after implementing the controls and is the level at which the benefits of the activity are realized and are within the realm of the leaders and participants to manage. The residual risk is where we will achieve optimal learning for the greatest number of students. It is important for leaders to understand that some participants may still perceive the residual risk of an activity as too high or above their risk tolerance. Students who perceive the residual risk as above their personal risk tolerance may not perform well because they are frightened and students who perceive residual risk as below their risk tolerance may be complacent.

Understanding the way that people view risk is important to effective adventure education experiences. Finding the balance between risk perceptions and risk tolerance requires continual attention.

### The Risk Assessment Triangle
A triangle (see graphic on next page) is a common visual tool for understanding the risks of a particular activity or event and organizing them either visually or in your mind. Triangles were initially incorporated into the NOLS avalanche curriculum through work by Jill Fredston and Doug Fessler from their book *Snow Sense*. Typically, the triangle is used to categorize the subjective and objective factors of risk assessment. The way in which someone organizes her thoughts when assessing risk can be done in many ways and tends to become individualized. Each person learns or adopts a method that works for them.

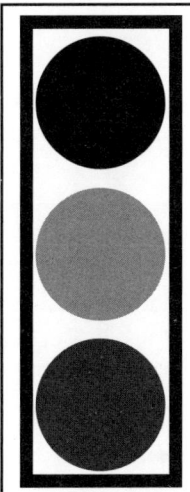

**RED LIGHT** = Danger: a significant hazard or high uncertainty exists.

**YELLOW LIGHT** = Caution: there is potential danger and/or uncertainty.

**GREEN LIGHT** = Minor or no hazard or risks

*A risk traffic light is a helpful tool for efficiently assessing risk in a given situation.*

## The Risk Traffic Light

This is a metaphor that is commonly used at NOLS. It too was initially incorporated into the NOLS avalanche curriculum from Fredston and Fessler, but has been adapted to other situations such as assessing grizzly bear risks. Instructors or program supervisors can, in specific circumstances, define the actual conditions for red, yellow, or green light situations. The traffic light concept is easily understood by students and provides a very simple, yet effective, method for students and instructors to communicate about risk and in determining when to adapt behavior to the conditions.

## Lemons

This is one way to consciously counteract the cascade of events or domino effect and potentially disrupt the causal chain of events that was discussed above. Lemons are specific conditions that alone may not be significant, but when combined with other lemons add up to be important warnings of higher risk. Think of decisions, acts, or events as possible lemons. Examples of lemons might be changes in weather, navigation errors, unanticipated obstacles or hazards, fatigue, minor injury, or haste in sticking to a schedule. As you proceed through the day reflect on the number of lemons you might have encountered and if a change of plans is warranted, this is also an aspect of situational awareness and mindfulness, which is discussed below.

## Situational Awareness

As stated previously, to manage risk and make good decisions we (instructors and students) need to strive to gain information and stay alert and adapt to changing situations and new or different information that arises. The ability to do this requires that we have the requisite technical skills and:

- Be observant of changing conditions—with individuals, the group, and the environment.
- Effectively make decisions based on those observations.
- Reflect (in real time) on those decisions to refine the course of action.

The ability to do this is called *situational awareness*, which can be defined as openness to the recognition of variables and their interaction or influence on decisions and actions. When you are maintaining situational awareness you are "in the loop." The loop, as coined by Colonel John Boyd, is the OODA loop, which stands for observe, orient, decide, and act. If you are not maintaining situational awareness you are considered "out of the loop."

### The OODA Loop

The OODA loop (see graphic on next page) is a continual process and each decision, no matter how inconsequential it seems, provides a test of the action and results in new data, new knowledge, and is the basis for a new or refined decision—it's a series of assessments, decisions, and actions.

*Observe:* Gather data—what is the condition of the environment, the group as a whole, and the individuals? What is the objective?

*Orient:* Synthesize data as it relates to your and the group's experience, training, and abilities, which are in turn influenced by the group's culture. This synthesis becomes knowledge and knowledge is used to make decisions.

*Decide:* Consider available options as they relate to the situation and your knowledge and select a course of action.

*Act:* Carry out the decision using leadership and technical skills to decrease the likelihood of a negative consequence. This is the test to see if the decision was correct; once the act is carried out, you begin to get new data or feedback and the loop begins again.

Individuals and groups that maintain situational awareness combined with a group culture where members are receptive to the idea that as circumstances unfold situations can change and decisions need to be modified are likely to be effective risk managers.

### Mindfulness

Mindfulness as explained by Karl Weick and Katherine Sutcliffe in their book *Managing the Unexpected: Resilient Performance in the Age of Uncertainty* (2007) is similar to situational awareness in that it requires that you acknowledge and recognize that situations might unfold differently than you may have expected. The idea that we have personal expectations is the significant difference between situational awareness and mindfulness.

We all have expectations, which are built into the roles we have in a group or society, the routines we follow in our day-day-lives, and the strategies we use to accomplish tasks. Expectations create orderliness in our lives, but they can also create blind spots when we unknowingly seek confirmation of our preconceived expectations. The classic example of this at NOLS is map reading errors when we have expectations of what the terrain will look like or how fast we'll travel and we interpret the map to those expectations, but in fact we might be miles off course. We have a natural tendency to be biased in seeking information to confirm our expectations.

Blind spots can hide small errors in our thinking or actions that can increase the potential for a significant incident—think of lemons. To avoid blind spots we have to heighten our awareness of details to discern if an event that was expected to happen fails to happen, if an event that was not expected to happen does happen, or if an event happens that was completely unthought of.

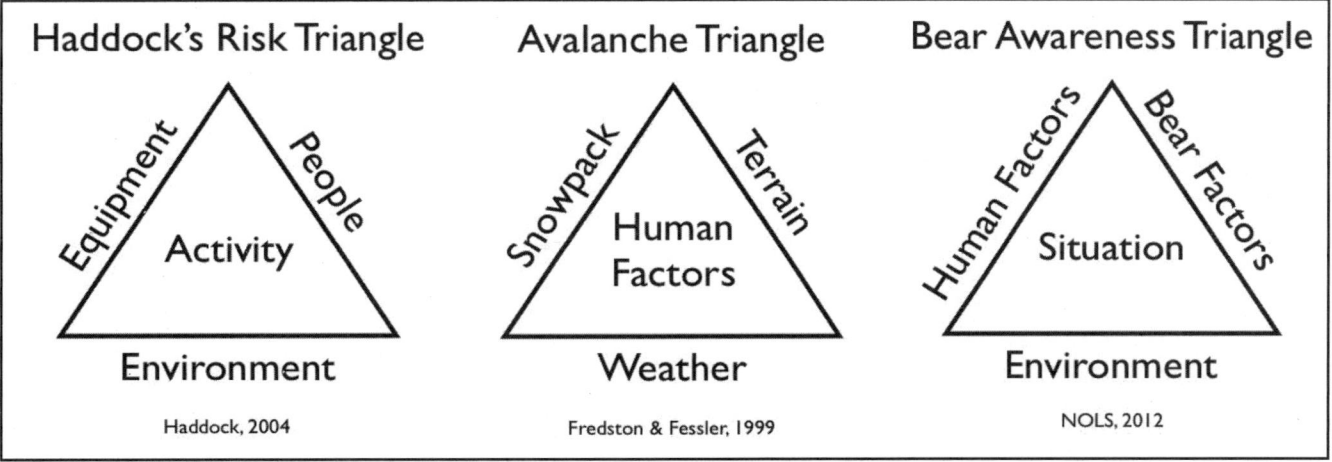

*Risk triangles visually represent the different factors that contribute to risk in different activities. They are a good way to gain understanding about the big picture before venturing into the backcountry, and are useful to continually reassess the situation while participating in an activity.*

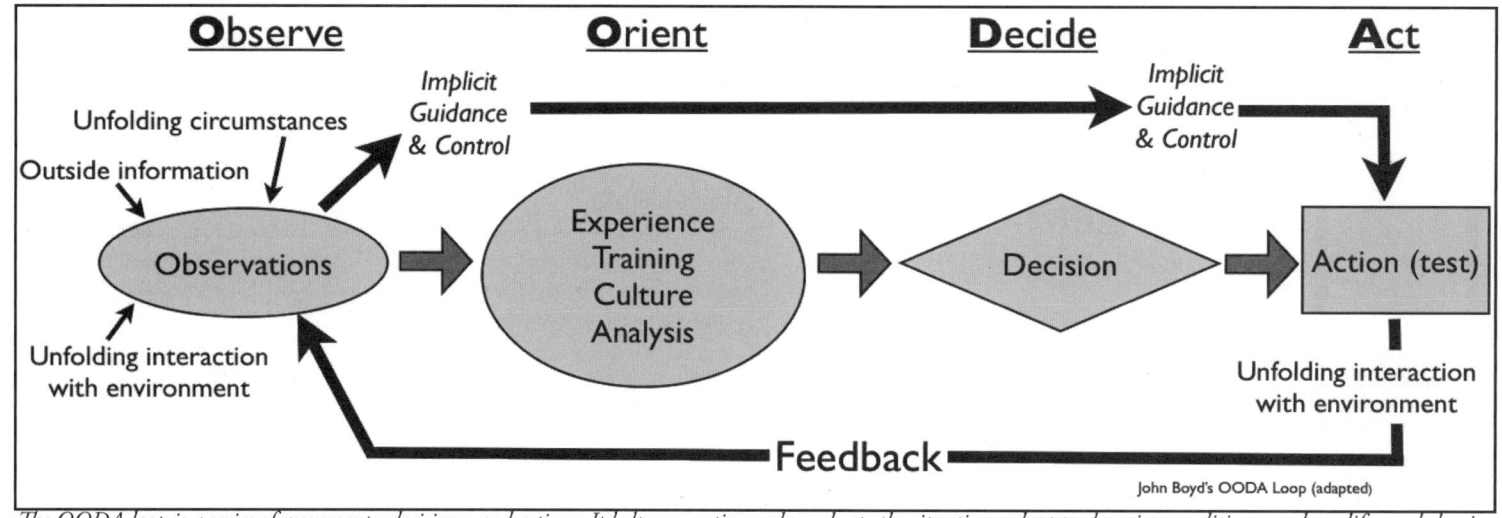

*The OODA loop is a series of assessments, decisions, and actions. It helps us continuously evaluate the situation, adapt to changing conditions, and modify our behavior.*

Written travel plans are an example of how we might form expectations on a course. You've studied the map, identified terrain obstacles, calculated distance and elevation gain in consideration of the group's strength, fitness, and the weight of their backpacks, and chosen a reasonable goal for the day. Now all you have to do is execute the plan. The potential problem is if you become too preoccupied with carrying out the plan (your expectations) you won't act *mindfully* and will let blind spots develop. Travel plans are good, and we need to use them, but we need to be alert to if or how our expectations are unfolding or if unexpected situations are arising and how the plan may need to be changed. Atul Gawande, a prominent surgeon and author, writes: "Recognizing that your expectations are proving wrong—accepting that you need a new plan—is commonly the hardest thing to do."

Mindfulness is a way to heighten awareness in order to seek anomalies from how you expected things to happen. Situational awareness is a way to interpret stimulus and respond to an event as it unfolds. Both allow you to adapt to changing circumstances and achieve the goal of managing risk. Wieck and Sutcliffe wrote: "Safe reliable performance 'is a dynamic non-event—what produces the stable outcome is constant change rather than continuous repetition." Reliable risk management performance, then, requires constant refinement and many small adjustments with no other obvious outcome other than successful attainment of your goals. Epic adventures might make good stories, while successful risk management is probably kind of boring.

### Teaching Considerations

Teaching risk management needs to be started early in a course. It is important to provide students with a framework to understand and assess risk, begin to develop their situational awareness and mindfulness, and to provide a lexicon to promote communication about risk to help them begin to assess and communicate about risk on their own. It needs to be a theme of a course so that students have well-developed risk management skills for independent student group travel. Presenting all this information in one class would be a mistake and it is not necessary to teach all the risk assessment tools. Rather, choose one assessment tool, teach in a progression, and reinforce assessment and communication through normal everyday experiences and a conscious use of debriefing and reflection. This will develop understanding and strong risk management skills in the students.

Make it an expectation that watching for hazards is everyone's responsibility. An outdoor leader understands that careless, thoughtless, or dangerous behavior affects personal as well as group well-being.

The examples instructors set are critical. Students emulate positive as well as negative role modeling. Often they lack the experience to recognize the latter. Students should observe us staying in control, practicing sound techniques, articulating thought processes, and demonstrating consistent hazard awareness. Stay engaged with your students and when students are traveling independently act mindfully when assessing their plans and abilities.

## Teaching Risk Management on Outdoor Educator Courses

There are three different levels of risk management that professional outdoor educators need to learn while at NOLS: NOLS' risk management practices, future supervision, and future administration.

### NOLS Risk Management Practices

Outdoor Educator students need the same clear expectations, education, and supervision to manage risk during their NOLS expedition as any other NOLS student. It may seem intuitive that these mature and experienced students need less education and supervision, but what they especially need is clear modeling of how we set the tone on our courses and supervise our students. Their maturity makes it easier to progress from the hard rules of day one to the independent decision making of day twenty, but they still need the complete progression. They need the full progression, both to manage the risks of the expedition and as a model to follow in the future. Faster progressions can only happen when students clearly meet our competency standards along the way.

### Future Supervision

This is a discussion of how these students will clarify expectations and supervise students in their own programs. It should be part of the thematic progression that keeps adding new context to the basic priorities of the course. It helps engage students to have some of them give their own stories of how they have applied risk management principles in their own programs in the past. We can be directive with the basic principles of supervision, but we need to get the students to add specific practices that work in their settings.

### Future Administration

We need to be careful that we don't inadvertently suggest that every program in the world adopt NOLS' field or administrative practices. For instance, less remote programs may not need the same first aid kits that NOLS uses. Less technical programs may not need the extensive staff training that NOLS is known for. Most programs don't have a designated evacuation coordinator. NOLS instructors can facilitate the discussion of administration of other programs, but the people who work in these programs have to brainstorm their own specific answers. Hearing what various programs do can help people develop approaches to risk management that fit their staff, students, setting, equipment, and goals.

NOLS conducted a research project with the University of Utah in 2003 to assess how other expedition-based programs manage risk, specifically so we could help our outdoor educator students who need to return to other programs (Szolozi, 2003). These students routinely ask NOLS which strategy to employ first in a small program: we can't advise them about that, but now we can at least tell them what people at other programs prioritize first.

### Risk Management Strategies Used by Expedition-based Programs (Szolosi, 2003)

| Risk Management Strategy | Importance rating (on a scale of 0-1,365) |
| --- | --- |
| 1. Field Staff Training | 1,025 |
| 2. Policies and Procedures | 1,001 |
| 3. Field Staff Instructor Judgment | 996 |
| 4. Supervision of Participants | 846 |
| 5. Pre-course Communication | 799 |
| 6. Ratios of Field Staff To Participants | 753 |
| 7. Field Staff Screening | 752 |
| 8. Course Debriefings | 746 |
| 9. Course Documentation | 685 |
| 10. Supervision of Field Staff | 672 |
| 11. Formal Wilderness Medical Training Requirement of Field Staff | 659 |
| 12. Participant Training | 622 |
| 13. Mentoring and Apprenticeship | 592 |
| 14. Emergency Action Plan | 576 |
| 15. Participant Screening | 561 |
| 16. Venue Evaluation or Location Scouting | 436 |
| 17. Internal Incident Review Procedure | 423 |
| 18. Internal Review of Safety Management Protocols | 420 |
| 19. External Review of Safety Management Protocols | 201 |
| 20. Critical Incident Stress Debriefing | 143 |
| 21. External Incident Review Procedure | 143 |

*The above list makes an excellent outline for discussing what these factors would look like for various programs.*

### Discussion Points for Outdoor Educator Course Students:
- What are your program goals?
- What types of available activities fit your students' maturity and program needs?
- How much training does the program leader need?
- How much training do the assistant leaders need?
- What sort of terrain is ideal?
- What equipment is available and how will you manage it?
- How will you manage evacuations?
- Should you use policies or judgment in controlling staff decisions?
- How will you manage a crisis if there is one?

There are some excellent resources on risk management for varied programs in the proceedings of the Wilderness Risk Management Conference, published annually by NOLS. These proceedings are available through the NOLS school store and in the NOLS staff libraries.

## Resources for Risk Management

- Ajango, D. (2005) Lessons Learned II: Using Case Studies and History to Improve Safety Education. SafetyEd.
- Cline, P. (2003) "Reexamining the Risk Paradox," Proceedings of the Wilderness Risk Management Conference. NOLS.
- Dzugen, J. (2005) in Ajango (above), Ch9: The Role of Perceptions, Genes and Culture on Risky Behaviors.
- Fredston, J. and Fesler, D. (1994) Snow Sense: A guide to Evaluating Snow Avalanche Hazard. Alaska Mountain Safety Center.
- Gass, Michael A. Ph.D. (1998) Administrative Practices Of Accredited Adventure Programs. AEE.
- Gregg, C. (2005) "Managing the Risk of Legal Liability." Proceedings of the Wilderness Risk Management Conference. NOLS.
- Haddock, C. (2004) Outdoor Safety: Risk Management for Outdoor Leaders. New Zealand Mountain Safety Council.
- Hale, Alan (1983) Annual Review-1983. National Safety Network.
- Hill, Kenneth (1997) Manging The Lost Person Incident. NASAR. (new edition expected ~ 2007.)
- Leemon, D. and Schimelpfenig, T. (2005) Risk Management for Outdoor Leaders: A Practical Guide for Managing Risk Through Leadership. NOLS.
- Leemon, D. & Merrill, K. (2002) Adventure Program Risk Management Report, V3. AEE.
- McCammon, I. Ph.D. & Schweizer, J. Ph.D. (2002) A Field Method For Identifying Structural Weaknesses In The Snowpack. Proceedings of the 2002 International Snow Science Workshop.
- Priest, S. and Gass, M. (2005) Effective Leadership in Adventure Programming. Human Kinetics.
- Raffan, J. (1984) Images For Crisis Management. JEE, Fall'84.
- Reason, J. (1990) Human Error. Cambridge U. Press.
- Ropeik, D. and Gray, G. (2002). Risk: A Practical Guide for Deciding What's Really Safe and What's Really Dangerous in the World Around You. Houghton Mifflin Company.
- Sagan, S. (1995) The Limits Of Safety. Princeton U. Press.
- Smithhammer, B. (2004) NOLS Sea Kayak Instructor Notebook.
- Szolosi, Andrew, Sibthorp, J. Ph.D., Paisley, K. Ph.D. & Gookin, J. (2003) University of Utah/NOLS Risk Management Study.
- Webster (2003) Merriam Webster's Collegiate Dictionary, 11th ed. Merriam-Webster.
- Williamson, J. (1997) Understanding The Meaning Of Risk. Proceedings of the Wilderness Risk Mgmt Conf. NOLS.
- Jackson, J, Heshka, J. (2011) Managing Risk: Systems Planning for Outdoor Adventure Programs, Direct Bearing

# Chapter Eleven
# Emergency Procedures

NOLS, due to its size and depth of resources, is capable of conducting self-sufficient expeditions and often does not require additional assistance to evacuate a patient (student or staff member) from the field. However, NOLS has extensive knowledge of evacuation resources should the need to seek help arise, e.g., use of a personal locator beacon, or need for a helicopter. The importance of self-sufficiency should be conveyed to our students when we discuss how to handle backcountry emergencies. Before students are allowed to travel independent of instructors, the basic procedures for handling an emergency should be understood. This instruction should also prepare students to handle emergencies that may arise on their future trips. A calm head, the ability to stay organized, and a well-thought out plan are more important than advanced medical training and a repertoire of technical rescue skills.

## Learning Objectives

Initially, students should be given a simple set of guidelines to follow in the event of an emergency while away from their instructors. This instruction should focus on the "front end" of the situation, which means keeping the patient and party safe, warm, dry, and well-fed until the instructors arrive to administer any additional first aid and carry out the evacuation.

## Basic Procedures

1) Stop and think. Survey the scene to determine if there are any risks to those responding. Think all plans through thoroughly. Neglected details can become time-wasting snafus, since errors tend to multiply over time.
2) Administer first aid to the patient. This includes:
   – ABCs, patient assessment, shelter, and treatment.
   – TLC and attention to patient's psychological needs.
   – Keeping a written medical record: mechanism of injury, chief complaint, vitals, and care given.
   – Making provisions for the patient to relieve themselves.
   – Getting the patient involved in their own care if possible.
3) Assume leadership and organize the group. Designate others to see that food, shelter, and hot drinks are available. Assign a scribe to keep medical records.
4) Make a plan to find the instructors. Designate two runners; the rest of the group will stay with the patient. Have written instructions for the runners, and send them with marked maps. Make sure runners are well-fed, properly equipped, and know where they are going.
5) If hiking is not feasible, students should consider staying put and waiting for the instructors to find them, but they must realize that this could take days.

## Additional Considerations

- Know the first aid training of your group and the qualifications and experience of any outside assistance available in the area (rescue groups, etc.).
- Keep your party occupied (scouting and preparing a landing site, preparing the evacuee's equipment, etc.).
- Consider the severity of the injury, the distance to the roadhead, the difficulty of terrain, your party's strength, and the weather when making preparations for an evacuation.
- Determine the best type of evacuation and have a backup plan. The options include walking out, riding a horse, carrying a litter, or flying out by helicopter.
- Helicopters have limitations:
   – They are used by NOLS for life or limb threatening injuries or when no other evacuation method is feasible.
   – They only fly in good weather with high cloud ceilings and winds less than 20 mph.
   – Pilots do not like to wait on the ground for extended periods of time in case the weather changes. Have the patient at the site before the helicopter arrives.
   – Know the helicopter rescue specifics for your area prior to your trip.
   – Helicopters can crash; don't use them lightly.

## Teaching Considerations

Teaching prevention is an important component of this instruction. Make students aware of hazards as you encounter them on the course. Without being morbid, share a few evacuation stories that illustrate valuable lessons. Model the safe behavior you expect from your students. As part of this instruction, review key hazard evaluation points you want your students to remember prior to hiking on their own.

Evacuations involving the entire course should be discussed with the students—including the patient if possible—beforehand so they understand what is expected of them and what they can expect from their instructors. Encourage them to ask questions and express their feelings regarding the upcoming challenge. It pays to have everyone oriented prior to making a litter carry or sending a group member out by helicopter.

## Finding Lost Students

During the first day or two of a course, students need to be taught what to do if they become disoriented or lost around camp (see *Staying Found* in Chapter 6). Before students begin hiking without instructors, more detailed procedures for staying found and what to do if they become lost need to be covered. Emphasis should be placed on maintaining composure, taking care of the group, preventing the situation from escalating, and being self-sufficient.

### Staying Found In and Around Camp

- Establish parameters for each camp, establish landmarks or handrails that define the perimeter of the camp and where students can go and still be considered to be in camp.
- When leaving camp (such as for a short day hike) with or without instructors:
   – Take a "life support pack" – minimal food and clothing to spend the night out.
   – Students must inform an instructor (or co-instructor) where they are going, when they plan to return, who is going, and why.
   – Orient to the cardinal directions and pick out landmarks along the route such as streams, cliffs, forested areas, and meadows. Note where the sun is, etc.
   – Time the walk to determine how long it will take to return.

### If Disoriented or Lost

- Stay calm. Go to a high vantage point to get your bearings and look for landmarks. If landmarks can be identified, travel along them back in the direction from which you came (backtrack). Listen for people talking. Look, listen, and yell.
- If the location cannot be determined and landmarks are not identified, stay put. Search parties will be sent out after the missing person(s) have not returned to camp when expected. Shouting or blowing a whistle may be helpful.
- Find a comfortable place to spend the night well before dark. It is hard to choose a good bivouac site without light. It is drier under evergreen trees or overhangs. It is warmer higher on hills (due to inversion) and out of the wind.
- Make efforts to be obvious to searchers. Stay in open areas; mark your site with clothing or fire. Stay on or close by trails.
- Look for water to drink and ways to keep warm. Covering up with leaves or pine boughs helps create a pocket of warmth. Get a nap in early in the evening because it may hard to sleep during the colder parts of the night.
- If you wake up cold during the night, get up and run around in a small circle to get warm, then try to doze off quickly so you can get in a short nap before the cold wakes you up again.

## Staying Found During Camp-to-Camp Travel

Before students begin hiking independent of instructors:

- Teach and model consistent use of travel plans – either time control plans (TCP's) or route and description (RAD) plans. These are valuable in supervising independent student travel and in organizing searches. Written TCPs or RADs are a matter of good habit and discipline and must be used for all ISGT travel.
- Teach that hiking groups need to be self-sufficient and have *all* the necessary and functioning equipment and food to be able to spend one or more nights apart from the main group in case they do not make it to camp.
- Teach that hiking groups need to stay together to avoid having an individual become separated and possibly lost during the day.
- Each ISGT group needs to carry with them a whistle and signal mirror. These can be put in the foot repair kits.
- Set clear expectations for what students should do if they are lost, delayed or otherwise cannot make it to the designated camp as planned.
- If students are disoriented due do a map reading error or weather and can accurately reorient themselves, they are expected to attempt to get to camp by noon the following day.
- If students are lost and unable to reorient themselves, they should stay put and do what they can to make themselves found. See Getting Found below.

## Responding to a Lost Group Incident

For our purposes, the course itself is the best immediately available resource for resolving the situation both in terms of the lost party realizing their error and taking corrective action to rejoin the rest of the group and the instructors and other course members organizing a systematic and efficient search.

The group is considered *overdue* if they do not arrive when planned or expected. Small scale hasty searches may be warranted at this time.

If the group hasn't arrived by noon the following day (day 1) they are considered *missing* at this point. Organized, and possibly extensive, search efforts should be undertaken at this time. Search procedures include the following:

- Determine point last seen (PLS) and mark it on a map.
- Mark any clues from the map and your knowledge of the terrain such as poorly marked trail junctions, difficult off-trail route areas, or likely accident areas.
- Establish some confinement, such as hiking back the intended route, leaving notes or markers at trail junctions. Make your campsite as visible as possible.
- Divide the search area into segments using geographic features, rivers, ridges, or lakes.
- Record your search efforts.
- Do not search at night.
- Consider any physical and/or emotional factors of individuals in the group or the group as a whole.

## Emergency Notification of NOLS Management

If the group is still missing by the morning of day 2 (refer to diagram) instructors are to notify NOLS via the evacuation coordinator. However, there may be circumstances that necessitate notifying NOLS sooner. These are listed in the text box in the diagram.

There are special circumstances for a lost individual. Occasionally a student will get lost in or around camp, and on very rare occasions a student might get separated from their travel group. These situations warrant a faster response by the instructors because an individual is likely under-equipped and less able to respond to the situation. Appropriate search efforts should begin as soon as reasonably possible; for example, if it is dark the instructors may organize a hasty search, but not have students begin searching until daylight. If the individual is not found within two hours of when the instructors learn he/she is missing or two hours past the first search efforts then NOLS management needs to be notified via the evacuation coordinator. The course will continue to search.

Once management has been notified, additional search resources may be mobilized. This can include NOLS staff or other students and may include non-NOLS agencies such as county sheriffs, land management agencies, state police or military. If the situation is resolved in the field, instructors must call management to inform them.

## Getting Found – Methods for Students When They Realize They are Lost

Students need to be taught that if they are in a group that is overdue or missing they need to do the following as appropriate for their situation:

- Establish leadership, keep a positive mental attitude, devise a plan for the day, and actively participate in becoming found and staying warm, fed, and hydrated.
- Do not split up, but make reasonable efforts to get reoriented. Use a compass and GPS to help get oriented.
- Backtrack the route to a point where location was last definitively known.
- Send out scouting parties to attempt to determine location. Scout in groups of two or more, have a plan of where each group is scouting, only scout for a short time (about 30 minutes), set a turn around time to return, leave at least one person at the point from which scouting starts.
- If location can be determined with certainty, and weather conditions and group strength are adequate, travel toward the group camp. Stay on established trails as much as possible. Avoid taking shortcuts that don't follow likely search routes or could further confuse the situation.
- If location cannot be determined, stay put.
- If possible, camp on or near established trails, on the shore of large lakes, or in open meadows. Be visible to ground searchers and possibly aircraft. Getting found supersedes conservation ethics.
- Attend to basic human needs: food, shelter, and water. Daily water is vital to survival. In arid environments water may be long distances away. It is better to expend the energy to find or get water than to ration it and run out while waiting for rescue.
- Build large smoky fires (not camp fires). These can often be seen by ground teams and from the air.
- Listen for sounds of searchers or other people. Make noise by singing, whistling, or shouting to attract attention.
- If separated for multiple days, expect an air search. According to pilots, bright flashes of light are most easily seen from the air. Signal mirrors are effective for signaling aircraft. Some compasses have mirrors. If lacking signal mirrors, bright flashes can be created with pot or pan lids, jewelry, or other metal objects.
- People are most visible when moving through an open area rather than standing still or in forested areas.
- In open areas, laying down or laying out brightly colored items such as sleeping bags, ground cloths, rain gear etc. will be more visible from an aircraft than standing and waving your arms. Geometric patterns are more discernible than bright colors from the air.

## Teaching Considerations

Students need to have been taught these principles before they actually need to use them. Safety of the group should be the foremost consideration. A few carefully chosen stories might help to convey these principles. There are incident accounts in the *NOLS Risk Management for Outdoor Leaders* book.

An effective teaching technique is to have students talk through a getting lost scenario, and write down the timeline. Make the scenario last approximately 24 hours, which is a typical length of time for groups to be lost. Throw in some complicating factors to spice up the discussion such as these actual NOLS occurrences:

- The lost group didn't tell the others what route they were taking.
- The lost group took a different route than they originally planned because they saw one that looked easier, then had an accident along that route.
- Two hiking groups became lost.
- One instructor became ill in camp and needed constant care while a student hiking group was lost.
- The lost group was both lost and became split up (now two lost groups and neither are well equipped).
- When the lost group initially got lost, they overcorrected and traveled really far and fast, the wrong way, and ended up 10 miles off route in just five hours. They thought they were getting closer to the X.

## Leadership Opportunities

Though it may sound cliché, the most important piece of equipment we bring to the wilderness is our minds. The best strategy is to think through any predicament and act slowly and deliberately. Staying found is a textbook example of good self-awareness, situational awareness, and self-leadership.

# Lost Group Response Action Chart

## DAY 0

Group fails to arrive at "X". Group is now **overdue**.

## DAY 1

- Designation of noon seems arbitrary, but has proven to be an appropriate amount of time to wait to allow the lost group to reach the X.
- Preliminary planning/organization of search efforts can begin before noon.
- If an individual is overdue the evening before, typically lost near camp, searching should start sooner, such as first thing in the morning.

Group fails to arrive at "X" by noon. Group is now **missing**.

Group arrives at "X" by noon. End Search.

Course begins search procedures. → Group found. End Search.

Group not found.

Search until end of day.

## DAY 2

Some factors may increase the urgency to notify NOLS management.

- Inclement weather
- Limited resources (small course size)
- Limited strength/endurance of course searchers (students/staff)
- Inexperienced or less competent students
- Lost group inadequately equipped
- Significant terrain/travel hazards
- Previous student medical problems (e.g. diabetes)

Course continues search procedures. → Group found. End Search.

Group not found. → NOLS management notified via phone or messenger party.

Search until end of day.

Begin planning for use of additional resources: e.g. aircraft (with NOLS staff aboard is preferable), NOLS staff as searchers or other agencies.

## DAY 3

Course continues search procedures as able. → Group found. End Search.

Group not found.

Prepare for media.

Implement use of additional resources.

Turn over search to other agency. Assist.

Search until end of day.

Notify parents/families.

Continue search until group is found.

---

This chart provides a rough guide to our response. The actual situation and circumstances may require a modification of this response.

During a 5-year period from 2001-2005 there were 32 reported lost person/group incidents. Twenty of the incidents occurred around camp and took a few hours to resolve. Six incidents were groups that were overdue and were out for one night. In each case the lost groups or people found themselves. Six incidents were groups missing (3 groups for 2 nights and 3 groups for 3 nights). In 4 of these incidents searchers found the groups and in 2 incidents the groups found themselves. In all cases there were no injuries. Significant incidents of lost students is uncommon.

*Emergency Procedures*

# Improvised Litters

With the increased use of high-tech resources like helicopters, satellite phones, and personal locator beacons, the skill of litter building may seem archaic. However, common sense tells us not to be overly dependent on complex technology.

## Learning Objectives
- Construct various types of litters.
- Understand the limitations and advantages of each type of litter, as well as the procedures for transporting a patient safely.

## Litter Construction Basics
Without sufficient padding, any litter will be very uncomfortable. Use plenty of clothes, sleeping bags, and ensolite pads for padding. Before you load the patient, test the litter out for comfort and function with a similar-sized healthy person. Take the time to build the litter right the first time. Each knot and lashing should be extremely tight in order to prevent loosening when the litter is moved. Consider how much of an interruption it would be to have to stop, unload the patient, and disassemble the padding. Any extra weight that must be carried on the litter should be placed at the feet.

## Rigid Pole Litters
Rigid pole litters are most efficient for long carries over moderate terrain. They are relatively comfortable and are good for patients with lower extremity injuries. They provide a rigid platform that protects the patient from accidental bumps, and they are easier to pass over or around obstacles.

Carry a pole litter by grabbing it around the edges. For longer carries it is easier and safer to use pieces of webbing tied to the litter that each carrier can loop across a shoulder and hold like a belay line with the opposite hand.

The disadvantage of a rigid pole litter is that it requires more materials and time to construct, it is difficult to maneuver in tight spots, and it is considerably heavier.

Rigid litters need to be built to last. It is worth spending the time to build a good one the first time. Use a person of similar size as your patient as your model for building the litter and to test moving it. While there are many possible designs, the following are some principles to go by:

- Main poles should be cut from live trees if possible. Use a multi-tool serrated knife blade to score the tree, and then break it. It should be at least 10' in length and 3" in diameter at the thinnest spots. If the poles taper, build the litter so that the thickest part of each pole is at the head and torso end (supporting most of the weight).
- The body of the litter can be constructed from the patient's pack and a tarp. The patient's pack can be lashed between the poles to provide stability for the torso. The shoulder and sternum straps can stabilize the patient on the litter. The patient's lower body may be supported by a tarp or tent, which has been carefully rolled over the poles to maintain support.
- Cross braces can be constructed of branches (at least 2.5" in diameter and 4' long). In a pinch, doubled up trekking poles can be used. Braces should run between the poles above the head, below the toes, and (for larger patients) just under the upper thigh of the patient. For transports in open terrain, the cross braces can extend a foot or so past the main poles and be used as handles. The braces should be lashed below the main poles as tightly as possible.

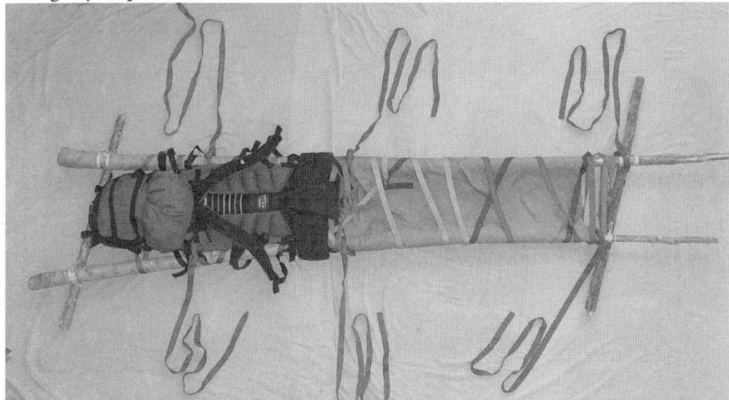

*This litter incorporates the patient's backpack, a ground sheet, long wooden poles, and some webbing.*

## Semi-rigid T-shirt Stretchers
For carries where time is more critical than the rigidity of the litter, semi-rigid litters can be constructed quickly with main poles of the same dimensions as above. Simply thread the main poles through the bottoms and sleeves of five or six T-shirts. Be sure the shirts overlap by several inches. The litter will sag considerably and the strength of the poles is critical here.

*This simple litter consists of two poles slipped through four T-shirts.*

## Rope Litters
Rope litters are quick and easy to construct with minimal materials. They are a good option when you are facing a quick move with a patient whose injury will not be compromised by lack of rigidity in the litter. Rope litters are more maneuverable than pole litters because of their flexibility.

The disadvantage of the rope litter is that it can be uncomfortable and confining during long periods of travel and is often more fatiguing to carry. The lack of rigidity in a rope litter and T-shirt stretcher limit the type of injury for which they are appropriate.

## Carrying the Patient
Safety of both the patient and litter bearers are the main criteria in how and where a litter will be carried. Unless shock is an issue or they request otherwise, carry the patient so that their head is uphill. Have one person guide the lifting and lowering of the litter. Warn the patient about what is ahead. Brief the team and patient about the carry before you begin and then debrief at the end of the move. Warm-up as needed. Expect to need more people to lift and lower the litter than to carry it.

In rough terrain, especially where there is a risk people may stumble and fall, try the caterpillar method. The litter bearers stand in line and pass the litter from person to person. The people in the back rotate to the front to continue the caterpillar until smooth terrain is reached.

## Teaching Considerations
Litter building is time consuming, but it is a great subject to teach when the group wants to be active and the weather restricts your options. Real litter evacuations require a great deal of preparation and thought, but these situations can provide excellent opportunities for students to learn more about emergency procedures, long-term patient care, teamwork, and leadership. If you intend to have students build their own litter, prepare materials beforehand in order to shorten the class.

Be careful of back strain when lifting the litter. As with a backpack, lift with the legs, lift in unison, and get bystanders to help lift it. The "sniffing position," nose up, helps straighten the back during the lift.

## Leadership Opportunites
In an actual litter evacuation, an open discussion prior to the carry can be beneficial to all the students and staff involved. Encourage the students to express their concerns and apprehensions about the carry before it starts. Instructors should address these concerns and detail any expectations they have of the students during the evacuation. Explain that for efficiency, leadership styles may need to become more directive during an evacuation. The patient should participate in the discussion if they are well enough.

It is easy for students to get caught up in the macho aspect of carrying an injured friend out of the mountains. Instructors need to be ready to park the litter when the team first shows signs of getting tired. On multiple day evacuations, it helps group morale to have a quick briefing each morning prior to the carry.

# Helicopter Evacuations

After completing a thorough patient assessment and writing a S.O.A.P. note, decide if the patient has a life or limb emergency that necessitates a helicopter evacuation. Keep in mind that helicopters can crash; they should only be considered when no other evacuation method is feasible.

## Considerations

- Helicopters usually only fly in good weather. Most will not fly in wilderness at night.
- Minimize the time the crew has to wait on the ground. Have the patient ready at the landing zone before the helicopter arrives.
- Communicate the coordinates of your suggested landing zone in both lat/long (DDM) and UTM. Tell them about any large land features identifiable from the air that may aid navigation. They may choose not to use your suggested site.
- Communicate hazards, weather, visibility, cloud ceiling height, air temp, and especially wind speed and gust range.
- Be considerate of weight, especially at high altitude or in hot weather when the air is less dense. Some aircraft may only be able to take the patient and not the patient's equipment. Plan accordingly and be prepared to pack out any additional gear.

## Creating a Landing Zone

- Select a site at least 40 paces in diameter and long enough for the aircraft to approach and take off at an angle 15 degrees off the ground. The helicopter should be able to clear any obstacle—trees, boulders, power lines, etc.—by at least 10 feet.
- The site should be relatively flat with a slope angle no greater than 10 degrees. The ideal path for takeoff should angle downhill.
- Wind direction is important. Orient the long axis of the site into the wind and provide a well secured and brightly colored wind direction indicator. They land and take off upwind because the helicopter tilts forward to move that way and gain the airspeed they need for smooth efficient flight.
- Choose a site located on a durable, hard surface that is free of debris. Remove any loose debris within a 100-foot radius. Loose objects can get sucked into the rotor. If possible, warn the pilot of the potential for brownout or whiteout conditions.
- In high winds, avoid landing zones downwind of obstructions that create turbulence—steady high winds are no problem.

## Signaling

Geometric shapes are more obvious from the air than most colors are. When the helicopter approaches, use a signal mirror to identify your location, but don't blind the pilot. If you use sleeping bags to mark your site, anchor them well.

## Landing Zone Safety

- Designate a landing zone officer to be responsible for safety during the evacuation and to communicate with the pilot. During the evacuation the aircraft may remain running, presenting additional risks and the necessity for a well-organized site and a clear plan.
- Establish a perimeter and a safety zone. The landing zone officer manages entrance into the perimeter.

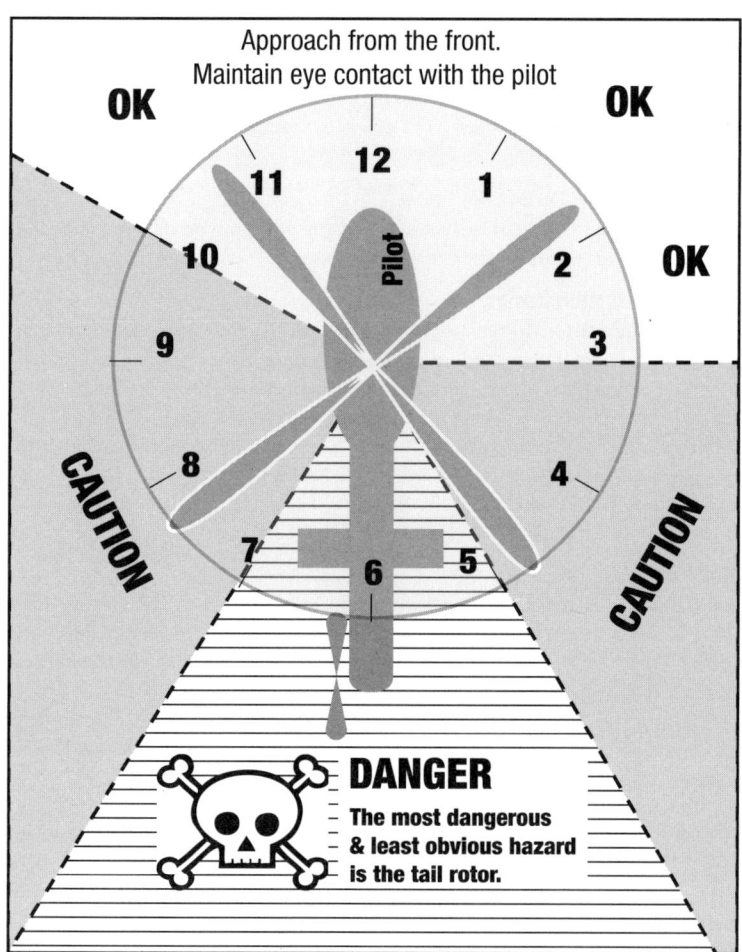

*The rotors on a helicopter present a serious hazard. Always wait for the crew to signal you before approaching the aircraft. Do not approach the rear of the aircraft.*

- Approach the aircraft only after the pilot has motioned you to do so. Keep your head down. When directed, approach toward the front of the helicopter to avoid the dangerous exhaust and tail rotor.
- Be prepared for blowing debris. Seek shelter behind rocks or trees if available.
- Move to the outside of the perimeter before the helicopter takes off. It may take several minutes for the crew to warm the engine up properly, check instruments, and secure equipment before they leave.

### Deep Snow

Boot pack a 20 foot square landing spot. If you have time, shovel more snow on top to elevate and strengthen it. Pack an approach trail at an angle around 2 o'clock. Set two heavy packs at the front edge of the landing spot (12 o'clock) so the pilot can tell distance during the whiteout as they land. Dry orange drink mix makes an excellent X marker on the snow, after it has been boot-packed. Most pilots won't trust your helipad to completely support their two ton helicopter and will load hot, keeping some lift in their rotors. Be especially careful of rotors when a helicopter settles into snow.

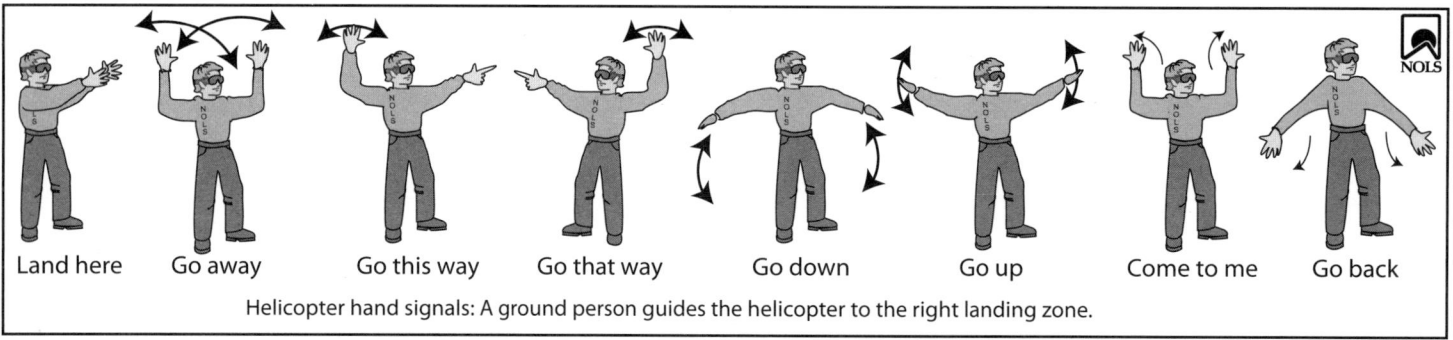

Helicopter hand signals: A ground person guides the helicopter to the right landing zone.

*It may be necessary to signal to the helicopter. Use these common signals. Remember to stay clear of the helicopter and it's dangerous rotors. Wear eye protection and be cautious of flying debris.*

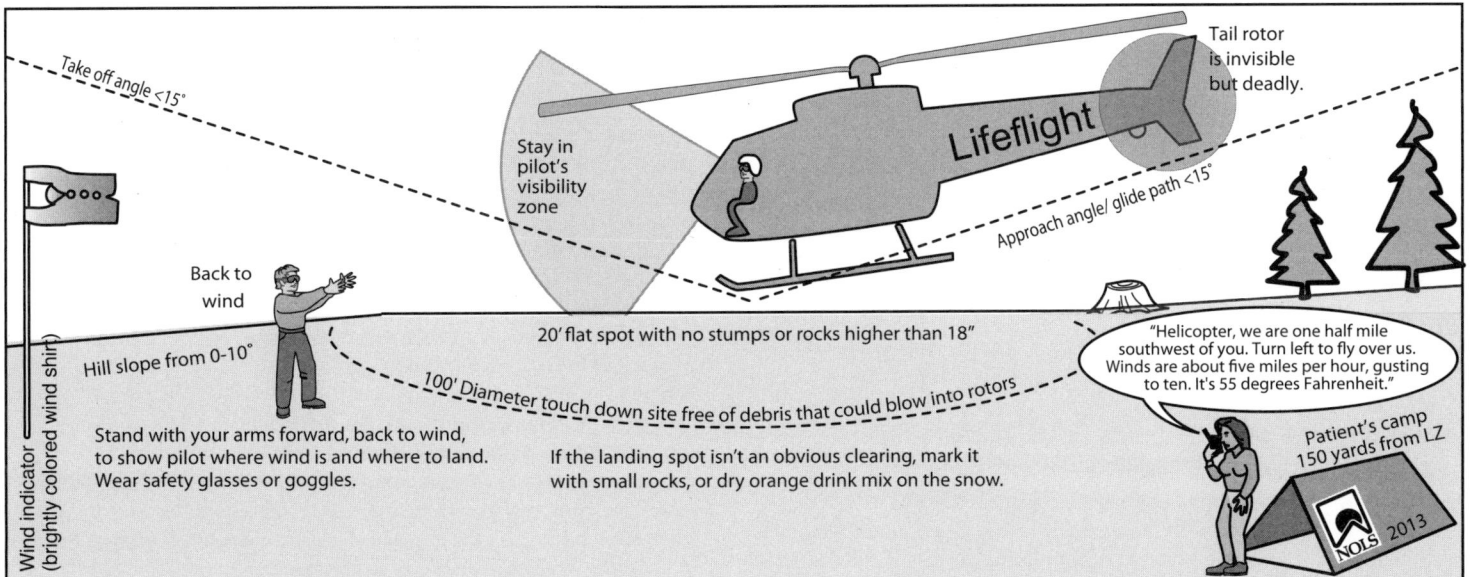

*It is important to select a good helicopter landing zone. Use this infographic to help with site selection. Remember, the pilot will make the final call whether a landing zone is suitable or not.*

## Helicopter Ambulatory Patient Pre-flight Briefing

(*Use this checklist to brief a patient before loading them in a helicopter*)

The motto for emergency operations is "Go slow to go fast." Rushing invites mistakes that delay us. Go slow and steady. Don't rush or run. Be calmly methodical. Do it right the first time.

The pilot is in charge of the helicopter operation, so follow their lead. Sometimes they bring a crew chief (helitac) to manage loading.

*Entry and Exit of Aircraft*
- Stay away from the tail rotor—it is invisible and deadly.
- Don't go further back than the rear cargo hatch.
- Load/unload under direction of the pilot or helitac crew chief.
- Approach/exit in front. Maintain eye contact with the pilot. Walk in a crouched stance—do not run.
- Approach upslope/exit downslope (main rotor is level so it is closer to the ground uphill).
- The pilot may have a reason for you to load from a certain angle.

*Airborne*
- Once in your seat, stay there (weight shifts change balance and can steer the helicopter).
- Keep seatbelts, gloves, and helmet chinstraps on.
- Don't touch the doors or windows.
- If the window is open, don't stick your hand out of it.

*Landing*
- Wait for helitac personnel to unload you.
- Leave seatbelt on until directed by pilot or helitac.
- Leave door closed unless directed to open it.
- Refasten seatbelt in the seat before exiting (so it won't flop around).

*Loading and Unloading Equipment*
- Equipment is generally loaded/unloaded by helitac personnel.
- If the crew asks for help loading, minimize how many people go near the aircraft.
- Carry long equipment parallel to ground and never above shoulders.
- Secure any loose items inside cabin (so they don't hurt anyone in a crash).
- Bear spray and stove fuel get loaded externally in the rear compartment or taped to a skid strut.

*Loading Hot (rotor still spinning)*
- Secure loose clothing. If it flies off, don't chase it.
- Watch for light objects that can catch wind and recirculate into the rotor.
- Don't toss things to each other (if the rotor bats it, it can become a dangerous projectile and can put the aircraft out of service).
- Step gently into the helicopter in case your weight tilts it.
- Let the pilot dictate the loading sequence.

# Chapter Twelve
# Course Management Skills

## Designing a NOLS Course
The primary goal of any NOLS course is learning to live and travel safely and responsibly in the environments encountered. There are certain goals that are consistent throughout all NOLS courses; they include developing competence in these areas:
- Personal risk management
- Camping skills (including LNT)
- Navigation and travel skills
- The seven NOLS Leadership skills
- Challenging adventures
- Hazard evaluation judgment
- Enjoyment of the environment and of fellow travelers

These goals are detailed more explicitly in the general expected student outcomes sent to every student with their specific course description. Instructors should refer to the student evaluation for the most specific expected student outcomes. There are also hidden outcomes that are inherent goals in good education:
- Furthering maturity in terms of personal responsibility, social skills, learning habits, organizational skills, and awareness of the world.
- Affirmation that learning can be very enjoyable.

It is the responsibility of the NOLS course leader to design a curriculum of classes and activities that accomplishes these goals. Patrol leaders are expected to help do this. The instructional checklist is offered as an organizational tool. It is not a "class list" because classes aren't always the best way to learn certain topics, and because it is not necessary to cover every topic on the list. The course leader reserves the ultimate judgment about how a course is run as long as the goals outlined above are accomplished and high standards of student competency are maintained.

## Course Priorities
Each NOLS course is unique due to variables such as route, group dynamics, fitness levels, and environmental conditions. Once the course is underway, it is common to find your plan for the course evolving and your priorities changing. It is important to be realistic about what you can accomplish in the amount of time you have. In general, priorities for instruction are:
1) Anything students need to know to stay safe on the course.
2) Classes and activities that support the bigger picture goals like furthering maturity and gaining positive "habits of mind." Excellent education needs to be personalized, so input from students about their priorities is necessary.
3) Achieving the core curriculum subjects: teaching transferable leadership skills, giving students the experience of mastering technical skills, and nurturing students' growth as environmental stewards and citizens.
4) The final priority is teaching the technical core: the specific decision-making, leadership, camping, technical, and environmental skills which are detailed on the evaluation.

It is a big curriculum; not every course will achieve all of the goals. In addition to all the teaching done on courses, it's important to simply have faith in the experience as a transformational one for most of our students. Remember, most students report on their program evaluations that "just being in the environments visited" was their most powerful teacher. So, don't forget to give your students the time, opportunity, and encouragement to do the things people go to the wilderness to do.

## Advice on Course Design
From seasoned course leaders to new CLs and PLs:
- Challenging activities are everything; classes support activities.
- Use the instructional checklist, but don't take it too seriously; organize around themes and topics.
- Be sure to organize some spectacular activities students will savor forever. Think of goals you can photograph.
- Ask new PLs and Is to teach what they are best at. Only ask folks to teach a new topic when they have a good experience base in that area. Generally, you should give the I first choice of instructional topics, then let the PL choose, then the CL picks up the slack.
- Ask your students to focus on developing their strong areas rather than their weaknesses.
- Don't overdo information. It's best to leave students a little hungry, rather than burned out. Teach them lots of appropriate things, but trim the stuff they can live without.
- Formal classes need a lot of depth and grounding in reality. Insist that your instructors have "meaty" material, not just canned outlines. Keep lectures concise.
- The three most important things that help students achieve technical mastery are practice, practice, and practice.
- Ask for high standards from your students, higher standards from your instructors, and model even higher standards yourself.
- The course has the CLs name on it. If you make your expectations clear to your fellow Is, life will be easier for everyone.
- If the staff needs help meeting your high standards, coach them early to set them up for success.
- Utilize teachable moments in lieu of classes when possible.
- Be sure your instructors are role modeling your own professional development. Try to get caught up in exploring and learning.
- When you give options, make sure everyone gets an option they value.
- Pay as much attention to your students' habits as you do their skills and knowledge.
- Make sure each group meeting is a special occasion so they'll be savored.
- Encourage reflection on accomplishments so students realize what they are learning.

## NOLS Student Supervision Practices
This section defines NOLS' expectations for supervising students while we concurrently develop their independence. Student independence includes camp-to-camp hiking days (ISGT) and multi-day student expeditions (ISGE). It also includes time that students are independent of direct instructor supervision while in camp.

### The Role of Independent Student Time
Our decisions to have students travel unaccompanied are significant and cannot be taken lightly. Instructors need to be engaged with their students throughout the course, need to be diligent in their teaching and coaching of students as they develop their travel, leadership, decision-making, and risk management skills, and need to be personally engaged and involved in facilitating ISGT experiences and supervising students as they design and execute their travel plans.

NOLS education is intended not only to prepare students to meet wilderness challenges on their own, but to lead others as well. Throughout NOLS history, the school has developed competent graduates capable of leading and conducting their own outdoor trips and expeditions. A foundation of the NOLS educational philosophy is to use the learning power of experience with the possibility of appropriate consequences to develop competency.

Leadership is a core value of NOLS. NOLS' use of independent student group travel has a profound effect in the development of desired leadership attributes in our students. Research into the educational outcomes from a NOLS course consistently correlates both daily and multi-day independent travel by student groups with higher student outcomes. Personal empowerment that comes from independent decision-making is the most significant course-level factor affecting all student outcomes.

Independent student group travel (ISGT) provides opportunities for students to display competencies necessary for wilderness travel, to better understand their abilities and limitations, to gain valuable experience upon which to further develop their self-awareness and judgment, and to accomplish a realistic and achievable goal.

### The Progression to Student Independence
Use a progression of classes, activities and experiences to build knowledge, skills, and competence. Carefully evaluate and assess student performance, and

gradually loosen supervisory reins to facilitate independent student experiences. The progression begins with students independently performing cooking and camp chores. A common next step is hiking without instructors during the day. The progression may culminate in a multi-day student expedition during which the students use their skills and knowledge to travel through the wilderness without instructors.

Many of our course types include the possibility of independent student group travel. Most commonly, these are either hiking for a day without instructors or the multi-day student expedition. However, there are NOLS courses where activities are too technical or the environment too harsh to allow student independence from direct instructor supervision. Defining technical terrain is subjective. The International Scale of River Difficulty and the Sierra Club classification of terrain and rock climbs are two common systems that can provide guideposts, but any definition is subject to many variables. Conservative, observation-based judgment that suggests the student is capable of managing the challenges is the best approach to evaluating terrain or routes for student travel.

## The Privilege of Independence
Participating in independent student group travel is an earned privilege rather than an automatic experience. Students who don't demonstrate adequate skills, effective group interactions, or decision-making can travel with the instructors while other students travel unaccompanied by instructors. Though not common, there are courses where instructors do not allow students to go on student expeditions or they shorten the experience. The route can be altered to fit the abilities of the students and some student expeditions may need a daily check-in with the instructors.

## Setting Up Student Independence
Familiarity with the terrain for both the students and instructors is a key element to successful independent student group travel. Specific knowledge of the intended route(s) may not be necessary, but students need to have had sufficient experience in the terrain type to be competent. ISGT groups don't do technical activities, e.g., rock climbing. They travel over familiar terrain types, e.g., they don't wade a river without a river crossing class and supervised practice, they don't cross a high mountain pass without first having done so with their instructors.

NOLS instructors deciding when and how to allow young people to venture into the world on their own face a challenge similar to parents. We balance the likelihood and cost of a beginner's error against the benefit of the activity. The degree of instructor presence depends on student ability, the level of risk, and the educational goals of an activity. We may let students cook with stoves after only one demonstration, while we teach and coach them through numerous river crossings before they attempt one on their own. We may let students lead themselves on a well-marked trail, and intervene the first time they cross an exposed high mountain pass or snow slope. Through the years, our teaching and coaching methods have balanced the advantages and disadvantages of allowing our students to develop responsibility and leadership through independent experiences.

Preparation for student independent travel requires that instructors use three key strategies:
1) Clear expectations and curriculum progression
2) Adaptive supervision—careful observation of student performance
3) Thoughtful decisions of when students are ready for independent travel

## Clear Expectations and Curriculum Progression
There are a number of tools we use to convey expectations of students preparing for and participating in independent student travel.

### Travel Plans and Route Briefing
Students should be oriented to their route through a route briefing, at first led by instructors and later led by ISGT leaders with instructor oversight. A written travel plan is an important and powerful tool to brief and teach students about hazard assessment and orient them to changing conditions. It is also useful for evaluating their navigation skills, and hazard awareness. These tools help students learn to anticipate distances and travel timetables, identify hazards and navigation challenges, and provide opportunities for collaboration between students and instructors to determine terrain hazards, contingency plans, and meeting places if the main plan cannot be achieved.

Students need to be given clear instructions on what to do in changing situations, such as: when hazards are encountered that were not anticipated, if situations arise that are beyond their ability to manage, and if the original plan has to change due to the changing conditions in the environment or within the group. Students also need to know our expectations about being overdue and emergency procedures to follow if someone is injured.

It is an expectation that each travel group will submit a written travel plan for all ISGT. Consider having everyone do an individual travel plan at some point in the course. This sidesteps the possibility that only a few interested students are doing all the daily travel plans.

### Camp Boundaries
Brief students on camp boundaries within which instructors do not have to be immediately on hand to supervise. While not as formal as the perimeter of a glacier camp marked with wands, this briefing can include how far students can roam unaccompanied during free time or for such things as fishing or solitude.

Point out natural boundaries beyond which you expect students to have told the instructors their plan, and that they bring a day pack, a map, a compass and a companion. Having students describe camp boundaries is a good way to develop this habit and awareness so they can use it during the student expedition.

### First Aid Skills
Students traveling independently need first aid skills. If instructors are nearby these may be simple skills such as stabilizing a patient and managing the ABCs. As their independence grows, so does their need for more skills. We have a specific scenario-based first aid curriculum appropriate to the length of ISGT. This curriculum is a prerequisite for participation in ISGT activities.

### Emergency and Lost Person Procedures
We address emergency procedures at a basic level when we tell a student what to do if they are disoriented around camp, or a group what we expect if they become lost or delayed. We tailor our overdue group instruction for the situation. We may use simple directives such as "stop walking and make yourself visible." As skill and experience increase we may add expectations on accessing support if the group is separated from staff.

*"We ran a few first aid scenarios and emphatically covered emergency procedures. One scenario, late in the course, went from the initial patient assessment all the way to having a runner party show up at our tent, documents in hand, with a plan and a good contingency. The students did a fantastic and thorough job at this, taking it very seriously, and assuring us that panic wouldn't arise if they found themselves in a tough spot."*

While on ISGT each student group knows the itinerary and travel plans of the other student groups, and the instructor group. Students are provided specific emergency procedures to follow if there is an incident. These include providing first aid to the patient, caring for the rest of the group, following emergency notification procedures, which depending on the situation may involve activating their PLB (or other electronic communication device) or sending a messenger team to locate and notify the instructors.

ISGT groups are formed to balance strengths and weaknesses of the team members. Each group travels with a full compliment of shelter, food, stove/cook gear, clothing, first aid kit, and a PLB or other communication device (as applicable).

Each ISGT group may follow the same route but depart at different times, or they may choose separate routes. The instructors plan their itinerary and follow it so that they are within a reasonable distance to any group at any time. This reasonable distance depends on specific local conditions. During multi-day student expeditions the upper limit is for the instructors to camp no further than 24 hours travel from any student group. Commonly, this time frame is much less. Instructors have to consider terrain features and student strengths and abilities when determining their camp locations. For example, instructors may shadow one group of students along the same route and be within be within visual contact of them at any given time, while a stronger, more competent group may follow a route farther away and be multiple hours away from the instructors.

*Curriculum Progression*

The curriculum progression of classes, activities and experiences is designed to build from basic outdoor living skills through travel and technical skills, from being a novice to being capable of more advanced skills, from leading yourself to leading others. The intent of this curriculum is, on courses where it is an option, to prepare the students for independent student travel.

## Adaptive Supervision

When students travel independently and in particular during multi-day student expeditions, the instructor team may use combinations of supervision techniques.

*"Students traveled with and without instructors throughout the course. By intermingling these types of travel days, students could work on new skills for a few days and then hike with instructors and be quickly reevaluated on their new skills."*

*Ghost Instructors*

Silent or ghost instructors accompany student groups, observing their actions but intervening if safety is compromised.

*"Progressively, the instructors 'stepped back' as we hiked with the students, saying less and giving more of the reins to the students, only stepping in if it became a safety issue. We could assess their map, travel, hazard evaluation and communication skills."*

This can become an awkward situation when student leadership is undermined or unclear. As much as we try to remove ourselves from daily hiking decisions, students can adeptly read when our body language says, "Hey, why are we going uphill when camp is down in that valley?" Clear intervention parameters need to be established to allow the students to experience their leadership but permit the instructor to take over if safety is in question.

*Shadowing*

Shadowing is when instructors travel within visual contact and intervene if an unexpected obstacle presents itself, if students need additional coaching or advice, or if instructors see a situation developing that needs their intervention.

*Leap Frogging*

There are a few variations of this, but essentially when the student and instructor groups pass each other at various times during the day or during a student expedition. For example, the instructor group leaves first then stops after a certain amount of time and lets the student groups pass by them. The instructors can check in with the students as they go by. Then the instructors catch up and overtake the students, providing another opportunity to check in. This is a common practice for supervising ISGT on canoe courses.

*Meeting at Hazards*

Instructors might leave camp before the students to assess terrain or a particular obstacle or hazard before the students arrive. By meeting at a river crossing, high pass, or boulder field, they can allow students to travel independently on familiar terrain and teach, coach, or supervise them at the new or unfamiliar terrain. This can happen by meeting groups at prearranged sites, such as the base of the big pass, or telling students to wait for the instructors if they are uncomfortable with a river crossing, or snow or boulder field.

*Debriefing*

We rely on daily debriefing of the student travel groups to evaluate and reflect on risk management and decision-making and to teach communication, conflict skills, and to assess the students' progress in developing their competency. Reflection and analysis of decision-making is an important educational tool because it offers an opportunity to look back to contributing factors that may have led to a particular decision. Incidents are often, though not always, a culmination of a series of small decisions that in and of themselves are not significant, but might lead to an incident.

*"We debriefed daily, addressing both teamwork and hazards with the most emphasis, and got a clear idea of how well and how safely they all worked together on the trail. It really built my confidence when one group debriefed themselves, and did a good job."*

## Thoughtful Decisions of When Students Are Ready For Independent Travel

Instructors observing competency demonstrated by students is the foundation for deciding if or when students are ready to travel independent of instructors. Our desire that they be ready is not the same as them actually being ready. Desire can be a subjective hazard in our decision process. We need to be able to articulate, with supporting examples, why we think they have earned independence. The length of most NOLS courses allows us to systematically apply a careful and specific teaching progression and provide the necessary time for observation to facilitate decisions on when to "turn students loose."

Instructors need to evaluate students' competency in leadership, expedition behavior, teamwork, communication, decision-making, core skills (travel, navigation, camping), and consider experience with relevant weather conditions and hazard awareness in deciding when students are ready to be independent.

*"I look for my students to be organized, on time, and motivated. Do they leave clean camps and kitchens? If students are assuming responsibility on the smaller scale I can consider them ready for larger responsibilities"*

*"When they show consistency in making safe decisions, understand risk factors, are solid campers and are developing an environmental ethic, then they're ready."*

*"We spent enough time with the students on the trail, assessing their map and travel skills, and their communication skills to know that the chances for success were high, and failure was unexpected."*

## Competence in Outdoor Living and Technical Skills

### Outdoor Living and Travel Skills

There is plenty of opportunity to observe competence in students in the core outdoor living (pack packing, organization, campsite selection, self care) and travel skills (map reading, navigation, negotiating various terrain, being an engaged member of a travel group). It becomes clear when students can be expected to take care of themselves and others without an instructor's presence.

A student's ability to travel through rivers, over high passes, and boulder fields develops throughout a course as they practice skills and become increasingly involved in the decision-making process. We evaluate and give them feedback on the limits of their skills, abilities, and experience. We can see if the student is aware of their surroundings and group, acting conservatively and consistently.

*"We held a skills clinic where every student had to start a stove, show us their location on a map, use a compass, tie a few knots and pack their day pack."*

*"Consistency with fundamentals will demonstrate both conscientiousness, and the setting of safe habits. Things like careful coiling, the dressing of every knot, the meticulous double checking of partners before starting a top-rope climb, accurate climbing communication, all reveal a commitment to fundamentals and safety which can be relied upon."*

### Weather Experience

On courses with potential for harsh weather, we may decide to stay closer as a group, especially if the expedition to this point has only experienced benign weather.

### Hazard Identification and Risk Management Experience

We can develop a good sense of our students' experience with and ability to identify hazards and manage risks such as weather, rock fall, moving water, animals and insects, etc. We can anticipate their performance when we're not around and adjust our level of supervision accordingly.

*"I do a hazard tour, walking around the area, identifying hazards and discussing risk management."*

*"After a formal class on hazard evaluation and risk management, I consistently weave a theme of speaking about the hazards and risk management strategies we're using. "*

### Leadership Skills

The NOLS Leadership Skills are a benchmark to measure student readiness. A student's self-awareness of his or her abilities and limitations, his or her ability to display reasonable judgment with mature communication and decision making skills, his or her tolerance for adversity and uncertainty, and his or her expedition behavior on a group and individual level can all be observed by instructors and used to assess readiness for independent group travel.

### Self-awareness
We can observe and assess whether a student is showing appropriate self-awareness of both physical and interpersonal abilities and limitations. Instructors need to be observant of strengths and weakness in students and if the individual and the group are cognizant of these differences. It may be easy for confident or charismatic students to speak up, but it may be difficult for less confident and more reserved students to speak up or express a contrary opinion about a route choice or other decisions. All students need to be coached to consider variability in his/her or other student's personalities and abilities.

### Decision-making Skills
We observe students interacting with others and reacting to the different challenges of a course. This gives us a lot of information on their decision-making, especially on month long and semester courses. We identify the leaders whose decisions we trust, and the "young immortals" who need closer supervision. Students making their own decisions need to both solicit input and be willing to speak up with their opinion regarding the goals and priorities for their ISGT travel group/student expedition, particularly in regards to risk management.

*"When they have experience—with instructors present—in a number of different hazard evaluation situations, and if they handle these decisions well, then they can be ready to be on their own."*

### Tolerance for Adversity and Uncertainty
Tolerance for difficult and uncertain situations is a necessary trait in outdoor leaders. However, tolerance does not simply mean enduring without question, it means being aware of the possibility of needing to adapt to changing situations; for example, abrupt changes in weather may be best tolerated by making camp earlier than planned. A student becoming fatigued or sick may have to be tolerated with a slower pace, sharing weight, and a positive attitude.

### Expedition Behavior
Likewise, we will have a sense of their expedition behavior. Tension within a group or poor expedition behavior is a risk factor for dissension and poor communication when times get tough.

*"Expedition Behavior, the ability to function in a group and as a team, is one of the more important prerequisites for participating in an independent student expedition"*

### Conclusion: Leadership and Independence
A goal of our curriculum is to develop students as leaders who make decisions and lead without the direct guidance of their instructors. The curriculum themes of wilderness skills, expedition behavior, leadership, Leave No Trace, and risk management all flow toward this goal. Our graduated levels of supervision parallel our leadership curriculum.

*"I like to use these four to five phases of supervision in leadership development; Role Modeling, Consultant, Guardian Angels, Autonomy, and if appropriate, Student Expedition."*

The expedition nature and length of most NOLS courses allows instructors to systematically apply a careful and specific teaching progression. It gives us the time for observation and evaluation to support our decisions.

## Guidelines for Conducting Solos on NOLS Courses
Solos can provide personal and educational reflective time. Reflection is a key part of a wilderness experience, yet it is difficult to schedule into a busy course. Reflection helps us take our accumulating feelings about nature, leadership, and ourselves and think about how these feelings might shape our future actions. In this sense, a solo can be an invaluable tool for transferring the lessons learned at NOLS. Tip: rather than telling students what they ought to think and feel on a solo, just tell them what you do on a solo and let each of them make their own choices.

### Learning Objectives
Goals should be established for solos. Solos have great potential, but solos don't inherently do anything. Many students who are just put on solos with no preparation and no guidelines can get bored, confused, and irritated. Discussing a variety of potential outcomes of a solo provides students with enough choices that they can make decisions they will own. Talk with participants about how they might best spend their time. Let them offer many of the ideas, if they will. It helps to include options like: think about things we've learned on the course; listen to nature; write in journals; write a letter to yourself that the branch will mail you in six months; take a breather; camp with less gear. Solos are an optional activity on NOLS courses.

### Solo Length and Duration
Solos are generally 24 hours in length and rarely 48 hrs in length. Solos of three days and nights are allowed, but other curriculum objectives need to be considered before allotting this much time to a solo. Even a two day solo needs extensive planning to be a worthwhile part of a NOLS expedition.

### Preparation
1) Brief students on the goals of the solo.
2) Inform students of expected behavior during the solo. Students must understand why any solo activity needs to be done conservatively. Solos are stationary. This means no day hiking, no visiting other students, no bouldering or climbing, no swimming, no building large fires, etc.
3) Instructions for ending the solo and returning to the instructor camp are established and made known.

### Supervision of Solos
- Instructors and students know how to get to each site.
- A method for distributing students to each site and reassembling after the allotted time is established and known to each student. Options may include: instructors assigning sites, instructors escorting students to sites, a responsible student being the farthest away and knowing where each site is along the route.
- Solo sites are mapped on an instructor map. Students may mark sites on their maps as well.
- Boundaries or distances between solo sites are established considering safety factors and achieving the desired outcomes of the experience.
- For solos longer than 24 hours a method for checking on students is arranged and known to all. One method that prevents direct human contact is to have cairns established where the instructor checks twice a day. The student places a 1" or smaller pebble on top of the cairn and the instructor takes it back off.
- A signaling method is agreed upon and known to all students to signal a need for help or to call off the solo activity if necessary. Whistles are effective for signaling; yelling may also work.
- Students' performance on the course along with maturity level and ability to be independent of instructors is considered when allowing students on solo. Some medical concerns, including certain allergies and possibly diabetes, may make being alone unsafe. These conditions should be carefully considered when organizing the solo.
- Some concern was raised in the past regarding being alone in mountain lion country. Having a means to make deterrent noise might be a consideration in planning solos.

### Solo Site Selection
- The terrain selected should be appropriate for the level of student skills and abilities.
- Instructors need to be familiar with the sites chosen for the solos to understand the physical layout, potential supervision issues, and educational possibilities of the solo sites.
- Solo sites are confined to a specific area such as a valley or canyon. Parameters are set for how widespread the sites can be. Scattering sites up a canyon for a quarter mile is a good general rule.
- Hazardous environmental conditions such as lightning or rainstorms flooding low lying areas are to be considered.
- There must be clear and specific guidelines as to when and how fires can be used.
- Consider access to water and other needed materials.
- Consider solo sites for physical hazards, potential exposure to dangerous animals or to unknown people in the area.

### Emergency Procedures for Solos
- The following emergency procedures are established and known to all students:
  - Go to the nearest instructor, if possible.
  - Otherwise, go to the nearest student for help.
  - As a last resort, blow 3 blasts on a whistle. Those hearing this distress signal should leave solo and provide help.
- Normal NOLS emergency procedures are followed once instructors are aware of the situation.
- The locations of first aid kits are known to all students.
- The instructor camp should be occupied at all times during the activity.

## Visiting Student Camps
It is important that instructors maintain a certain presence in student camps. Every instructor team should make the rounds to student camps roughly once per day. At a minimum this means one instructor walking through camps and checking in as they pass. But it might also include dropping in for a hot drink, coming to dinner, or even camping with that tent group. This needs to happen more often earlier in a course or with younger students and less often later in a course.

Some instructors say they are too tired at the end of the day to "make the rounds" on more technical courses. Sometimes intense technical or physical training is a critical part of an excellent NOLS course, but we still need to coach and supervise our students in camp. If we instructors can't handle the intensity and still do our job, we need to back off on the agenda to an activity level we can excel at.

The NOLS curriculum includes camping and leadership skills and habits that can only be practiced in camp, and we have an obligation to oversee this aspect of the NOLS experience. It isn't the CLs job to do this; it is the CLs job to make sure this happens.

### How and Why We Supervise Camps?
Observe student competence to assess who is excelling and who isn't so you can give higher quality feedback to students. This may include minor coaching in the moment, like helping them light the stove. Any coaching should feel to the students like you are there to help them, not walking by with a clipboard looking for opportunities to correct their behaviors and make written notes for their permanent record. While assessment may help us give better written evaluations at the end of the course, the primary use of assessment is to coach the student to keep improving: a NOLS course is a course of instruction, not a test.

Impose our values: any visit is an opportunity for us to impose our values on our students. While this is categorically both paternalistic and arrogant, the NOLS values include expedition self-sufficiency, reflecting on beauty in wild areas, and role modeling what we stand for (See the NOLS "Core Values" document if you want more detailed information on our values). The dangers of imposing our own values are self-evident, and our culture is so guarded about imposing our values on others that there is little need for concern about this becoming a problem in the foreseeable future.

Maintain rapport to help your entire expedition team feel more cohesive. By checking in to see how everyone is doing, by soliciting input for logistical decisions, and by modeling that you put your own time and energy into group maintenance functions, we are helping glue together our own expedition, and we are modeling valuable leadership habits our students can mimic on their own expeditions.

Provide supervision: think "safe learning environment." We need to supervise well enough to quell bad habits before they degenerate into old bad habits, enough such that anyone who is considering antisocial behavior doesn't think they will be able to get away with it. A more positive view of providing supervision is to look for opportunities to develop good habits. But one reality of being a teacher is providing adequate adult supervision so our students feel safe and not like some camper left to fend for themselves like in *Lord of the Flies*.

Protect students: an ever-growing part of teacher and camp counselor education is protecting our charges from other humans. These rare predators occasionally include fellow students, staff, and strangers. We are protecting students from being molested, harassed, assaulted, battered, or harmed in any way. These things don't happen often at NOLS, but when they do happen they are so destructive that we need to be vigilant in preventing them. We have an increased obligation to protect minors in our care.

### How Do Students React to Our Presence?
The typical student gleans information from us and appreciates our presence. Some may easily take us for granted and not appreciate how much they learn from us, but most students actively appreciate our occasional presence in their camps.

Some students drop the conversation when an instructor enters their camp: this is a bad sign that either it is unusual that an instructor is present or else they are discussing something they don't want an instructor to hear. If it happens once, it isn't significant. If it happens regularly, it is significant.

That rare troublemaker who likes to bully their way to the top of the pecking order will have fewer opportunities to slowly manipulate their way to King Rat position if responsible adults are maintaining a presence. These folks have typically done this before and the more likely you are to show up in their camp, the more they are going to mind their manners. At NOLS we are very good at positively motivating students, and we clearly value teaching with carrots more than with sticks, but we need forceful tools in our supervision toolbox for some students. Students who aren't meeting expectations need more supervision and sometimes need more directive approaches. If our supervision or intimidation is stifling bad behavior, that is good for the group. It is generally better for an unruly student to go home with 30 days of forced acceptable behavior than it is for them to go home with 30 more days of self-directed antisocial habits.

### How Can We Change Our Routine?
Certain circumstances make us realize we have been missing important opportunities to supervise student behaviors. It would be awkward if all of a sudden students felt like we were babysitting them. If we had been maintaining a presence during the whole course, our sudden presence wouldn't be felt as "different." But if we don't visit camps for the first week, then find out that camp life is less than ideal (messy campers, dysfunctional teams, last minute risers), we need to shift gears and try to repair the bad habits we have inadvertently allowed to develop.

SGEWIs: small group expeditions with instructors are valuable in helping students to consistently master important skills and habits. You can't get much curriculum crossed off the old instructional checklist on one of these, but you reinforce skills and make improvements that foster the mastery our alums are known for.

## Staff Guidelines for Grades and Diplomas at NOLS
Timely, specific, growth-oriented feedback is a NOLS leadership skill. We should explain performance expectations early during our educational expeditions, and use ongoing feedback to coach student performance. Upon this foundation, we also provide students with a formal written evaluation and a letter grade.

The written evaluation and grade become a record of the student's performance that they can use for continued growth. The evaluation and grade serve as NOLS' record if a student applies for another course or asks us to be a reference (many do). Most of our students (75%) use their NOLS course as part of their formal education. The evaluation and grade are needed for their college credit, an important service to students.

Evaluations should give concise feedback that will be clearly understood by our students, their parents, and by other institutions. NOLS uses letter grades with accompanying narratives that describe student behaviors observed during the course.

General performance expectations are listed in the student's Course Description and again in more detail on the student evaluation. Staff are encouraged to edit written expectations to match their specific course experience. Staff use the below system to let students know how well they performed each of these outcomes.

+ = Excellent
√+ = Good
√ = Satisfactory
Δ = Inconsistent/unsatisfactory. The symbol delta indicates change.
N/A = Not applicable to this student's performance or experience.

## Teaching for Success

NOLS staff must design courses so the typical student can potentially earn an "A" in any category. We expect staff to decide what "A performance" looks like, then design a curriculum of activities in which students can potentially progress to excellent performance. It is the instructor team's job to create opportunities, clarify performance expectations, and coach students towards our high standards; it is the student's job to perform in specific situations. Letter grades should reflect this performance.

A NOLS course is a course of instruction, not a test. When most students arrive at NOLS they are inexperienced and nervous, so it usually takes them a few days to settle into routines and get into the flow of the expedition. Student performance at the end of the course is more significant than performance at the start of the course.

Effort vs objective performance is a timeless dilemma in student evaluation. Luckily, we can easily include effort as part of our leadership and EB grades, while we remain objective about actual performance in other categories.

Rather than curving grades, we judge students by how well they accomplished the expected outcomes. An entire group might earn low or high grades, based on performance.

## NOLS Letter Grades

NOLS grades for are just as inflated as the national norms. This means we are using the grading system our students are calibrated to. This reflects a huge adjustment of NOLS' grading practices over the past decade.

> **A**: excellent performance of expected student outcomes
> **B**: good performance of expected student outcomes, is reliable & consistent
> **C**: satisfactory performance of expected student outcomes
> **D**: inconsistent performance of expected student outcomes
> **E**: unsatisfactory performance of expected student outcomes
> *The symbols + or - may be used to adjust a grade by 1/3 point.
> **An A+ will usually not transfer on a transcript, but may still be used to honor truly exceptional performance.

Grade inflation is a national reality that is problematic. Despite significant efforts to thwart the grade inflation trend, students still generally receive higher grades than the letter descriptions describe. The institutions that are fighting this trend ask staff to use integrity in only giving students the grades they earn and encourage the use of contracting and other performance clarifications. Clear expectations help make the student feel like their own choices determine their grade rather than their instructors' choices.

Contracting is telling students specifically what they need to do to earn various grades and is generally done at the start of a course. Because of the experiential nature of our programs, contracting may need clarification as the course progresses, like at mid-course check-ins.

## Grade Stress

Some people stress themselves about getting grades. There is nothing we can do about that. Grading can be tough on students and staff but is a critical part of education we need to tolerate.

A college student with a high grade point average (GPA) may be disappointed if they come to NOLS and work significantly harder than usual, then earn a lower than normal grade. We especially see this pattern in students who arrive weak physically but study hard. Or they may be able to recite the 7 leadership principles but may not apply them with finesse. The problems this creates include the pride of the student and the significant effect on their GPA. What is important for staff is that at these moments of challenge by our students, we feel like we set the course up so everyone could earn an A and that we coached this student effectively. This is exactly when we want students to feel that it was their own choices that resulted in earning a B or C, not our choices. This problem won't go away unless we lower our standards and start giving the same easy A's that breed this expectation.

## Who Earns a NOLS Diploma?

NOLS diplomas are earned by students who complete NOLS courses that cover the core curriculum and meet basic expectations as defined in the expected outcomes. Diplomas and college credit are not earned by students who are expelled for any reason. Students who earn below a C- (C minus) in overall performance may only receive a diploma at the branch director's discretion. Branch directors need to be involved with any case where a student does not receive a diploma. This standard is similar to the graduation requirement at most universities, where you might pass a course doing "D" work, but you need a "C" average to earn a diploma (See semester concerns on next page). A student who does not earn a NOLS diploma can sometimes still earn University of Utah college credit. A student who leaves a course for non-disciplinary reasons and completes at least 80% of the course may receive a diploma at the branch director's discretion. Branches should contact the NOLS Registrar for help with specific cases.

To be fair to our students, they need to hear and/or see the standard for passing at the orientation, and they need feedback that tells them how they are performing and what they need to do to pass. Students who don't graduate should be so aware of their status during the course so that the end result is no surprise.

All students on a single course should be evaluated using the same criteria. For example, all AKW students don't need the same grading standards, but all students on "AKW 7/12-A" need identical grading standards. The reason for this flexibility is so staff can adjust their grading strategy around the specific events that define the expedition.

## Consistency in Individual Categories

Instructors need to be generally consistent in their use of checks, pluses, and deltas. We use the symbols check, delta, and plus to indicate that student performance of individual outcomes has been satisfactory, unsatisfactory, or excellent. An "A" performance ought to have almost all pluses in that category. A "B" performance ought to have some pluses. A "C" performance ought to have about as many pluses as deltas. Another "C" student might have all checks if they have completed all those expected student outcomes satisfactorily. A "D" performance ought to have some deltas to explain specifically what expected student outcomes were subpar. An "E" performance should have almost all deltas for that category.

Program supervisors should look for consistency in this area, especially within each course. Exceptions will occur when performance of specific outcomes was merely inconsistent, or good, rather than unsatisfactory or excellent. Staff should err on the side of giving clear feedback to individual students but should be able to explain inconsistencies in this area.

## Overall Performance

The overall performance (OP) grade is the most important one on the evaluation. It is important that the grade given reflects student performance as judged by the instructors. It is also important that this summary grade has some correlation to the other grades on the evaluation. If a student gets an overall performance grade of "C," that ought to be a rough average of the other grades in the subcategories. It is acceptable for staff to weight some categories more than others based on the experiences that defined the course. At NOLS, Leadership and EB are so fundamental to our identity that they always need to have a significant role in determining Overall Performance grades. Just be sure to use the same system to grade each student in your group. Program supervisors are expected to watch for consistency in grading.

Written comments should explain what went well, lessons learned, and suggested next steps. This is also an area to comment about a student who makes great strides in the bigger pictures of education. If they learn to take more responsibility for their own learning, or just act more mature in some way, written comments along these lines can be invaluable to students.

## Group Grades Are Not Okay

Plan ahead with a system to assess individuals in each category we grade. It isn't acceptable to give your whole course the same "group grade" in any category without making individual assessments.

## Pass/Fail Option

On 25+ courses, students may be given the option to get graded on a pass/fail basis. Just ask your students to let you know within the first day whether they want letter grades or pass/fail. Some prefer the lighter atmosphere of pass/fail. Others desire letter grades for personal or professional reasons. Problems may arise if someone changes their mind at the last minute. This is a student option, not an instructor option, so it is not okay for staff to announce to their students that the course will be graded pass/fail.

### Adventure Course Grading
NOLS courses for 14-15 yearolds have special grading guidelines that reflect the more fundamental learning needs of adolescents.

### Instructor Course Grading
These courses use the above guidelines with some additional parameters in the letter grade definitions. These meet the specific feedback needs of instructor candidates.

### Semester Grading
Diplomas are earned by NOLS semester students who achieve an overall grade of C- (C minus) or better. Branches may average grades straight across the board or weight some sections more heavily because they were longer or because they were last. It is important that the same grading strategy be used for every student in a semester group and that they know the grading strategy ahead of time.

University of Utah grades are based on how semester activities align with the U/UT course titles. A skills practicum grade might be based on one section. Environmental Studies is usually an average based on every section's Environmental Studies grade. Contact the NOLS Curriculum Manager if your branch needs help creating a worksheet for calculating overall semester grades.

### Separations and Grades
Students who leave a course early may earn some college credit if the branch thinks they have completed enough of the curriculum to earn credit for one of the U/UT course titles. An example of this would be a student who only completes the climbing section receiving a grade just for the climbing skills practicum. This credit is at the discretion of the staff and may not exceed 2 semester hours for every 10 days at NOLS.

### Student Evaluation Appeal Process
When a student formally appeals their grade, the Curriculum Manager may pull together an evaluation review committee, including three instructors who didn't work that course, and we check to see if grading is consistent with our guidelines. If there are questions for the instructors, we get those answers first. We don't second guess the grades judged by the instructors who actually observed student performance in the field, but we sometimes look for grading consistency within a group of students.

### Flexibility
Grading is a critical student service. Our overall grading system is controlled by NOLS HQ and we try to keep it fairly consistent. But other parts of evaluations are controlled by our branches. If a branch wants to experiment with new grading systems, these systems need to be worked out in advance with the Curriculum Manager, and they need to be part of a test that helps NOLS assess their service to our students. These tests have helped us provide better service to our students in the past, so we hope to keep growing in this area.

# Chapter Thirteen Helping All Students Succeed by Closing the Gap Between Behaviors and Expectations

Despite our efforts to provide students with clear expectations about expedition behavior and a positive learning environment, we occasionally have students who are not motivated, exhibit behavior that is below our expectations, have emotional issues, or mental health conditions. Less than four percent of our students have reported incidents of these types of behavior on courses, though there are likely more students that need help.

Types of behaviors that interfere with success are not isolated to any one demographic group. The challenge for instructors is that the rare student who is exhibiting behaviors that fall below expectations may demand a disproportionate amount of time and energy and may negatively influence a course experience for everybody.

This chapter provides instructors with strategies to find greater success for students who don't meet our expectations. We can do this by being aware, skilled, and willing to coach students past hurdles. And, if a student cannot complete a NOLS course, we can manage their separation from NOLS with skill and sensitivity without dropping our responsibilities to educate the other students on the course.

Our student management toolbox includes clear expectations on expedition behavior and a positive learning environment. It has the communication and conflict management skills of our leadership curriculum. It has clear, consistent, and reasonable consequences that help our courses run smoother, and allows us to spend more time learning and having great adventures.

This chapter presents guidelines, not rules. Every situation has unique variables and specific circumstances. The goal is to identify the threshold for unacceptable behaviors to guide decisions on how to respond. Some decisions are clearer than others because of NOLS policies or legal factors, but judgment will also be necessary in most cases.

## The Management Spectrum

The level of reaction should match the level of infraction. We view behaviors as a continuum from acceptable, safe, and legal to unacceptable, unsafe, and illegal.

If a behavior is illegal or threatens safety, we likely need a swift and strong response. If it is unacceptable, but not a clear threat to health and safety, a measured response, restating expectations and consequences and giving the student a chance to change, is often warranted. For example, for a student whose performance is below expectations, the performance continuum might look like this:

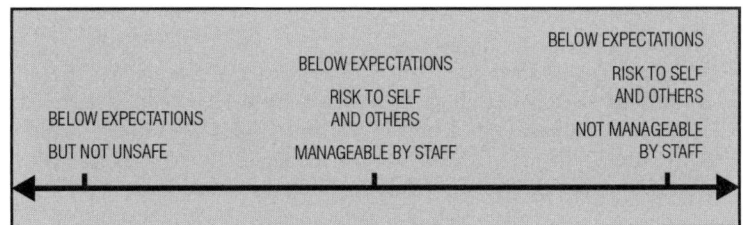

The parallel response continuum might look like this:

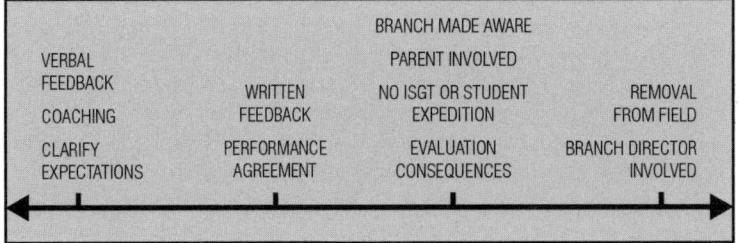

## Instructor Response Methodology

### Establish Expectations

The NOLS catalog, website, and other materials inform students about what they should expect on a NOLS course. The admissions department further informs students and reviews applications of students with physical, mental health, or behavioral issues that may be inappropriate for NOLS.

Set your students up for success by clearly stating expectations for behavior once they arrive. The standard for setting expectations is a Positive Learning Environment (PLE) exercise that is thorough and thoughtful. The PLE exercise forms a foundation for conveying our community values, culture, and behavior expectations. The core of PLE is teamwork and treating fellow expedition members with dignity and respect. Clearly define expedition behavior, and what our boundaries are for acceptable behavior.

Despite these efforts, some students become overwhelmed physically or emotionally by the wilderness or the close living situation, simply become homesick, decide NOLS isn't what they thought it would be, or exhibit disruptive behaviors that couldn't be detected during the admissions process. If you become aware of this before you go into the field, talk with the student. The branch program staff can help, perhaps by calling family or a therapist. This may provide useful background and involves branch staff and the family early in this process.

### Build Rapport

At the heart of positive student behavior is building rapport with each student on your course. One study by NOLS and the University of Utah quantified effective instructor traits and behaviors that include patience, knowledge, empathy, having fun, and creating a supportive learning environment (Schuman, 2009). To create accountability in this area NOLS added the following to the instructor qualifications: "Foster an inclusive, supportive course culture, and strive to build rapport with all students. Recognize exceptional student experiences begin with a safe learning environment and positive connections to instructors." Good rapport can help instructors and students find solutions more effectively.

### Intervene Early and Often

It is critical to promptly and consistently set boundaries for appropriate behavior. Group habits and norms develop within days. If you do not follow the norms set in your positive learning talk, students will be confused and will lose commitment to the PLE.

Early intervention includes simple, timely feedback describing the behavior, and stating why it is unwanted or inappropriate. If the behavior is severe, or has been repeated, it may be time to add consequences.

It is best to operate from personal observations and interactions. It can be awkward and difficult to intervene based on secondhand reports, but may be necessary if the behavior is severe. Mentors can give students a personal touch and facilitate early identification of issues and steps for intervention.

Consider the waterline model if you are having difficulty connecting with a student as a method for addressing the situation (see the *NOLS Leadership Educator Notebook*). Stay focused on observed behaviors and setting expectations. Refrain from commenting on personality and character. Waterline interventions used by staff include:

### Structure

- Revisit expectations from orientation, course catalog/description and PLE.
- Describe behaviors below threshold and consequences (evaluation, non-participation in course activities, ISGT, student expedition, grade, diploma, credit, evacuation, or expulsion).
- Use a performance agreement.
- Describe desired behaviors. Be as specific as possible.

### Group

- Be consistent with everyone on the course.
- If the group is non-supportive of a member, visit the course norms and the team expectations.

### Interpersonal
- Teach conflict management (see *NOLS LEN*).
- Revisit structure.
- Teach feedback skills.

### Intra-personal
- Revisit PLE, perhaps with a written performance agreement.
- Reinforce desired behaviors with positive feedback.
- Use a mentor, instructor, or peer coach.

### Student Check-ins
Formal check-ins between a student and an instructor should happen before day seven of a course. They are a chance to give the student feedback, praise their good work, recognize improvement, and coach and assess the student's comfort with the course. Consider framing check-ins with the seven leadership skills. Early check-ins provide an opportunity to address poor performance before it becomes a habit and give the student time to change.

### Follow-up
The magnitude of the situation will dictate the frequency and level of the follow-up. Follow-up may include a daily check-in with documentation of what was discussed, a chat with the student every couple of days, or positive feedback to reinforce appropriate behavior. On multi-section courses, consider having a check-in with the student along with outgoing and incoming instructors.

Once you state expectations and consequences, it is important to honor that agreement. A string of second chances undermines credibility and the PLE.

## Student Performance Agreements
A written Student Performance Agreement (SPA) is a valuable tool for documenting behavior and setting expectations. It specifically describes the student's behaviors that need to change. For example, "display a positive attitude" would be better stated as "will work to eliminate the following actions that express negativity: rolling eyes and sighing, reading his book during meetings, sitting apart from the group during meetings." Include measurable positive actions such as "will cook one meal a day, will either set-up or take down the shelter each day, will clean tent group cooking utensils once every two days" instead of "will do his share around camp."

Include specific measurable proportionate consequences in the SPA. These may range to inability to participate in course activities or separation from the course. They may describe how the student can earn a passing grade for the course, participate in independent student expedition, and receive a diploma or college credit. SPAs are also valuable because you ensure that you understand the situation, can express and evaluate it clearly, and coach the student for success. The SPA should be retained and turned in with the student's evaluation in the course paperwork.

Our records from 2006 to 2013 indicate that the use of an SPA correlates with positively changed behavior in the categories of safety and judgment (82%), inappropriate physical or verbal behavior (77%), and poor performance (88%). Percentages refer to the number of cases in which the SPA resulted in a positive change and the student graduated. SPAs are not typically used in cases of alcohol or drug use violations, but are used and are effective in cases of tobacco violations (92% effective). See below for comments about SPAs and motivational incidents.

### Measuring Success and Probability of Success
The student needs to acknowledge the situation. This is the first step toward an agreement that will enable the student to change their behavior and remain on the course.

A student who is not succeeding must be willing to change their behavior. Though a student who says they will change may be saying it because we want to hear it, we need to trust his or her sincerity and look for actions that will support their efforts to change.

Use a Student Performance Agreement to set a specific timeline for an observable change in the student's behavior. Provide tangible examples of behaviors that are unacceptable as well as of behaviors that will demonstrate change.

Consider the expedition's ability to support and include the person as they try to succeed. If the group has been so negatively impacted that it can no longer support any changes, consider more serious consequences.

It is important to consider the quality of the group's experience and the impact on the instructor team's energy in their ability to continue to manage the student. There is a point at which the line must be drawn and a student who is not succeeding cannot continually impact the group.

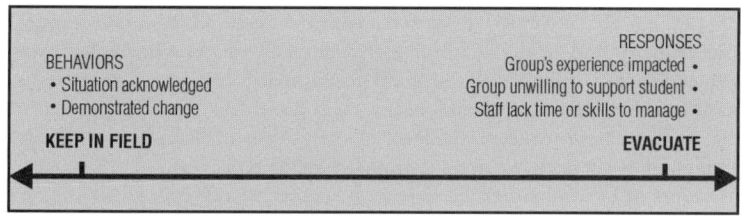

### Removal from the Field/Expulsion
If you think the situation warrants expulsion it is ultimately the branch director's decision. Be thorough in recording the details of the behavior (there likely would have been an SPA used by this point). You can use the satellite phone to inform the management of the situation and your recommendation. If you have been thorough in your process and documentation, it is rare that the branch director will disagree with your recommendation. Once a decision is reached and a plan made, tell the student that they will be evacuated and why, and that an instructor will accompany them.

## Documenting Student Non-Medical Incidents
Use the following guidelines for thoroughly and concisely documenting student behavior or motivation issues. There are three priorities in documentation:

*Truth:* Be factual, write down what you know happened, or quote/paraphrase from students. Avoid speculation.

*Clarity:* Be clear and organized with details, write legibly, use dates, time of day, full names and page numbers. Read it to another instructor to verify its accuracy and check the overall tone.

*Brevity:* Be concise and clear with important messages. Avoid rambling and redundant documentation.

Once you identify a student as having behavioral or motivational issues, the following should occur:
1) Keep a daily student performance log outlining significant interactions and events with that student.
2) Use a Student Performance Agreement (SPA).
3) Have daily check-ins with the student. If the concern is resolved, document that it has been resolved.

When all reasonable efforts to help a student succeed have been exhausted, and the decision is to evacuate the student and recommend separation from the course, documentation is critical. If the reasons for evacuation are unclear, the process muddled, or the documentation incomplete, management may not support your recommendation, parents can get angry, and there is a possibility the student will be returned to the field. The following needs to be included in the paperwork that leaves the field:

- **Field evacuation form** (attach any additional notes)
- **Student performance log**
- **Student Performance Agreement**
- **Written response from the student** (not required, but should be offered)
- **Additional documentation** (e.g., written statements from other students)
- **Student evaluation form** (If a student is leaving for misbehavior or poor performance, the grade/number on the specific category of safety, EB, or leadership and the overall grade should reflect their performance, e.g., a "2" or a "1".)

All paperwork should be sealed in an envelope and given to the person leading the evacuation party, not to the student.

Non-medical incidents may have related medical concerns, but an incident needs to be defined as a medical or non-medical incident—it cannot be both. Clearly identify the main reason for the evacuation. Some students can tolerate physical exertion, pain, or discomfort better than others, but simple fatigue, a nagging injury, or illness can be legitimate medical reasons for evacuating a student even if the symptoms don't seem serious. Avoid making judgments that a student's injury or illness isn't severe enough to be evacuated.

# Conclusion

The majority of our students match our expectations of behavior and performance, but sometimes students are more significantly challenged by the course than they may have expected or other factors result in their behavior not meeting our expectations. These students need to be treated fairly and these strategies and tactics will provide instructors with methods for responding to these situations to help the student succeed or evacuate them in a sensitive and reasonable way.

# NOLS' Responses to Specific Behaviors

The following information provides a detailed treatment of behaviors that students might exhibit. All instructors should have read and be familiar with this material.

## Motivation

There are students who do not want to be on their NOLS course. Perhaps it wasn't their idea to enroll, they've found that wilderness living is not to their liking, it may be more work and discomfort than they bargained for, or not the experience they anticipated. Motivational incidents are the leading type of non-medical incident at NOLS (30%).

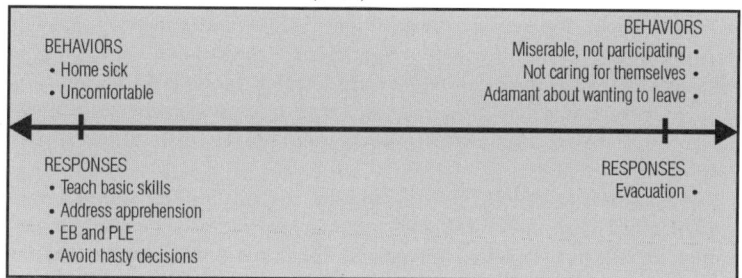

We are disappointed when students choose to leave early and we try to convince them to stay. How you do this depends on what is driving the student to want to leave. If they are apprehensive or uncomfortable, then provide reassurance and encouragement and teach skills to increase their comfort. Early in a course a student can be homesick, or overwhelmed by the experience. They may say, "my parents sent me," or "this wasn't my idea." Even though some students are convinced to go on a course by their parents, many of them turn out to be successful students. If we recognize apprehension, homesickness or discomfort, we may be able to help them put this in perspective and anticipate fun and accomplishment as the course evolves. Use the following advice about how to manage student anxiety:

- Have students talk about their fears. This is the first coping step of acknowledging the fear; learning this is normal and may be shared by others.
- Give students little stepping-stones to confront their nervousness one step of intensity at a time.
- Likely all students have some anxiety and non-dominant, underrepresented groups might have more. By showing how we help others cope with their fears we set students up for success in leading others.

Ultimately, we cannot force students to stay on the course, but we can create the atmosphere for an exciting, supporting, comfortable, and rewarding experience. It's the student who decides to participate.

Student performance agreements are rarely used with students who want to leave—usually because the students are very adamant about leaving—but SPA's are still worth trying as a way to help these students find reasons for staying.

Avoid hasty decisions regarding evacuation. Provide adequate time to coach the student and for them to develop a tolerance for adversity before making a final decision.

For adult students you can do your best to change their mind, but ultimately it's their decision. If the student is under 18, and sometimes when the student is between 18 and 21, we have had some success by involving parents early in a discussion. This typically involves using the satellite phone to call from the field to the branch or in some cases calling a parent directly. We've headed off a few motivational incidents by identifying the concern, sometimes before the course leaves for the field, talking with the student and parent, and picking up some valuable background and some ideas of how to help the student. If the student still desires to go home, involving the parent in the process has proven helpful for the parent to accept the decision.

A motivational incident is not an emergency and should not inconvenience a course. It is fine to wait for the scheduled re-ration or pickup to send the student out. The trip insurance that students purchase through NOLS does not apply in non-medical situations and there is no tuition refund.

## Misbehavior

Intervention is required for behavior that disrupts other students' experience, does not support good expedition behavior or a positive learning environment, disregards instructions, and/or becomes a course quality or safety concern. Misbehavior may range in severity from innocuous to offensive and include inappropriate verbal or physical behavior, use of drugs, alcohol, or tobacco, violation of our sexual relationship policy, or refusal to adhere to LNT practices. It can include a student who has a lack of connection to the course, which manifests in negative comments, sarcasm, tardiness, and other disruptive behaviors or a student with anger management issues.

### Behavior That Clearly Warrants Expulsion

There are few absolutes, but below are examples of behavior that will almost always warrant expulsion:

- Violation of the drug and alcohol policy in the field. We define field time as beginning when the student steps on a vehicle for transport to the field, and ending when the students steps off the vehicle at headquarters, or an intermediate location designated by the branch administration, as the end of the course or section.
- Illegal drug use or substance abuse in town.
- Intentional violation of risk management instructions, practices, or policies.
- Behavior that causes harm or intends to do so—threats or physical assaults.
- Damage to NOLS' reputation (for example, committing such a serious offense that we lose the privilege to operate in an important area).

### Behaviors That Warrant a More Flexible Discipline Response

- Reasonable suspicion of drug, alcohol, or tobacco use, in the field but no actual physical or behavioral evidence.
- Irresponsible use of alcohol in town; possession or use of alcohol by minors in non-field situations.
- Tobacco use in the field or in town.
- Psychological conditions that affect safety of self or others, or are detrimental to the quality of the course.
- Abusive language, inappropriate physical contact, or other forms of poor expedition behavior.
- Minor theft or other minor unlawful conduct.
- Disregard of instructions that have a detrimental effect on the group.
- Embarrassment to NOLS' reputation, which might affect privileges, access or stature in the community.
- Outdoor skill performance below expectations.

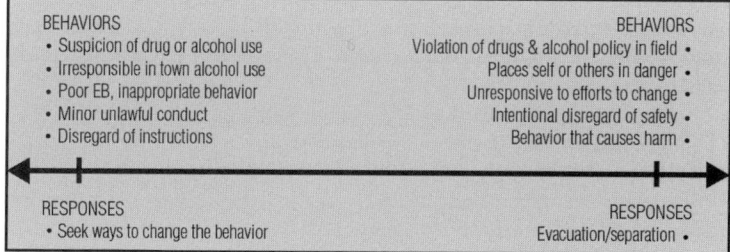

### Safety Concern—Disregarding Instructions

A student who intentionally disregards instructions, does not follow risk management practices, repeats the behavior, the behavior is malicious, or puts them or others at risk is a serious situation. Strong intervention with immediate verbal feedback and a written performance agreement is warranted. A student who does not or cannot follow directions because of poor performance, i.e., they don't understand or perceive a hazard, is also significant, but can be handled with more compassion.

*Evacuation threshold*: If a student refuses to adhere to risk management instructions and procedures and places themselves or others at risk, they can be removed from the field. Likewise, if they refuse to adhere to LNT instruction, they can be removed from the field. If a student's performance does not improve or they cannot be adequately supervised they can be evacuated.

## Inappropriate Behavior

There is a range of inappropriate behavior from poor expedition behavior and undermining of the positive learning environment to harassment.

Persistent poor expedition behavior and not upholding the expectation for a positive learning environment should be managed with verbal feedback, by revisiting expectations, using a student performance agreement, addressing it on the student evaluation, and lowering their grade. More serious transgressions may result in denial of the privilege of independent student travel and student expeditions and denial of diploma. Minor, isolated, or infrequent poor expedition behavior may warrant a student performance agreement or other proportionate consequence.

*Evacuation threshold*: Inappropriate verbal, or physical behavior and/or disregard for the positive learning environment are grounds for expulsion and separation.

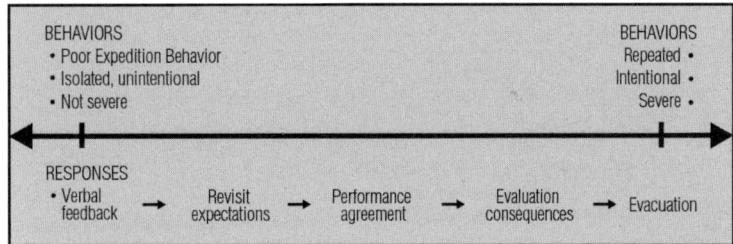

The NOLS Human Resource & Inclusion Director manages the NOLS Harassment Policy and the most current version is in the NOLS Employee Guidelines, which can be found on NOLS Rendezvous on the Human Resources page. The following information is from the 2014 version of the NOLS Harassment Policy.

NOLS is committed to an environment free from all forms of harassment by anyone including supervisors, coworkers, students, or visitors. Harassment may include words or actions concerning an individual's race, color, sex, national origin, religion, age, disability, marital status, or sexual orientation. The conduct is not welcomed and may be severe or pervasive enough to create a hostile work or learning environment. Anyone found harassing another will be subject to disciplinary action, up to and including dismissal from employment or expulsion from a course. Examples of behavior that could be harassment:

- Telling or e-mailing sexual, racial or ethnic jokes
- Slurs based on race, religion, or national origin
- Seeking sexual favors in return for grade or employment benefit
- Inappropriate touching or gestures
- Unwanted romantic or sexual attention
- Sexually suggestive or obscene visual displays or notes
- Unnecessary and conspicuous nudity
- Gender-based humiliation/intimidation

Harassment can occur between same gender, female to male, male to female or in a variety of relationships such as instructors and students, supervisors and employees. Factors that are considered when determining whether behavior is harassing, include:

- Severity (for less severe behavior, how much it is repeated)
- Whether the behavior is wanted or unwanted.

It is important to examine the effect on the offended person, as opposed to the intent of the offender. We encourage staff and students to address issues promptly; preferably clearly, directly, and privately with the individual involved. Students should report it to an instructor or branch administrator. If more follow up is desired, the concerns should be raised with the branch director.

## Drug, Alcohol, or Tobacco Use

The use or possession of alcohol, illegal drugs, abuse of prescriptions drugs or other substances is not allowed in the field or classroom and the person(s) violating this policy will be expelled as soon as reasonably possible.

*Evacuation threshold*: People using drugs or alcohol in the field will be evacuated and separated.

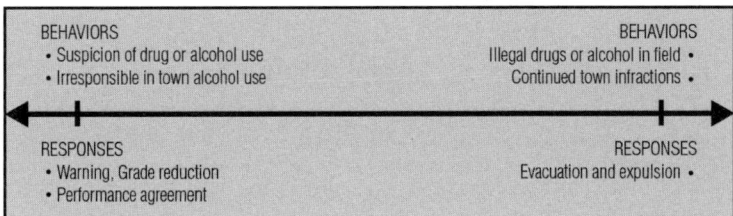

Some alcohol use may be permitted while in town or after class time by students of legal drinking age as determined by the branch director. In non-field situations alcohol use by a minor or alcohol abuse by anyone where they disrupt a group or cannot participate in scheduled activities requires disciplinary action. Typically this involves a written warning with a student performance agreement, lowering grades for expedition behavior and leadership, possibly denying a diploma and/or loss of college credit. Repeated offenses can lead to dismissal from the course. Severe incidents, such as abusive behavior, property damage, potential alcohol poisoning, or need for hospitalization may require intervention by law enforcement and will result in immediate dismissal from NOLS.

The best way to handle this is to catch the students in the act or in possession of drugs or alcohol. Realistically, we more often deal with suspicion and rumor, and we have to actively investigate. Signs that people may be smoking marijuana or drinking alcohol on your course include the following:

- If you smell marijuana in a tent, in a snow shelter, on someone's hair or in the air.
- If groups of people tend to disappear after meals (and are not obviously watching birds or identifying flowers).
- If people are going for a little hike in their free time when the weather doesn't make that very attractive.
- If a couple of people ask to stay behind to hang out while coming off a peak or hiking somewhere.
- If the same individuals seem to be unaccounted for occasionally.
- Students who stop what they're doing or seem awkward when you approach a group.
- If a student tells you that others are drinking or smoking, but won't tell you who they are and doesn't want to "rat" on the other students.
- If some people seem to have changing attention spans (they're always spacey, though this is hard to assess).
- Groups with ongoing poor expedition behavior.

Most of these signs are meaningless alone, but if you see a repeated pattern you need to investigate. If this is on a semester, and you don't confront the situation, it will likely grow as more and more students see what the others get away with, or the unwanted behaviors undermine expedition behavior and the course tone.

One tactic is to go about a normal routine while keeping an eye out for behavior patterns. Take and trade notes on your observations with co-instructors. Visit camps more often, or put your tent near the student tents. Some people refer to this level of supervision as *maintaining a presence*.

You may let the group know of your concerns and observations, and remind them of our policy, or approach people directly with your suspicions. Both of these tactics could drive the behavior underground. If you feel there are enough signs, you may need to move to active surveillance and seeking ways to catch students in the act.

Searching packs is a more aggressive tactic, but we reserve the right to search student's property (packs) if there is suspicion that illegal or unsafe acts have occurred or are likely to occur. This is stated clearly in the pre-course information. It does need to be managed well. If your assumptions are wrong, or even if they're correct but you don't catch the people misbehaving, you may have initiated an adversarial relationship and may need to take active steps to retain the safe learning environment and rapport. You may also call the branch to discuss the situation and seek the program team's advice. You may not catch the offender, and you might not have enough observations to confront people, but you may determine whether there are enough other behavioral concerns to warrant evacuation and you don't need to catch them in the act.

## Smoking or Chewing

The NOLS Alcohol, Drug, and Tobacco policy states that:

*"NOLS courses and facilities are tobacco free (includes smoking and chewing tobacco). The use of nicotine replacements (unless prescribed by a physician) and electronic cigarettes are not allowed. Students found to be violating the tobacco policies will be put on a performance contract. Continued violation may warrant the student being expelled."*

This policy is clearly told to students in the pre-course information and orientation. As the policy indicates, we allow a little more leniency for tobacco use than for alcohol or drug use. Isolated violations of our tobacco policy can be managed with a student performance agreement. Repeated offenses become insubordination and can result in expulsion from the course.

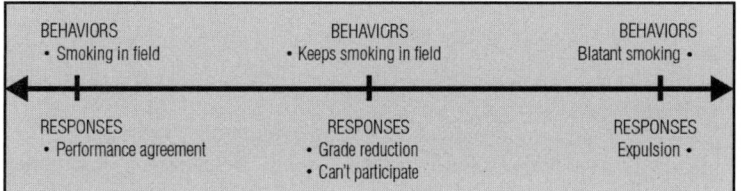

## Sexual Relationship Guidelines

The following is from our *Position Statement on Sexual Relationships Between Students*. Sexual and/or exclusive relationships between students can be detrimental to group dynamics of a NOLS expedition. They may detract from the educational mission of the course and can be a health and safety issue. We have received complaints from students who have been exposed to other students' sexual activity and complaints of sexual and/or exclusive relationships negatively affecting expedition behavior. In addition, NOLS has varying levels of legal responsibility for minor students involved in sexual relationships.

The policy is not black and white—there is a spectrum of considerations and responses. At one end of the spectrum we have acceptable student sexual relationships with no need for intervention. On the other end of the spectrum we have unacceptable student relationships that should result in evacuation.

If both students are adults (18 or older), in a consensual relationship, meeting expectations for the course, and not affecting the expedition negatively, we should allow them their privacy. They should be expected to keep engaged with the rest of the group and course objectives. When a married or already established adult couple comes to our course, we should allow them the opportunity to have their own tent, if logistically reasonable, and maintain our expectation that they mix with the group.

*Evacuation threshold*: If there is a non-consensual sexual relationship (including sexual assault) evacuate immediately. If there is a sexual relationship between an adult and a minor, even if there is reason to believe it is consensual, immediate evacuation is usually necessary. Otherwise, our response may vary depending on the severity of the act, the age, power difference, and the existing laws of the local area.

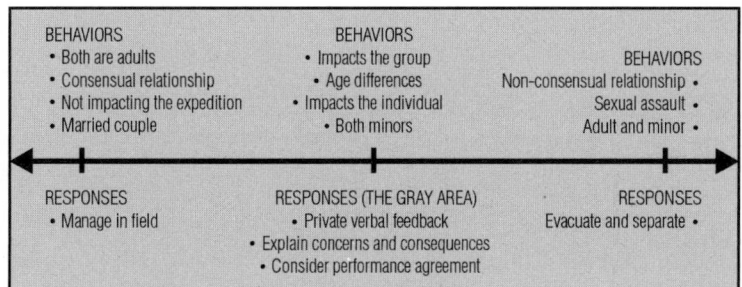

*Sexual Relationships Between Minors*

When two minors are involved in what appears to be a consensual sexual relationship, we need to determine if evacuation is warranted. Consider the following factors in your decision: their ages, age difference, the sexual act, local law, and the relationship's effect on the students and the group. If a minor is expelled, parents will be notified of the reason for expulsion. Under some circumstances, we may have an obligation to notify law enforcement authorities if we become aware of misconduct.

*Evacuation threshold*: Factors arguing for evacuation include younger students (14 yrs. vs. 17 yrs.), a greater than one year age disparity, penetration versus fondling/kissing, a relationship negatively affecting the students or the group, and a relationship clearly in violation of the local law. If the behavior does not warrant an immediate evacuation, but does not change despite a warning, we recommend evacuating both students.

*Gray Areas Require Different Responses*

When two adult students are involved in a sexual or exclusive relationship that is affecting team dynamics, intervention can include talking to the individuals or the couple and separating them during hikes, tent or cook groups, and/or student expeditions. The response should be proportional to the severity of the behavior or degree of non-compliance with our stated expectations.

We inform our students in their course information about our general expectations regarding relationships. In addition, during the positive learning environment orientation, you should reinforce that sexual or exclusive relationships, which are detrimental to expedition dynamics and any sexual relationship involving a minor may result in expulsion.

*Evacuation threshold*: Exclusive or sexual relationships between students may be grounds for evacuation and separation.

## Poor Performance

Occasionally we have a student who simply cannot perform basic skills, or requires an inordinate amount of supervision. We become concerned for the safety of the student or of other expedition members. This might be due to fitness, learning ability, motivation, or a combination of these and other factors. They might be a wonderful person who just can't master basic skills. They require extra supervision and staff time, and the challenge is how much time can be or should be devoted to this student at the expense of the others. Should this student participate in independent student group travel or even wander unaccompanied out of sight from camp?

NOLS courses can accommodate slower, weaker, ill or injured students by altering route and shifting weight. This is part of Expedition Behavior. However, some courses begin immediately in difficult terrain, with little time for getting fit, and some students cannot catch up.

Sometimes failure to perform basic tasks can be a safety concern. Address concerns with verbal feedback and coaching. Try different teaching strategies. Document with a performance log, a student performance agreement, and the student evaluation. Specifically describe skills that are below expectations.

*Evacuation threshold*: If the student cannot care for himself and/or perform basic outdoor skills, if their inability to perform presents risks to others, and if the instructor ability to supervise is stretched, the student may need to be separated. It's rare, but does happen.

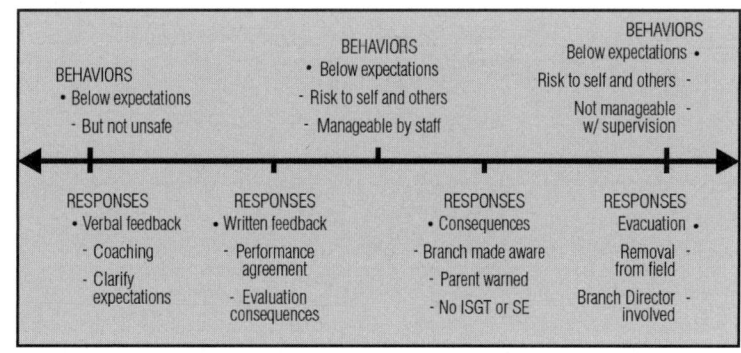

*Attention Deficit Hyperactivity Disorder (ADHD)*

ADHD is a neurological syndrome that is characterized by distractibility, impulsiveness, and restlessness. It manifests itself differently in each individual.

It is not appropriate for us to diagnose or label learning disabilities, but understanding strategies for teaching to students with ADHD may be useful for addressing poor performance. The following list of points on teaching to students with ADHD may be helpful:

- Use written outlines and underline key points or phrases.
- Announce what you will teach, teach it, then review major points.
- Recognize that memory can be an issue: use mnemonics, index cards, cues, rhymes, and codes.
- Make eye contact.
- Make a game out of learning—try teaching via a skit, a puzzle, planted questions and answers, a story, a reading. Vary the techniques as much as possible.
- Teach shorter topics (a series of mini classes) and practice in the smallest groups possible.
- Choose a classroom that has the least amount of distraction or additional stimuli.
- Ask your student what will help them learn.
- If a student is being taught classes one-on-one, explain the situation to the group.
- Students with ADHD need to find enjoyment in the classroom.
- Repeat directions, write down directions, speak directions, and repeat directions.
- Seat a student with ADHD near a teacher—they might drift off less often.
- When possible, make a predictable schedule. A student with ADHD will need time to switch gears and a routine can help.
- Breakdown large tasks into categories.
- Try to keep a student with ADHD engaged in the learning process and create a comfortable fun atmosphere for learning.
- Underscore success.
- Use feedback and provide social coaching.
- Simplify instructions, choices, scheduling. Provide structure. Give clear rules.
- Provide opportunity for lots of physical exercise.
- Stress preparation—a checklist of what to bring to a class, how to Storm-proof camp, etc.
- Most importantly look for the special talent that each person has to offer a group. Embrace and enhance it.

Most students with ADHD are successful at NOLS. The application process may not be able to fully determine their ability to perform until they arrive and are in a field setting.

## Mental Health Concerns

Poor performance on a course might be due to psychological conditions that adversely affect the person's ability to perform or may result in some unusual behaviors. These may include mood swings, or poor control of emotions; something simple trips off an emotional display. The person may respond to normal events by elevating them to crisis level. They may spend excessive time daydreaming. Students may express thoughts of suicide or threaten to or actually injure themselves. Their self-perception may not match what you observe in their behavior.

*Evacuation threshold:* If students (or co-workers) exhibit behaviors that the instructors cannot manage in the field then the person should be evacuated. Mental health incidents are considered medical incidents, though instructors don't need to be overly concerned about whether it is a medical or non-medical incident—respond to the behaviors and signs and symptoms, not the label.

Many students with a history of mental health conditions are successful students, though there are some who cannot manage their condition while on a course. Often these students will let instructors know they are having difficulty and ask to leave. On very rare occasions a student may start to exhibit signs or symptoms of a mental health disorder that they have no history of. It is not within the scope of instructor's responsibility to determine if a student has a mental health condition, rather the individual's behaviors and actions should be observed and documented in an objective fashion. Instructors should approach the student and discuss the behaviors and determine if they can be managed in the field or not. Often this determination evolves over time so it

will require close observation. Evacuation decisions revolve around assessing the chance of harm to the student or other course members, the ability of the staff to manage the condition, as well as more obvious situations such as disassociation, disorientation, incoherence, mention of or actual self-inflicted injury, and extreme emotional reactions or mood swings.

Some ways of assessing behavior include looking for patterns that repeat, looking for multiple clues in combination, and using performance as an indicator of mental health. Trust your perceptions and instincts.

*Indicators of a Potential Mental Health Concern*
- Showing poor judgment.
- Disoriented, incoherent, or dissociated.
- Overly optimistic or pessimistic, neither of which is reality based.
- Losing it emotionally. Anxious when nothing is wrong.
- Withdrawn and isolated. Do they withdraw as you approach?
- Showing tangential speech, pressured speech, or inability to focus on one topic. Do they repeatedly return to fixate on the same topic or activity?
- Reporting that thoughts are racing, or that they can't keep up with thoughts. Is their internal experience overwhelming?
- Emotionally down, followed by an abrupt turnaround.

After you have noted a number of the above indicators, consider the following questions and procedures:
- Are they a danger to self or others (suicide or just general safety)?
- Does the condition outweigh the confidence of the instructor team to deal with it?
- Does the harm to the group outweigh the benefit of keeping this student on the course?
- Does the student's behavior vastly differ from what you expected from the paperwork?
- Remove the student from the next activity (e.g., class, peak climb, top rope day). Evaluate how it felt not having them around.

*Suicidal Thoughts*
If suicidal thoughts are suspected, talk to the student. It may be challenging to open this conversation, but talking about suicide does not cause people to commit suicide. Ask the following five questions:
- Are you thinking of harming or killing yourself?
- Have you planned how you would do this?
- Do you have the means with you now to carry out this plan?
- When are you thinking of doing this?
- Do you have a history of past suicide attempts?

## Chapter Thirteen References

- Schuman, S. et.al. "Instructor Influence of Student Learning at NOLS." Journal of Outdoor Recreation, Education, and Leadership. Volume 1, Issue 1. 2009